Selected Correspondence of Bernard Shaw

Bernard Shaw and Barry Jackson

Bernard Shaw and Barry Jackson

Edited by L.W. Conolly

UNIVERSITY OF TORONTO PRESS
Toronto Buffalo London

Published by University of Toronto Press Incorporated
Toronto Buffalo London
Printed in Canada
ISBN 0-8020-3572-8

 Printed on acid-free paper

National Library of Canada Cataloguing in Publication Data

Shaw, Bernard, 1856–1950
Selected correspondence of Bernard Shaw

Includes bibliographical references and index.
Contents: [v. 4] Bernard Shaw and Barry Jackson / edited by L.W. Conolly.

ISBN 0-8020-3572-8 (v. 4)

1. Shaw, Bernard, 1856–1950 – Correspondence.   2. Dramatists, Irish –
20th century – Correspondence.   I. Title.

PR5366.A4 1995   822'.912   C95-930151-8 rev

The Press acknowledges a generous subvention from Mr John Wardrop.
We also thank the Academy of the Shaw Festival for its support.

University of Toronto Press acknowledges the financial assistance to its
publishing program of the Canada Council for the Arts and the Ontario Arts
Council.

This book has been published with the help of a grant from the Humanities
and Social Sciences Federation of Canada, using funds provided by the Social
Sciences and Humanities Research Council of Canada.

University of Toronto Press acknowledges the financial support for its
publishing activities of the Government of Canada through the Book
Publishing Industry Development Program (BPIDP).

For my mother

With love and gratitude

Contents

General Editor's Note

This volume is the fourth in the series entitled *Selected Correspondence of Bernard Shaw*. The first two volumes – *Bernard Shaw and H.G. Wells*, edited by J. Percy Smith, and *Theatrics*, edited by Dan H. Laurence – appeared in 1995. The third – *Bernard Shaw and Gabriel Pascal*, edited by Bernard F. Dukore – was published in 1996. The hiatus between the third and fourth volumes was caused in large part by the illness and subsequent death of the founding General Editor of the series, J. Percy Smith. It is an immense privilege and pleasure to have worked with Percy Smith (when we were colleagues at the University of Guelph) in the planning and implementation of this series, originally conceived by Dan H. Laurence and made possible by the generosity of John Wardrop and the support of the University of Toronto Press. As General Editor and the editor of the first volume in the series, Percy Smith set formidable scholarly standards, standards that have been maintained by the distinguished Shavian editors of the *Theatrics* and *Pascal* volumes. It now falls to me, Percy Smith's successor as General Editor, to do my best to honour his memory by living up to those standards.

The volumes in this series are of two kinds. Percy Smith's inaugural volume, *Bernard Shaw and H.G. Wells*, represents an example of the first kind: correspondence between Shaw and another individual of distinction in his or her own right. Bernard Dukore's edition of the correspondence between Shaw and film producer Gabriel Pascal is another example of this kind, as is the present volume, *Bernard Shaw and Barry Jackson*. Other such volumes are in preparation: Shaw and the Webbs, Shaw and Lady Astor, Shaw and William Archer, for example.

This approach replicates other sets of Shaw correspondence published prior to this series: Christopher St John's *Ellen Terry and Bernard Shaw: A Correspondence* (1931), or Alan Dent's *Bernard Shaw and Mrs. Patrick Campbell: Their Correspondence* (1952), among others. The advantage of this approach, of course, is that it gives the reader two voices rather than one, with all the stimulation that can arise from complementary or adversarial views on issues, events, or people. Such an approach also allows for insights into the nature of close personal and professional relationships, with all the emotional and intellectual drama that usually accompanied such Shavian associations. While matching the epistolary Shaw in full flow is a tough challenge, people like Wells, Pascal, and Jackson – hardened professionals all – were not easily intimidated by Shaw's sharp wit, searing logic, or intellectual aggression. Thus the sparks sometimes fly, from which light as well as heat is produced.

This attempt to capture Shaw's *dialogue* with friends and colleagues differs, of course, from collections solely of Shaw's letters to individuals, be they single individuals as in C.B. Purdom's *Bernard Shaw's Letters to Granville Barker* (1957) or Samuel Weiss's *Bernard Shaw's Letters to Siegfried Trebitsch* (1986), or hundreds of individuals as in Dan Laurence's monumental edition, *Bernard Shaw: Collected Letters* (4 volumes, 1965–88). And both of these approaches differ again from the second kind of volume in this series, Shaw's letters to a variety of individuals *on a particular subject*. Thus, Dan Laurence's *Theatrics* provides the opportunity to explore Shaw's ideas on theatre and theatricality. Similar volumes on Shaw and publishers and Shaw and musicians are in preparation.

And so through a variety of approaches the magnificent edifice of Shaw's correspondence is gradually constructed, drawing, in this series, largely on previously unpublished letters, and, in many instances, opening up new insights into Shaw's life and achievements, as well as the life and achievements of his correspondents. All but two of the letters in this volume, for example, are here published for the first time, and their appearance enables us to recognize much more clearly than had previously been the case the significance of the relationship between Bernard Shaw and Barry Jackson, a relationship that deserves to be celebrated, I believe, as one of the most consequential in the history of twentieth-century British theatre.

Introduction

The Birmingham Repertory Theatre

On 16 October 1923 Charlotte Shaw, Bernard Shaw's wife, wrote to Barry Jackson, director of the Birmingham Repertory Theatre, to tell him that a recent stay in Birmingham and nearby Malvern had been 'like a lovely, elusive dream.' The Shaws had holidayed in the spa town of Malvern and then had stayed in Birmingham with Jackson to attend rehearsals and the subsequent opening at the Repertory Theatre on 9 October 1923 of the British premiere of *Back to Methuselah*, an occasion, says Mrs Shaw, that 'was probably the crown of G.B.S.'s career,' a '*big thing*' (Letter 2). It was also a most *unlikely* thing. Shaw scarcely knew Barry Jackson, and Birmingham would not have sprung to many people's minds in 1923 as a likely venue for the British premiere of a major new play by Shaw. The world premiere of *Back to Methuselah* had taken place in February 1922 in New York; Birmingham, theatrically speaking, was hardly in the same league. Of all the 'rotten towns' on the major British theatrical circuits, Birmingham, said Shaw, 'was notorious as the rottenest.' 'If anyone had told me twenty years ago,' he continued (writing in 1924), 'that I should one day write a cycle of plays as far beyond all possibility of performance in the beaten way of trade as Wagner's *Ring* was in Germany in 1866, and that this theatrical monstrosity would be first performed [in England], and promptly performed, in Birmingham, I should have marked off that prophet as the most extravagant lunatic in the world' (Matthews, 168).

How, then, had this '*big thing*' come about, this enormous production

of Shaw's five-part play, spread over four days, in a small provincial theatre tucked away on an obscure street behind a Birmingham railway station? And what was it about this encounter between Bernard Shaw, the
world's most famous living playwright, and the 'lunatic' Barry Jackson,
barely known outside Birmingham, that led to one of the most produc-
tive professional relationships in British theatre in the twentieth century, arguably as important as Shaw's earlier and much-celebrated
relationship with Harley Granville Barker?

When Barry Vincent Jackson – the 'Barry' came from family admiration of Irish actor Barry Sullivan –. was born in Birmingham on 6 September 1879, Shaw, a generation older (born in Dublin, 26 July 1856),
was living an unremarkable and unpromising life in London. After leaving Dublin, a pedestrian clerical job, and his alcoholic father in March
1876 to join his mother and sister in London (they having departed
three years earlier in the footsteps of Mrs Shaw's singing teacher, Van-
deleur Lee), Shaw had struggled to give direction to his life. He had
ghostwritten some music criticism for Lee, he had started a novel, and
he was soon to become an unenthusiastic employee of the Edison Telephone Company. The novel, *Immaturity*, was completed a few weeks after
Barry Jackson was born, but Jackson had passed his fiftieth birthday
before it was published (in 1930). Shaw's employment in an administrative department of the Edison Telephone Company lasted only from
November 1879 to July 1880. In the immediate future lay more unpublished novels, little or no income, and strenuous efforts at self-education
and entry into circles of London's intelligentsia.

In a different way, and in very different circumstances, Jackson too
struggled as a young man to find a satisfying direction to his life. Unlike
Shaw, Jackson was born into wealth, his father, George Jackson, having
established a successful chain of grocery stores throughout the Birmingham region. Theatre and the arts, as well as business, featured prominently in the Jackson family. Visits to professional theatre in Birmingham
and on European travels were complemented by amateur dramatics at
the spacious Jackson home in a fashionable suburb of Birmingham and
by the plays in George Jackson's well-stocked library. Barry Jackson's
enthusiasm for theatre was equalled by his interest in painting, and he
had hopes of becoming a professional artist. His father, however, took a
more pragmatic approach to a career for his son, and in August 1898

apprenticed him to a Birmingham architect. At the same time, Jackson enrolled in evening courses at the Birmingham School of Art. At age eighteen, then, Jackson's future certainly did not lie in the grocery business, but art, theatre, and architecture were still contenders.

It took more than four years for Jackson to settle on his vocation. During those years, 1898–1902, he continued to train as an architect, and maintained his interest in painting and sketching (as he did for the rest of his life). Yet he also developed his keen interest in theatre by writing plays (unperformed), designing sets for them, and reading voraciously in his father's library. By 1902 George Jackson, increasingly ill with arthritis, agreed that his son should choose whatever career appealed to him, and that career was theatre.

By 1902 Shaw's professional future was even more sharply defined, despite the uncertain beginnings. The 1880s and 1890s had been filled with a kaleidoscope of activities and interests, fuelled by almost manic energy and determination. There were more unpublished novels, but there was now some regular if unspectacular income from music, art, theatrical, and literary criticism. He had joined the Fabian Society in 1884 and had rapidly become a much sought-after lecturer and writer on social and political issues. He had been elected (in 1897) to political office, albeit in the unglamorous role as Vestryman of the Parish of St Pancras. And he had met (1896) and married (1898) Charlotte Payne-Townshend, the 'green-eyed Irish millionairess' (*Collected Letters*, I, 418), who gave his life stability and financial security. Most importantly, with the encouragement of critic William Archer he had found his artistic vocation and profession. Like Jackson's, it was in the theatre.

Shaw's first play, *Widowers' Houses*, opened in an Independent Theatre production at the Royalty Theatre, London, on 9 December 1892. It was not a box-office success. There was just one more performance – a matinee on 13 December – but Shaw was undeterred and now began to immerse himself in theatre as playwright, critic, and vigorous adviser to directors of his plays. His trenchant drama reviews appeared in the *Saturday Review* from January 1895 to May 1898 and the plays began to appear at regular intervals. By the time that Barry Jackson had determined, sometime in 1902, that theatre would be his profession, close to a dozen Shaw plays had premiered in London, New York, Aberdeen, Chicago, and the English provinces: *Widowers' Houses* (1892), *Arms and the Man* (1894), *Candida* (1895), *The Devil's Disciple* (1897), *The Man of Destiny* (1897), *The Philanderer* (1898), *You Never Can Tell* (1898), *Caesar and Cleopatra* (1899), *Captain Brassbound's Conversion* (1899), *Mrs Warren's Profession* (1902), and *The Admirable Bashville* (1902). Some of these early productions were single performances for legal copyright purposes, and only *Arms and the Man* (fifty performances at the Avenue Theatre, London) and *The Devil's Disciple* (sixty-four performances at the Fifth Avenue Theatre, New York) had significant runs. Shaw was a confirmed playwright, but not yet a household name, and in Birmingham the young Barry Jackson had yet to see a Shaw play.

That event took place on 5 December 1906 when Jackson saw an amateur production of *You Never Can Tell* at the King's Head Institute in Birmingham.[1] Jackson's theatrical enthusiasm was by now gathering momentum. Since giving up architecture he had occupied himself by organizing and presenting several productions in the family home, supported by a group of interested friends, including John Drinkwater – later to become a successful playwright, but at this time working as an insurance clerk. Drinkwater first acted with Jackson in a production of *Twelfth Night* as Fabian, with Jackson as Feste. In addition to Shakespeare, Jackson sought out rarely performed plays from the English repertoire, one of which was *The Interlude of Youth*, a medieval morality play that he presented in September 1907. Among the invited audience was a local vicar, Arnold Pinchard, who invited Jackson to remount the play in his parish hall in central Birmingham, a performance that duly took place on 2 October 1907. It was this occasion that prompted Jackson to move his theatrical group to a more formal status. He called them the Pilgrim Players, a name chosen for its alliterative rather than Bunyanesque or colonizing associations. The Reverend Pinchard (surely a name that Shaw might have invented) became a regular member of the company.

For the next five years the Pilgrim Players, funded by Jackson (now independently wealthy following the death of his father in 1906), performed a variety of plays (twenty-eight in all), classical and contemporary, in various locales, indoors and outdoors, mostly in Birmingham and area, but also as far afield as London and Liverpool. Among the contemporary plays was Shaw's 1909 suffragette sketch *Press Cuttings* (performed on 25 February 1910), the first of Jackson's many productions of Shaw, and, in 1912, Shaw's *How He Lied to Her Husband*. Shake-speare, Beaumont and Fletcher, Fielding, Goldsmith, Wilde, St John Hankin, Drinkwater, and Jackson himself were other playwrights featured in the repertoire of the Pilgrim Players. It was, said a press release in December 1907, the company's intention to 'put before the Birmingham public such plays as cannot be seen in the ordinary way at theatres' (*Birmingham Post*, 6 December 1907, quoted by Trewin, *The Birmingham Repertory Theatre*, 9). For Jackson 'the ordinary way' meant both the usual light fare of commercial theatre and production values that sabotaged the directness and simplicity of presentation that he believed good plays needed and deserved.

The Pilgrim Players was an amateur company in that most of its members held regular daytime employment, but sometime around the end of 1909 Jackson persuaded Drinkwater to give up his insurance job to become the salaried secretary of the company, and during the 1910–11 season Jackson rented administrative offices for the company in Birmingham and began paying small salaries in recognition of the commitment its members were making. For the 1911–12 season the Pilgrim Players also began calling themselves the Birmingham Repertory Company. The next step was inevitable: the creation in Birmingham of a fully professional repertory theatre along the lines of those already established in Manchester (1907), Glasgow (1909), and Liverpool (1911).

Jackson took the plunge in June 1912 when he announced the purchase of a site for a new theatre in central Birmingham on the unlovely and prosaically named Station Street behind New Street Station, one of the city's two principal railway hubs. Construction began in October 1912, and the opening production of *Twelfth Night* in the 464-seat, steeply raked, quietly elegant theatre took place only four months later, on 15 February 1913. It was the formal beginning of what critic J.C. Trewin, who knew them all, called 'the leading Repertory Theatre of the twentieth century' (Trewin, *Birmingham Repertory Theatre*, xii).

Shaw was not among the celebrities at the opening night of the Birmingham Repertory Theatre, but he was sensitive to the import of the occasion. As a playwright he had already benefited significantly from, and contributed enormously to, a like venture undertaken by actor, playwright, and director Harley Granville Barker and theatre manager J.E. Vedrenne at the Court Theatre in London from 1904 to 1907. The

Birmingham Repertory Theatre will celebrate its hundredth anniversary in 2013, while the Barker/Vedrenne initiative at the Court lasted only three seasons. But Jackson and Barker (the artistic force behind the Court seasons, with Vedrenne providing sympathetic but cautious managerial acumen) had in common a commitment to art before commerce and an intense dedication to the plays of Bernard Shaw. While Barker and Vedrenne introduced to the theatre-going public challenging work from playwrights other than Shaw – Greek, European, and British – Shaw's plays dominated. Of the 988 performances in the Court enterprise, 701 were of plays by Shaw, ranging from eight for *The Man of Destiny* to 176 for *Man and Superman*. The Court seasons had given Shaw national prominence and laid the foundation for even greater national and international acclaim from subsequent plays such as *Fanny's First Play, Pygmalion, Saint Joan, Heartbreak House, Back to Methuselah*, and *The Apple Cart*. The Court seasons had also consolidated the close and mutually supportive friendship between Shaw and Barker, a friendship that was to remain close until ended by Barker's second marriage in 1918. The vacuum created, however, by the loss of Barker to American heiress Helen Huntington would be filled by Barry Jackson.

But not yet. The occasion that precipitated the friendship and collaboration between Bernard Shaw and Barry Jackson was the Birmingham Repertory Theatre production of *Back to Methuselah* in 1923, some ten years after the theatre's opening. Shaw may have known of Jackson, if only peripherally, through the Pilgrim Players' production of *Press Cuttings* in 1910 and *How He Lied to Her Husband* in 1912, and when the Repertory Theatre opened in 1913 Shaw wrote to Jackson to advise him against too rapid a turnover of plays in the repertory system, a mistake made, in Shaw's view, at the Court (Trewin, *Birmingham Repertory Theatre*, 18; the letter seems not to have survived). Shaw was perhaps aware as well that in an ode written by John Drinkwater to mark the opening of the theatre, 'Lines for the Opening of the Birmingham Repertory Theatre' (read from the stage by Barry Jackson), he (Shaw) was praised as 'the cleanser of our day/Whose art is both a Preface and a Play' (Drinkwater, 45). And during the decade that culminated with the *Methuselah* production, Jackson had selected at least one Shaw play every year for the BRT repertoire. Only Shakespeare could match that. Eleven Shaw plays were produced between 1913 and 1923, some more than once (there were six productions of *Candida*, four of *Arms and the Man*), and the production of *The Inca of Perusalem* on 7 October 1916, directed by John Drinkwater, was a world premiere.[2]

There were other world premieres in this first remarkable decade of the Birmingham Repertory Theatre – thirty-six of them; Drinkwater and John Masefield were particular favourites of Jackson. Further, there were eight British premieres, mainly of European writers – Chekhov, Tolstoy, Björnson, Andreyev. Remarkable too was Jackson's commitment to young actors, directors, and designers. Because no established star was going to leave London for a repertory season in Birmingham, Jackson found his own talent. In the early years he helped build the careers of designer Paul Shelving, and actors and directors such as Gwen Ffrangcon-Davies, Cedric Hardwicke, Felix Aylmer, and H.K. Ayliff. He cast a young Edith Evans in *Back to Methuselah*, and later in the 1920s he gave opportunities to unknowns such as Laurence Olivier and Ralph Richardson. Margaret Leighton, Peter Brook, Albert Finney, John Neville, Donald Pleasence, Paul Scofield, Derek Jacobi, Michael Langham – these and many more leading figures of twentieth-century British and international theatre were subsequently to be grateful to Barry Jackson and the Birmingham Repertory Theatre for believing in them at early and crucial stages of their careers.

So there were values and initiatives at the Birmingham Repertory Theatre in that first decade that would surely have met with Shaw's approval: risk-taking with new plays and playwrights; seeking out and supporting new theatrical talent; introducing audiences to challenging foreign works; placing artistic considerations above commercial return; and, of course, showing an obvious predilection for Shaw's plays. Moreover, in addition to his work in Birmingham, Jackson was making inroads into London theatre. One of the drawbacks of the repertory system, as Shaw and Granville Barker had found at the Court, was that successful productions had to be taken off even if there was still audience demand for them. Jackson's way of dealing with this was to move successful BRT productions to London for longer runs. Thus it was with Drinkwater's new play *Abraham Lincoln*, which opened at the BRT on 12 October 1918 and broke tradition by being allowed to run for a month (a week or two was the norm). Because of the likelihood of a continuing audience interest, Jackson (in a cooperative venture with Nigel Playfair, owner of the Lyric

Opera House, Hammersmith) moved the production to London, where it opened at the Lyric on 19 February 1919 and ran for an impressive (and lucrative) 466 performances. In 1922 Jackson took two more BRT productions to London: Rutland Boughton's *The Immortal Hour* (Regent Theatre, 13 October 1922), and his own children's play, *The Christmas Party* (Regent Theatre, 20 December 1922). Jackson continued this strategy throughout the 1920s and 1930s, but the lack of a permanent London base eventually made it uneconomical.[3]

There was plenty of evidence by 1923, then, albeit mostly focused on Birmingham, of Barry Jackson's accomplishments. Shaw had also gained some first-hand knowledge by a visit to the BRT in September 1916, when he saw Goldsmith's *The Good Natured Man* on the 19th, having attended a production of his own *Fanny's First Play* at the Theatre Royal the previous evening. He left Birmingham on the morning of 20 September without, somewhat surprisingly, meeting Jackson. Nor did Shaw attend the world premiere of *The Inca of Perusalem* three weeks later, though he was certainly aware of it (*Collected Letters*, III, 496). The first meeting between Shaw and Jackson did not in fact occur until 15 March 1923. Hubert Humphreys, a Birmingham resident and acquaintance of Shaw, saw and was impressed by the BRT production of *Heartbreak House*, which opened on 3 March 1923, directed by H.K. Ayliff. Humphreys had had several discussions with Shaw about the London production of *Heartbreak House* (Court Theatre, 18 October 1921), a production that had not been well received, closing after a disappointing sixty-three performances. Humphreys happened to see Shaw in London during the BRT run ('I accidentally met Shaw in the street') and 'went into ecstasies' over the Birmingham production, so much so that Shaw decided to see it for himself. He attended a matinee performance on 15 March, and that, according to Humphreys, 'was the first time Barry Jackson ever met him.'[4]

The credit for this first meeting between Shaw and Jackson may not, however, belong entirely to Hubert Humphreys. Four days after the BRT opening of *Heartbreak House* the theatre's general manager, Bache Matthews, sent Shaw copies of reviews and invited him to see the production. Shaw's secretary, Blanche Patch, replied on 10 March 1923, asking Matthews to reserve a ticket for Shaw for the March 15th matinee (Birmingham Central Library, MS 2129/4/1). Shaw's engagement diary

shows that he arrived by train in Birmingham (from London) that day
at 1:35 pm, saw the matinee at 2:30 pm, and took either a 6:00 or 6:20
pm train back to London.

Several years later, in 1938, Shaw gave his own account of that first
meeting with Barry Jackson. The chance meeting with Humphreys and
the letter from Matthews had been forgotten by now, as had his 1913 letter to Jackson about the repertory system. And while it was certainly true
that Jackson had indeed been producing Shaw's plays 'for years,' there
had been only one premiere (*The Inca of Perusalem*), not 'some.' Shaw's
memory, then, of his early relationship with Barry Jackson was a bit
shaky by 1938, but there is no reason to doubt the main features of
Shaw's recollection.

> I had written and published a play, or rather a cycle of five plays, called
> *Back to Methuselah*, in which I had discarded all thought of production until
> perhaps fifty years after my death in a theatre like the Festival Playhouse,
> which made Wagner's *Ring* possible at Bayreuth, should such a one be
> established in England. Meanwhile I was induced, on some pretext, to
> attend a performance at the Birmingham Repertory Theatre. Here, at the
> end of the performance [of *Heartbreak House*], I was accosted by a strange
> young man who seemed to have some grudge against me which good man-
> ners were obliging him to conceal. He said he was Barry Jackson. I had
> never heard of Barry Jackson, and possibly betrayed that fact unguardedly.
> I found out afterwards that he had been producing my plays for years, in
> some cases giving the first performance, only to see that distinction
> ascribed to others in my published records. My secretary had arranged all
> these exploits as a matter of routine without calling my attention to them.
>
> I felt my way cautiously, gathering that he had built the theatre and
> owned it, until he said that he wanted to produce *Methuselah*. I asked him
> was he mad. He intimated that though not sane enough to keep out of the-
> atre management he could manage more or less lucidly. I demanded fur-
> ther whether he wished his wife and children to die in the workhouse. He
> replied that he was not married.
>
> I began to scent a patron. 'How much a year are you out of pocket by this
> culture theatre of yours?' I said. He named an annual sum that would have
> sufficed to support fifty laborers and their families. I remarked that this was
> not more than it would cost him to keep a thousand ton steam yacht. He

said a theatre was better fun than a steam yacht, but said it in the tone of a
man who could afford a steam yacht.

That settled the matter. The impossible had become possible.[5]

Shaw's recollection of a quick settling of 'the matter' of a BRT production of *Methuselah* was confirmed many years later by Jackson. At some
point in the early 1950s (the date is uncertain) Jackson gave a lecture in
France about Shaw in which he said that once he had assured Shaw that
he had no financial worries Shaw gave permission to do *Methuselah* at
the BRT 'like a shot.'[6] It's a story with a good punch line, but it wasn't
quite like that. The conversation between Shaw and Jackson took place
on 15 March 1923. Some six weeks later, on 2 May 1923, Bache Matthews wrote to Shaw, clearly at Jackson's behest, to remind him of the
conversation and to repeat the request for permission to produce *Back
to Methuselah*. At the meeting with Jackson, Matthews pointed out to
Shaw, 'you did not give any definite reply, but as you did not refuse at
once, I venture to ask you the same question.' There must have been a
prompt and affirmative response this time, since on 5 May 1923 Matthews wrote again to Shaw, thanking him for 'your postcard of yesterday'
and saying that he would now send a copy of the play 'to the Censor and
when we get it through, if we do, I will get in touch with you again.'[7]

As it happened, there *were* a few problems with the censor (see Letter
1) as well as some difficulties in rehearsal caused by a difference of opinion between Shaw and Edith Evans about how the Serpent in Part I
should be played – Shaw wanting a property snake with the below-stage
voice of Edith Evans, Edith Evans wanting to be both voice *and* snake.
Ms Evans (supported by the director, H.K. Ayliff) had her way.[8]

In the end all went well, and for having made the impossible possible
Shaw remained forever grateful to Barry Jackson. From the stage of the
Birmingham Repertory Theatre on 12 October 1923, at the end of Part
V of *Back to Methuselah* (and the completion of the full cycle) Shaw
described the production of this play as 'the most extraordinary experience of my life ... perhaps the crown and climax of my career as a dramatic author' (Matthews, 110–11). It was also, to that point, the crown
and climax of Barry Jackson's career as a theatrical producer. Jackson,
like Shaw, was to go on to other triumphs, but it was his bold decision to
produce *Back to Methuselah* that gave the Birmingham Repertory The-

atre a profile and stature that set it apart from other repertory theatres in Britain, as well as according it an artistic credibility that no London theatre of the time could match.

That credibility, coupled with a need to generate more revenue than provided by the small size and challenging repertoire of the Repertory Theatre, encouraged Jackson to take more productions to London, including *Back to Methuselah* itself (Court Theatre, February 1924), followed by some fifty more over the next twelve years. The *Methuselah* production perhaps also gave Jackson the confidence to take further financial and artistic risks, such as continuing with the experiment he began in Birmingham just a few months before *Methuselah*, when, in April 1923, he mounted a modern-dress production of *Cymbeline*, directed by H.K. Ayliff and designed by Paul Shelving. The experiment heralded what theatre historian Claire Cochrane has called 'a radical psychological change in twentieth-century attitudes towards Shakespeare, which is still felt in present-day productions' (Cochrane, 3). In the case of *Cymbeline* the controversy generated by discarding traditionally costumed Shakespeare was tempered by the provincial Birmingham location, but two years later London felt the impact when Jackson opened his modern-dress *Hamlet* at the Kingsway Theatre (25 August 1925), again directed by Ayliff and designed by Shelving, with a relatively inexperienced BRT actor, Colin Keith-Johnston, as Hamlet. Other modern-dress Shakespeares followed, not all of them successful by any means. The BRT *Macbeth* (Court Theatre, 6 February 1928; BRT, 3 November 1928), directed and designed again by Ayliff and Shelving, was deemed a failure, caused as much by the shortcomings of Eric Maturin as Macbeth ('a pitiful and ridiculous performance,' according to Shaw: Letter 143) as by the design concept. Yet whatever the ups and downs of particular Jackson modern-dress Shakespeares the breakthrough had been made. It did not take long for other directors and producers to appreciate the benefits of modern-dress productions on uncluttered sets – which was, after all, as some critics pointed out, simply reverting to the Elizabethan way of doing things.

Perhaps the most significant outcome of the BRT *Methuselah* production, however, was the bond of trust it created between Jackson and Shaw. Shaw's respect for Jackson is demonstrated by his proposing a knighthood for Jackson in 1924. In his letter advocating the honour,

Shaw praises Jackson's accomplishments at the Birmingham Repertory Theatre: 'He has revived everything in the opera and drama of the 17th and 18th centuries that had been forgotten by the ordinary theatres and that is still full of life; and besides this he has experimented freely and boldly with modern work which no commercial manager would touch, and carried it to such success that he has been able to bring it to London.' This work, Shaw continued, 'has been done for its own sake at great labor and expense, and with the foregone certainty that its profits would be purely public and cultural, and its losses personal, pecuniary, and considerable ... [I]t is the duty of the Government to give official recognition of the public gain, and official encouragement to others to face the same loss, by conferring an appropriate honor on one who has set so valuable an example.' The recognition was doubly appropriate, Shaw argued, because it would also acknowledge other theatrical accomplishments in the provinces: '[I]t is now evident that the work of Mr Barry Jackson, even more than that of Miss Horniman in Manchester, Lady Gregory in Dublin, and Mr Archibald Flower in Stratford-on-Avon, has carried the British Drama and the British theatre forward with a rush while London has been marking time or creeping forward timidly in the footsteps of others.'[9]

In view of later tensions between Jackson and the Flower family, benefactors of the Shakespeare Festival in Stratford-upon-Avon, Shaw's associating Jackson with Flower was ironic, but that problem was twenty years ahead, and for now Jackson could enjoy the honour of being Sir Barry. He may or may not have known that Shaw was largely responsible for the knighthood that was officially announced on 3 June 1925; Shaw's initiative is not mentioned by either of them in the extant correspondence.

The bond between Shaw and Jackson grew rapidly in the 1920s. There was continued public acclaim for Jackson's achievements, but running the BRT, together with London productions, wasn't all smooth sailing. Only two letters from Jackson to Shaw from the 1920s have survived, but there are several from Shaw to Jackson, as well as a number from Charlotte Shaw to Jackson, that reveal that the pressures on Jackson were considerable. These surfaced publicly in 1924 when, only a few weeks after the elation of the *Methuselah* premiere, Jackson announced that he was closing the Birmingham Repertory Theatre at the end of the 1923–4 season because of lack of support from the Birmingham public.

According to Trewin (*Birmingham Repertory Theatre*, 78), attendance at Georg Kaiser's *Gas* in November 1923 averaged only 109 a night, 'fewer than those engaged in the performance and the business of the theatre.' The crisis was averted by a commitment from 4000 subscribers for the 1924–5 season (ibid., 82), but the economics of running a small theatre in an industrial city that was intensely sceptical about the value of the arts was an ongoing worry for Jackson, despite his personal wealth. He carried on subsidizing the Rep for another ten years, but then, in 1934, having lost in all some £100,000, he called it a day. A fund-raising appeal brought in only £3000 of a £20,000 target, and in January 1935 Jackson handed over ownership and management of the Birmingham Repertory Theatre to a board of trustees – but with himself as governing director. This arrangement meant, in effect, that Jackson was relieved of financial responsibility for the theatre, but retained full artistic authority for the rest of his life.

During the thirty-seven years (1913–50) of Shaw's lifetime that Jackson controlled the Birmingham Repertory Theatre, years marked from Jackson's point of view by despondency and frustration as well as by triumph and satisfaction, Shaw, as the correspondence in this collection attests, was ever ready to advise, support, and criticize Jackson and to discuss, debate, lecture, harangue, and argue about matters theatrical – finances, Sunday openings, entertainment tax, amateurs and professionals, audience behaviour, and, naturally, Jackson's productions of Shaw's own plays. These productions continued steadily; there were very few Shawless seasons at the BRT under Jackson, and there might have been more distinction still for Jackson had he not turned down a chance to produce the British premiere of *Saint Joan* (see Letter 7) and if Shaw had not thoughtlessly given the rights for the first licensed performance in England of *Mrs Warren's Profession* to another producer (Letter 13).

Barry Jackson was unfailingly modest and self-effacing about his achievements at the Birmingham Repertory Theatre. 'Of the why and wherefore of the Birmingham Repertory Theatre, it is impossible to say much. In the world of art things happen, and that is the beginning and the end' (Matthews, xii). Well, not quite. It has been left to others to assess the importance of what Jackson accomplished at the BRT. Many tributes came, as they are wont to do, after Jackson's death, but one of the simplest and most telling was given directly to Jackson while he was still alive to appreciate it. It came from playwright James Bridie (O.H. Mavor). As war in Europe was becoming imminent in 1938, Bridie wrote to Jackson on the occasion of the twenty-fifth anniversary of the Birmingham Repertory Theatre: 'If we are to be bombed, a thorough razing from Piccadilly Circus to Drury Lane and down to the Strand would do less harm to the Theatre than one bomb on Station Street, Birmingham.'[10] As it happened, the BRT, unlike many of its London counterparts, escaped serious bomb damage (see Letter 114), and apart from a one-year hiatus, stayed open throughout the war.

Barry Jackson founded the Birmingham Repertory Theatre before he even met Shaw, and Shaw played no direct part in helping or persuading him to keep it open when the end looked close in 1924 and, again, in 1934 (Letter 60). There was, nonetheless, some considerable reassurance for Jackson in knowing of Shaw's respect and admiration for what he was doing at the BRT, and some comfort in having Shaw as a trusted confidant when he needed one. And for Shaw, Jackson could be relied on not only to produce his plays with integrity and enthusiasm, but also to continue to set the best example there was in England of enlightened artistic patronage.

Jackson and Shaw, then, were good for each other as far as the Birmingham Repertory Theatre and the London spin-offs were concerned. It was a mutually supportive and beneficial relationship. It was not, however, the kind of relationship that Shaw had enjoyed with Granville Barker at the Court, each inspiring the other to accomplishments that they could not have achieved separately. That kind of partnership between Shaw and Jackson did not materialize until Jackson embarked on his second great theatrical adventure, the Malvern Festival, and this time Shaw was at his side from the beginning. That beginning was a suggestion made by Jackson to Shaw in Jackson's home town of Malvern, Worcestershire, in 1928 (see Letter 27) at a time when both men were in the theatrical doldrums.

The Malvern Festival

Shaw's only play since the production of *Back to Methuselah* had been *Saint Joan*, written in 1923, and performed in New York in December 1923 and in London in March 1924, to great acclaim. Thereafter silence, theatrically speaking, for five years. There were numerous revivals of his plays around the world, especially in celebration of his seventieth birthday in 1926, but no new play. Shaw was busy with various projects, particularly *The Intelligent Woman's Guide to Socialism and Capitalism*, published in June 1928, as well as accepting the Nobel Prize for Literature in 1925 (but not the money) and declining a knighthood in 1926. But the inspiration and motivation to write for the theatre again were missing.

For his part Barry Jackson was continuing to present an eclectic program at the Birmingham Repertory Theatre and to seek opportunities for London transfers, some of which achieved considerable commercial success – Eden Phillpotts's comedy *The Farmer's Wife*, for example, ran at the Court Theatre (where it opened on 11 March 1924) for an astonishing 1329 performances. Jackson also continued to seek and find young talented actors; in the BRT's 1927 modern-dress production of *All's Well That Ends Well*, Parolles was played by Laurence Olivier. All was not well, however, with Jackson. In a letter to Shaw on 8 June 1928 (Letter 24) he bemoaned the state of British theatre, particularly its being 'absolutely permeated with purely financial interests,' and worried again that the Birmingham Repertory Theatre would have to close. In his reply (Letter 25) Shaw offered little consolation. After rehearsing a series of problems and unlikely solutions, he concluded, 'It is no use: I give up.'

In the summer of 1928, then, Barry Jackson had grave doubts that he could continue – or *wanted* to continue – his work at the Birmingham Repertory Theatre and in London, and Bernard Shaw seemed to have abandoned playwriting. They both needed some kind of stimulus to regenerate their theatrical batteries. The stimulus was the Malvern Festival.

In an article on the Festival in the New York magazine *Theatre Arts Monthly* (March 1931) Jackson described for American theatre-goers – he was always eager to attract visitors from North America – how the Malvern Festival came about. Regular theatre-going, he argued, in an urban setting of 'a bustling city,' after an 'exhausting day,' did not allow for full appreciation of the 'beautiful thing' that drama is, or should be. The Greeks, Jackson argued, had made 'enjoyment of the drama ... a basic part of life.' While that ideal might no longer be attainable, drama might still, he hoped, 'be made a central part of at any rate holiday life,' especially in an attractive town and area such as Malvern ('a veritable gem'). Jackson had, then, the concept – immersion in drama for a week or more in the summer; he had the setting, Malvern, which was also, fortuitously, where he lived; he had access to a theatre – the 900-seat Malvern Theatre in the centre of town; and he had the playwright around whose work the Festival would be built – Bernard Shaw: '[I]t was admiration and reverence for his work that largely inspired the whole conception of the Malvern Festival.' Thus, despite his concerns over financial losses in Birmingham and London, Jackson did not hesitate to come up with the necessary funding.

In association with Roy Limbert, lessee of the Malvern Theatre (an association that would gradually sour), the first Malvern Festival,[11] which lasted two weeks, opened on 19 August 1929 with the British premiere of Shaw's *The Apple Cart*, directed by BRT stalwart H.K. Ayliff, with another BRT stalwart, Cedric Hardwicke, as King Magnus. The conversations Shaw had had with Jackson the previous summer about what Shaw thought of as 'the Malvern Bühnenfestspiel' (after Bayreuth – with himself as Richard Wagner) had inspired him, at last, to write another play. By mid-November 1928 he told Jackson ('you ought to be the first to know') that he had completed 'the first two acts of a five act play' (Letter 27) and on 6 January 1929 (Letter 29) Charlotte excitedly reported to Jackson that the play was finished: 'I myself think that as a successor to St Joan it is as good as it could possibly be.' Shaw, too, was again excited about the production of a new play, so excited in fact that he couldn't wait until the following August for the Malvern production and instead gave the world premiere, without consulting Jackson, and much to Jackson's chagrin, to the Teatr Polski in Warsaw, where it opened (in Polish) on 14 June 1929.

Still, the irritation that Jackson felt about what he considered to be a serious discourtesy on Shaw's part did not impede the development of the Malvern Festival or Shaw's new enthusiasm and energy for playwriting. Jackson mounted (and funded) nine Malvern Festivals, of increasing length and variety (concerts, lectures, films, exhibitions, social events), from 1929 to 1937. The 1929 program was Shaw and nothing but Shaw, and although there were no more all-Shaw programs, his plays were absent only in 1931 and 1933. After Jackson dropped the Festival it was continued to the outbreak of war by Roy Limbert, and for one season (1949) after the war, again directed by Limbert. Limbert included Shaw in all three of his seasons.

Including *The Apple Cart* and *Shakes versus Shav*, a puppet play, the Malvern Festival produced seven Shaw British premieres, of which two (*Geneva*, 1938, and *In Good King Charles's Golden Days*, 1939) were also world premieres. Jackson was directly responsible for the premieres of *The Apple Cart* (1929), *Too True to be Good* (1932), and *The Simpleton of the Unexpected Isles* (1935), and although Limbert was in charge of Malvern for *Geneva*, Shaw began the play in February 1936 and told Jackson about it before he had even started writing ('Tomorrow I intend to begin a new play in the [Panama] Canal without the faintest notion of what it is about': Letter 82). Even for *Buoyant Billions*, produced at Malvern (British premiere, 1949) *twelve* years after Jackson's last Festival, it was from Jackson that Shaw sought advice: 'Read it and tell me whether I ought to burn it or not. At 90 I cannot trust my own judgment. Certainly not Limbert's, for he must take anything he gets' (Letter 153).

Of the fourteen plays that Shaw wrote after the five-year hiatus that followed *Saint Joan*, seven, as we have seen, premiered at Malvern. Jackson did early productions of two others at Malvern (*On the Rocks*, 1936, and *The Millionairess*, 1937), and all of the remaining five (*Village Wooing*, *The Six of Calais*, *Cymbeline Refinished*, *Farfetched Fables*, and *Why She Would Not*) were discussed in one way or another with Jackson, often before anyone else got to hear of them. 'Tell Barry Jackson – but no-one else,' he instructed his secretary, Blanche Patch, while on his 1932–3 world cruise, 'that I am now well into a more considerable political play [*On the Rocks*] ...' (see headnote to Letter 51), and in one of the last letters that Shaw wrote he told Jackson of another play, *Why She Would Not*, 'a pitiful senile squeak,' 'provoked,' he said, by Jackson (Letter 182).

The relationship, then, between Jackson and Shaw during and after the Malvern years went much beyond the usual producer/playwright professional business necessities of the kind that Shaw conducted with Limbert and someone like Charles Macdona (frequently referred to by Shaw in his letters to Jackson). To a large extent, Barry Jackson was the *raison d'être* for Shaw the playwright in the last two decades of Shaw's life. As with Harley Granville Barker at the Court, Shaw was intensely engaged with Jackson at Malvern in the business of creating good theatre, and good theatre for its own sake, for there was nothing in these last plays that made easy watching (quite the contrary), and certainly no money in them for Jackson. Furthermore, just as at the Court Shaw did not restrict himself to the role of playwright, at Malvern too he immersed himself in the production process, attending (and frequently taking over) rehearsals, and discussing with Jackson (and often disagreeing with him) textual revisions, program notes, the role of the press, play selection ('Volpone is a filthy cruel play ... curiously unreadable ... but on the stage it has terrific vitality that forbids one to bury it': Letter 69), and casting (witness the prolonged efforts to find the right Joan for the 1936 Malvern *Saint Joan*: Letters 78–91, *passim*).

That Barry Jackson was the inspiration for Shaw to return to playwriting in 1928 after five years of inactivity is indisputable. It may seem farfetched (to borrow a word from Shaw) to claim that without Jackson Shaw's last play would have been *Saint Joan*. But in the absence of Harley Granville Barker it is hard to know who else in England could have stimulated and sustained Shaw's renewed theatrical energy.

For Jackson there was the satisfaction of creating at Malvern a theatrical milieu quite different from anything that had been attempted before in England. Unlike the nominal festival at nearby Stratford-upon-Avon, the Malvern Festival celebrated innovation and experiment, not just with Shaw, but with the whole range of English drama. There is palpable excitement, for example, in Jackson's claim in the *Theatre Arts Monthly* article quoted above that 'there is no one alive who has witnessed all the plays to be performed at the next [1931] Malvern Festival.' The plays ranged from an anonymous Tudor play through Nicholas Udall, Thomas Heywood, George Etherege, Sheridan, and Bulwer Lytton to James Bridie.

Summer festivals of eclectic theatrical fare, albeit usually more timid fare than Malvern typically offered, are now commonplace. Like modern-dress Shakespeare, they began with Barry Jackson.

Jackson seems to have been at his happiest, artistically and socially, at each summer's Malvern Festival. He enjoyed seeing the fruits of his adventurous programming, and he revelled in the company of Shaw and other arts luminaries – Edward Elgar, Laura Knight, J.B. Priestley, James Bridie, and many more (he rented a local girls' school to accommodate his many guests, though the Shaws stayed at a local hotel). According to critic George W. Bishop, a Festival regular, Shaw too was at his happiest in Malvern: 'He climbed the hills and swam in the pool, he wandered about snapping members of the company with his miniature camera, he went to the garden parties, and on most evenings he was at the theatre, sitting with Mrs. Shaw in the seats reserved for him in the centre of the dress circle' (Bishop, *My Betters*, 109). At the start, money didn't matter, and Jackson also put to one side the difficult working relationship with, in Jackson's view, a plebeian Roy Limbert and municipal politicians and local residents who didn't entirely embrace Jackson's cultural commitment to Malvern. As the losses piled up in Birmingham, however, Jackson began to seek help, and at the end of the 1936 Festival he told the Malvern Urban District Council that he had lost £800 in that season alone and was not prepared to continue without some guarantee against the loss as well as improvements to the theatre (adequate air conditioning, among other things). The result was an immediate row with Limbert and no subsidy from the Council (Elkins, 131–4). Jackson carried on for one final season of intriguing eclecticism (discussed with Shaw in Letters 95–7) and then, with considerable and understandable bitterness – some of it directed towards Shaw for maintaining his Malvern involvement (Letter 101) – left it all to Limbert. With the help of two Shaw world premieres Limbert kept going until 1939, but struggled against ongoing municipal parsimony when he tried to revive the Festival after the war (Letters 167, 175, 176). He succeeded – again with the help of a Shaw premiere (*Buoyant Billions*) – in 1949, but that proved to be the last of the Malvern Festivals as Barry Jackson had conceived them.

At the end of the 1937 Malvern Festival Jackson left for a much-needed vacation in Russia. Shaw gave him some advice about what to see there and assured him that 'the heat of a Russian summer will wipe away all Malvern's tears' (Letter 99). On his return, Jackson's theatrical agenda was relatively uncluttered: no Malvern, no London productions. The Birmingham Repertory Theatre could have his full attention, which it did, in a relatively routine way, throughout 1938 and 1939 ('routine' meant that there were ten new plays produced at the BRT in these two years).

The outbreak of war in September 1939 caused an immediate, but brief, closing of all theatres in Britain (a 'dastardly funk,' Shaw fumed: Letter 108), and then the BRT had to adjust to presenting plays in a city that was a prime bombing target and to doing so with a company whose human resources were depleted by war service. As the bombing intensified in the autumn of 1940 (including a raid on 24 October that destroyed the theatre's major storage facility) and audiences dwindled, Jackson found it impossible to continue and the theatre closed in December 1940. 'We stuck it out for eighteen months and then had to give in,' Jackson told playwright St John Ervine. 'With diabolical ingenuity Hitler arranged a coup to coincide with every first night; this with the black out, the evacuation and ever growing staff difficulties made conditions anything but easy.'[12] The last play performed before the closure was *Pygmalion.*

The Birmingham Repertory Theatre reopened a year later with a resident company run by Basil Langton, and Jackson's own BRT company started up again in November 1942. There were fewer new plays at the Rep during the war, but Shaw remained in the repertoire with *Heartbreak House* (1943), *You Never Can Tell,* and *Getting Married* (1944), and *Man and Superman* (1945). Shaw and Charlotte retreated from London to their country home in Ayot St Lawrence, from where they both (sometimes aided and abetted by Blanche Patch) regaled Jackson with war stories (they were not entirely safe from enemy action even in the Hertfordshire countryside), and Shaw expounded upon sundry matters theatrical, including the BRT productions of his plays.

Jackson and Charlotte Shaw corresponded regularly from the time of the 1923 production of *Back to Methuselah* at the Birmingham Repertory Theatre until her death in 1943. Only a small portion of that correspondence can be included in this edition, but these letters chart the growth of a relationship that is interesting in its own right and also shed valuable light on the Jackson–Shaw relationship. At times Charlotte simply deals with the routine logistics of daily life: arranging tickets for Jackson to see *Saint Joan* (Letter 10) or asking him for Malvern tickets for friends such as T.E. Lawrence (Letter 36). Or she reports to Jackson on things domestic (holidays in Yugoslavia, Letter 36, or the difficulties of securing Shavian food in wartime, Letter 115: '[A]ll the articles of food G.B.S. likes best are gradually disappearing, & I feel at this rate he will disappear too!'). But, more importantly, she engages, sometimes on Shaw's behalf, sometimes independently, in discussion of matters theatrical: Jackson's fascinatingly entitled play *The Marvellous History of Saint Ber-*

nard (Letter 15); a possible London production of Sean O'Casey's *Juno and the Paycock* (Letter 19); Sunday opening of theatres (on which she supported Jackson against Shaw, Letter 114). When Charlotte died on 12 September 1943 Shaw sent Jackson a note (Letter 135) telling him, 'You were – and are – one of her special friends.'

Charlotte, then, played an important role in sustaining the Shaw–Jackson relationship for some twenty years. She did not live, however, to witness the third phase of the relationship: Jackson's controversial term as director of the Shakespeare Memorial Theatre at Stratford-upon-Avon.

Stratford-upon-Avon

There have been various accounts of Barry Jackson's work at Stratford, but none has recognized Shaw's behind-the-scenes, multifaceted role as adviser, badgerer, consoler, and confidant to Jackson as he battled entrenched interests at a moribund institution, eventually being ousted by forces that could muster more guile than Jackson was capable of.

The first Shakespeare Memorial Theatre opened at Stratford-upon-Avon in 1879, but was destroyed by fire in 1926. A new theatre (still in use, though much renovated) opened on the same site on Shakespeare's birthday in 1932. The new theatre and its summer Shakespearean Festival season were directed by William Bridges-Adams (a BRT alumnus) until 1934, when he was succeeded by Ben Iden Payne. Payne kept the theatre and the Festival running during the early years of the war before being succeeded for brief periods by Milton Rosmer (1943) and Robert Atkins (1944–6).

The Shakespeare Memorial Theatre was overseen by a large board of governors, many of whom were only marginally involved. Authority rested mainly with a smaller executive group, chaired from 1879 by a member of the Flower family, whose generosity towards the theatre (they donated the site for the 1879 building and continued to be major patrons) was made possible by their successful brewing business in Stratford-upon-Avon. Archibald Flower was chair of the Governing Council from 1903; he was succeeded in 1944 by his son, Lieutenant Colonel Fordham Flower. By then, the reputation and relevance of the Shakespeare Memorial Theatre was, by general consensus within the profession and with the critics, at a low ebb, though its finances were in good shape. The money was there, but it was not being spent to improve the inadequate theatre facilities or to boost the quality of Shakespearean production – quality, such as it was, 'buried in deadly sentimentality and complacent worthiness,' as Peter Brook put it (Trewin, *Peter Brook*, 24).

It was to the credit of Fordham Flower and his colleagues that they saw the necessity for change at the SMT, and the announcement in October 1945 that Barry Jackson would become director for the 1946 season was widely welcomed. Jackson's experience and accomplishments at Birmingham and Malvern were seen as exactly the right prerequisites for new leadership at Stratford, leadership that would, it was hoped, give Stratford the kind of national and international prominence that hitherto had escaped it. Jackson, somewhat surprisingly, had not consulted Shaw about the appointment; Shaw learned of it from the press (Letter 142). Perhaps this explains the rather prickly nature of their correspondence in the early months of Jackson's appointment. Fending off Shaw, however – including his efforts to have his own work performed in the Stratford winter season: 'As the modern Shakespear I consider that a season of Shaw plays in the off season should be a permanent feature there,' he later told Jackson (Letter 177) – provoked Jackson into articulating very clearly his priorities for reform. These included administrative restructuring that gave Jackson control of the Memorial Theatre year-round (not just for the summer Festival as had previously been the case); programming changes that staggered opening nights throughout the summer season rather than crowding them all into the opening week; using more than one director for the season; undertaking repair and renovation to the physical fabric and production facilities of the Memorial Theatre; and – Jackson's Birmingham hallmark – attracting new talent to Stratford, including the likes of Peter Brook and Anthony Quayle (Quayle's presence subsequently becoming a source of great distress to Jackson). To accomplish all this meant spending money and, for the first time in Stratford's history, running a deficit. While Jackson's reforms succeeded in revitalizing Stratford and attracting increased critical and public interest, the 'Old Gang' (Letter 169) of the Governing Council were unhappy with the pace, cost, and depth of the reforms. Jackson's problems were compounded, moreover, by an uncomfortable personal relationship with the Council's chairman,

Fordham Flower, a relationship about which neither spoke publicly but that was complicated not only by Jackson's uncompromising commitment to reform but also by his discreet but widely known homosexuality. (When Peter Brook dined with Jackson and his partner Scott Sunderland in Birmingham in 1945 he described them as 'an old married couple' [Brook, 35].)

Shaw's involvement in Jackson's problems at Stratford began in December 1947 when Jackson asked Shaw for 'a word of advice' about his contract (Letter 160), which was to end in October 1948. There followed six months of private and public controversy about Jackson's appointment, culminating in an announcement on 11 June 1948 that Jackson would be replaced as director of the Shakespeare Memorial Theatre by Anthony Quayle who, apart from his theatrical experience, had also, like Flower, a military background – and was a married man (twice). Shaw, now ninety-one years old, was ready to do battle in the press on Jackson's behalf, but Jackson preferred to keep his sense of grievance private, using Shaw, rather, as a friend who would listen sympathetically to his version of the events that led to his dismissal.

There is a remarkable frankness in Jackson's letters to Shaw at this period, a frankness not only about the Stratford debacle, but also about the Malvern Festival (Letters 166, 175). These letters document for the first time Jackson's deep distress over the ways in which his association with Malvern and Stratford ended. They also supplement and, in some instances, challenge existing accounts of why Jackson behaved as he did. What has been described, for example, as Jackson's 'hasty resignation' from Stratford (Beauman, 187) was in fact no more than a straightforward and considered statement that the executive committee of the Governing Council had decided not to extend his contract (Letter 163). Jackson's letter to Shaw following the announcement of Quayle's appointment (Letter 173) is particularly important in giving Jackson's version of the events that led up to that announcement. In all of this unpleasantness Shaw did his best to keep Jackson's spirits up: 'No man,' he told Jackson, 'has less reason to look back on his life as wasted' (Letter 176). Shaw's career was not over, and he wanted to make sure that Jackson's did not come to a premature end. Shaw would have liked Jackson to return to the Malvern Festival, but he was realistic enough to know that that would not happen. What Jackson needed and got from

Shaw was the encouragement to return to the Birmingham Repertory Theatre with a fresh sense of purpose – the prospect of a new municipal theatre (Letter 174), a prospect that Jackson tirelessly pursued but, sadly, did not live to see fulfilled.

When Harley Granville Barker died Shaw wrote an appreciation in the *Times Literary Supplement* (7 September 1946) in which he quoted a remark by Granville Barker to the effect that Shaw and Barker's father were the same age (see notes to Letter 146). Just over two weeks after the *TLS* article was published Shaw wrote to Jackson in Stratford-upon-Avon about a disagreement they were having over off-season availability of the Shakespeare Memorial Theatre (Letter 149). In the letter Shaw tells Jackson, 'Keep your eye on your father and he'll pull you through.' Shaw as a father figure to both Harley Granville Barker and Barry Vincent Jackson is an arresting thought. Jackson was never to Shaw the 'beautiful young genius' that he dubbed Barker (Letter 25). Still, the almost thirty years of correspondence in this collection make an impressive case for seeing Jackson – this 'quiet Coriolanus' of the British theatre, as J.C. Trewin perceptively called him (*Birmingham Repertory Theatre*, 82) – as an equally creative and inspiring partner and progeny.

Notes

1 In the personal papers of Barry Jackson in the Birmingham Central Library (MS 978/2) there is part of a program for this production, annotated (in an unknown hand) 'the first Shaw play Sir Barry ever saw.'

2 Shaw was not publicly acknowledged as the author of *The Inca of Perusalem*, playbills referring to the author only as 'a member of the Royal Society of Literature.' Nor did the Birmingham critics seem to catch on to the author's identity.

3 There is a full listing of Jackson's London productions in Trewin, *The Birmingham Repertory Theatre*, 241–3, and extended commentary on many of the productions can be found in G.W. Bishop, *Barry Jackson and the London Theatre* (London: Arthur Barker, 1933). Bishop's book is handsomely illustrated (in colour) with Paul Shelving's designs for Jackson's productions.

4 Typewritten note, undated, from Hubert Humphreys to Dan H. Laurence; private collection of Dan H. Laurence.

5 Birmingham Repertory Theatre, 25th anniversary souvenir program (1938), 6–7.
6 The transcript of the lecture (undated) is in the Birmingham Central Library, MS 2129/1/3.
7 Shaw's postcard has been lost, but copies of the Matthews letters are in the Birmingham Central Library, MS 2129/4/1.
8 See *Collected Letters*, III, 845–8. Edith Evans and Ayliff both wrote to Shaw on 4 September 1923, Evans reporting that she was 'almost broken-hearted' by Shaw's preference, and Ayliff reporting 'severe attacks of discouragement' (British Library, Add MSS 50519 ff. 50–2). The British Library attributes the Ayliff letter (which is unsigned) to Jackson, but the letter goes into the kind of production detail that is more likely to have been in Ayliff's domain. Another copy of the letter is at Hofstra University, where it is attributed to Ayliff (*Collected Letters*, III, 847).
9 Shaw to Lady Lavery, 10 December 1924, Cambridge University Library, MS Baldwin 159 f.256.
10 Birmingham Central Library, MS 978/74, 21 January 1938.
11 The 'Malvern Festival' was the accepted name, but the 'Shaw Festival' was also used. Shaw noted in his engagement diary on 19 August 1929 that 'the Shaw Festival opens,' and while the 1929 souvenir program is headed 'Malvern Festival,' the individual play programs are headed 'Shaw Festival.'
12 Letter from Barry Jackson to St John Ervine, 25 January [?1947], HRC.

Sources for Introduction and Letter Notes

Beauman, Sally. *The Royal Shakespeare Company: A History of Ten Decades.* Oxford: Oxford University Press, 1982.
Bishop, G.W. *Barry Jackson and the London Theatre.* London: Arthur Baker, 1933.
– *My Betters.* London: Heinemann, 1957.
Brook, Peter. *Threads of Time.* London: Methuen, 1998.
Cochrane, Claire. *Shakespeare and the Birmingham Repertory Theatre 1913–1929.* London: Society for Theatre Research, 1993.
Collected Letters. Bernard Shaw: Collected Letters. Edited by Dan H. Laurence. 4 vols. London: Reinhardt, 1965–88.
Drinkwater, John. *Poems 1908–1914.* London: Sidgwick & Jackson, 1917.
Elkins, Dennis R. 'Sir Barry Jackson: The Definitive Amateur of the English Theatre.' PhD thesis, University of Colorado, 1993.

Mander, Raymond, and Joe Mitchenson. *Theatrical Companion to Shaw.* London: Rockliff, 1955.

Matthews, Bache. *A History of the Birmingham Repertory Theatre.* London: Chatto & Windus, 1924.

Trewin, J.C. *Peter Brook: A Biography.* London: Macdonald, 1971.

– *The Birmingham Repertory Theatre 1913–1963.* London: Barrie and Rockliff, 1963.

Weiss, Samuel A. *Bernard Shaw's Letters to Siegfried Trebitsch.* Stanford, CA: Stanford University Press, 1986.

Other Sources

Many other sources, Shavian and non-Shavian, printed and in manuscript, have been consulted during the preparation of this edition. Several are cited in the headnotes or notes to the letters, but I do as well want particularly to acknowledge the guidance and insights gained from previous editions in this Shaw Correspondence series: *Bernard Shaw and H.G. Wells,* edited by J. Percy Smith (1995); *Bernard Shaw Theatrics,* edited by Dan H. Laurence (1995); and *Bernard Shaw and Gabriel Pascal,* edited by Bernard F. Dukore (1996). T.C. Kemp's *Birmingham Repertory Theatre,* 2nd ed. (Birmingham: Cornish Bros., 1948) has to some extent been superseded by J.C. Trewin's history of the BRT (above), but is still helpful, as is Dorothy Laming's 1970 Ohio State University MA thesis, 'Sir Barry Jackson: The Malvern Festival (1929–1937).' Vivian Elliot's article 'Genius Loci: The Malvern Festival Tradition,' in *SHAW: The Annual of Bernard Shaw Studies* 3 (1983), 191–218, is a useful survey of the main theatrical and social features of the Festival. Michael Holroyd's biography *Bernard Shaw* (5 vols, London: Chatto & Windus, 1988–92) has been an invaluable source of information, and it would have been impossible to provide detailed information on London productions of Shaw and other playwrights without the huge scholarly achievement of J.P. Wearing's multivolume *London Stage* calendars, 1890–1959 (Metuchen, NJ: Scarecrow Press, 1976–93). Dan Laurence's splendid two-volume *Bernard Shaw: A Bibliography* (Oxford: Clarendon Press, 1983), together with the supplement published in *SHAW: The Annual of Bernard Shaw Studies* 20 (2000), has made it possible to provide relevant bibliographical details and to identify a number of ephemeral newspaper articles. Among manuscript sources, Shaw's engagement diaries and business papers held at the British Library of Political and Economic Science are extremely helpful for locating Shaw's meetings and travels and for tracking productions of his plays and his royalty income.

Editor's Note

The letters collected here do not by any means cover the full range of the interests and accomplishments of either of the correspondents. There were many aspects of Shaw's professional life that Jackson was not involved in, and some of Jackson's activities are barely mentioned by Shaw – more likely, though, because letters have been lost than because of a lack of interest from Shaw. Jackson's two visits to Canada, for example (on a 1929 lecture tour, and then with a full production company in 1931–2) do not feature prominently in this collection. Nor does Jackson's pioneering series of radio broadcasts from a studio at the Birmingham Repertory Theatre, beginning in November 1931 with Irene Vanbrugh in A.A. Milne's *Mr Pim Passes By* and later including transmissions to Canada, South Africa, and Australia. Given Shaw's fascination with radio it is hard to imagine that he took no interest in this important initiative by Jackson. Most of the letters address professional matters, either ones immediately to hand or ones of a more generic kind. It is Charlotte's letters – and Blanche Patch's too – that often introduce issues of a more intimate and domestic nature, but Shaw's whimsy, especially about the Ayot acorns (Letters 62, 65, 93, 94, 100), is a welcome break from heavier subjects.

Of the 183 letters included in this collection, only two have been previously published (Letters 24 and 25). A few of the letters have long been available in collections in the British Library (111, 120, 140), the British Theatre Museum (1), and the University of Texas at Austin (64), but the bulk of them, 176, were acquired by the Birmingham Central Library in 1998 from the estate of Tom English, Jackson's secretary at the time of his death, and form an appropriate complement to the archives of the Birmingham Repertory Theatre already held by the Library. Barry Jackson corresponded regularly with Shaw for nearly thirty years. He kept the letters he received from Shaw, and he also kept drafts, typed copies, or carbon copies of letters he wrote to Shaw. All but a few inconsequential pieces of this correspondence are published here. There are 120 letters from Shaw to Jackson, 35 from Jackson to Shaw. The imbalance is probably explained in part by Shaw's epistolary energy and in part by Jackson's taking more care to save Shaw's part of the correspondence than his own. Even so, it is clear from references in the extant correspondence and from significant gaps in the chronology, that many letters on both sides have been lost, though it is sometimes possible to reconstruct the content of missing letters. Jackson also corresponded frequently with Shaw's wife, Charlotte, and, to a lesser extent, with Blanche Patch, Shaw's secretary. He preserved much of that correspondence as well, though not, apparently, copies of his letters to them. Seventeen letters from Charlotte Shaw to Jackson, and nine from Blanche Patch are here published for the first time. They all provide, I believe, interesting and unique insights into the professional and personal lives of Shaw and Jackson. The views of both women also have their own considerable intrinsic interest and value.

Jackson's side of the correspondence is mostly typed, and his handwriting does not, in any case, provide significant difficulties. Shaw sometimes wrote his letters in longhand, sometimes had his secretary type them from his shorthand, and sometimes typed them himself. Again, no particular difficulties of transcription arise, though as Shaw got older his typing got shakier and handwritten corrections are frequent. I have maintained the idiosyncrasies of Shaw's spelling ('Shakespear') and punctuation ('musnt'), and have used the intrusive *sic* as sparingly as possible. Any editorial conjecture is given in square brackets. In a very few instances I have silently corrected obvious typographical errors, and I have occasionally omitted material of peripheral interest in letters of Charlotte Shaw and Blanche Patch to Jackson; ellipses mark such omissions.

The letters are printed in chronological sequence, with headnotes providing both the context for each letter and a connecting narrative. Notes at the end of each letter identify people mentioned in the letters, as well as clarifying various theatrical, historical, political, literary, and other references and allusions. The subject of each such annotation is given in boldface type. I have attempted to make the notes as complete as possible, but in a few instances I have, reluctantly, had to concede defeat. As with previous volumes in this series, certain features of the letters (e.g., addresses and dates) have been standardized. The recipient of each letter (usually Shaw or Jackson) is identified in boldface type at the head of each letter. The author of the letter is also identified in those relatively few instances when it is *not* Shaw or Jackson (i.e., either Charlotte Shaw or Blanche Patch).

Acknowledgments

I gratefully acknowledge permission of the Society of Authors, acting for the Estate of Bernard Shaw, to publish the Shaw letters in this volume, with particular thanks to Jeremy Crow of the Society of Authors for his interest and support. I am equally grateful to the Sir Barry Jackson Trust and its chairman, Mr R.S. Burman, for permission to publish the Jackson letters and for the award of a grant that greatly facilitated my research for this book. The letters of Charlotte Shaw are published by kind permission of the Trustees of the will of Mrs Bernard Shaw. My thanks are due also to the Birmingham Central Library for permission to publish the Shaw, Jackson, Charlotte Shaw, and Blanche Patch letters held by the Library. Siân Roberts, senior archivist at the Birmingham Central Library, was generous with her support and guidance at all times, as were her staff. Other letters in this edition are published with the permission of the British Theatre Museum, the British Library, the Harry Ransom Humanities Research Center at the University of Texas at Austin, and Cambridge University Library.

In addition to the libraries just mentioned, my research has benefited from the collections and the help of staff at the British Library of Political and Economic Science; the Shakespeare Centre, Stratford-upon-Avon; the Malvern Public Library; Birmingham University Library; the Robarts Library, University of Toronto; Trent University Library; and the University of Guelph Library. My thanks go to all of them. A special word of appreciation is due to the staff of Archival and Special Collections at Guelph, who for many years have cheerfully and efficiently responded to my many requests for materials from the Dan H. Laurence

Shaw Collection and other impressive theatre archives held there. I am most grateful to Bernard Katz, former head of Archival and Special Collections at Guelph, and Lorne Bruce, his successor, for their support.

Suzanne Rancourt and Kristen Pederson of the University of Toronto Press have also been unfailingly generous with their help and support, and I thank them both most warmly. Anonymous reviewers of this book for the University of Toronto Press and the Humanities and Social Sciences Federation of Canada made helpful suggestions and saved me from a number of embarrassing slips. I am very grateful to them. I am equally grateful to John St James, my editor at UTP, for drawing attention to other errors, inconsistencies, and omissions.

Much of the research for this book was undertaken at Robinson College, Cambridge. I have been privileged to be a member of Robinson College for over twenty years, and I express my deep appreciation to the Warden, Fellows, staff, and students of the College for providing me with such a welcoming and congenial home away from home.

It is a pleasure to thank others who have been generous with their help and advice. The late J. Percy Smith, friend and mentor, sadly did not live to see this book published, but his guidance during its formative stages was invaluable, and his influence and inspiration will never wane. Like all other Shaw scholars, I am deeply indebted to Dan H. Laurence, unstinting as ever in sharing his unequalled expertise in matters Shavian. Whenever I came to a dead end in my research, Dan Laurence was there with solutions and advice, as he has been for so many Shaw scholars before me. My colleagues at the Academy of the Shaw Festival (Niagara-on-the-Lake, Ontario), Ronald Bryden and Denis Johnston, have been a constant source of insight into Shaw and his period, as have productions of plays by Shaw and his contemporaries at the Shaw Festival, outstandingly led by artistic director Christopher Newton. And Michel Pharand, University of Ottawa, has shared his deep Shavian knowledge and enthusiasm with me on memorably convivial occasions, occasions frequently invigorated by the stimulating and discerning company of Colleen Franklin and Barbara Conolly. My thanks as well to Kathryn Yam and Jason Belleghem for invaluable help.

Joel Kaplan and Sheila Stowell at the University of Birmingham were enthusiastic supporters of this book from the beginning. I am particularly grateful to Professor Kaplan for inviting me to the University of Bir-

mingham to give a seminar on Shaw and Jackson in February 1999, and
for facilitating my association with the Sir Barry Jackson Trust.

I have discussed my work on Shaw and Jackson from its inception with
Eugene Benson, Emeritus Professor of English at the University of
Guelph. He has advised, cajoled, corrected, and encouraged me on this
project throughout the four years it has taken to complete it. Our scholarly collaborations have thrived for almost two decades and we have discussed and debated matters great and small in places as diverse as
lecture halls in Ahmadabad and dining halls on an Alaskan cruise ship.
Long may such occasions – enhanced (and sometimes refereed) by
Renate Benson and Barbara Conolly – flourish.

This book would not have been undertaken if my brother-in-law, Alan
Taylor, and his wife, Gillian, had not spotted a news item in a Midlands
newspaper in March 1998 announcing the acquisition of the Shaw–Jackson correspondence by the Birmingham Central Library. I thank both
of them for bringing the article to my attention, and for their keen
interest in my work as it progressed from that starting point. The interest of other family members has also been deeply appreciated.

My son James, a fellow academic, challenged me to get this book completed before he finishes *his* next book. I did, and I thank him for the
incentive. My daughter Rebecca, and my wife Barbara, talented editors
both, assisted greatly with solving the mysteries of word-processing,
repairing my (alleged) stylistic quirks, and alerting me to the needs and
sensitivities of publishers. My love and thanks to all three.

Abbreviations

Type of correspondence

ACCS   Autograph 'compliments' card signed
ADS   Autograph draft signed
ALCS   Autograph letter card signed
ALS   Autograph letter signed
ALU   Autograph letter unsigned
ANS   Autograph note signed
APCS   Autograph postcard or 'compliments' card signed
APCU   Autograph postcard or 'compliments' card unsigned
(c)   Carbon copy
TDU   Typed draft unsigned
TEL   Telegram or cable
TLS   Typed letter signed
TLU   Typed letter unsigned
(tr)   Typed transcription or copy

Sources of the correspondence

All the letters printed here are in the Bernard Shaw–Barry Jackson Collection at the Birmingham Central Library (BCL) unless otherwise indicated. The following abbreviations are used for other collections:

BL   British Library

BTM   British Theatre Museum, Covent Garden, London

HRC   Harry Ransom Humanities Research Center, University
of Texas at Austin

Letters

1 / To Barry Jackson   10 Adelphi Terrace WC2
                                                   25th June 1923

[ALS: BTM]

The first letter deals with an all-too-familiar issue for Shaw: censorship. Under the terms of the Stage Licensing Act of 1737, confirmed by the Theatre Regulation Act of 1843, it was necessary for every new play intended for public performance in Great Britain to be licensed by the Lord Chamberlain, a senior, though largely ceremonial, officer of the royal household. The Lord Chamberlain, through an official known as the Examiner of Plays, had the authority to deny a licence altogether, thus effectively banning a play (as had happened with Mrs Warren's Profession *in 1898), or requiring changes to the text before issuing a licence. Shaw fought vigorously against this bizarre form of censorship, but the legislation remained in force until 1968. It was necessary, then, for* Back to Methuselah *to be submitted to the Lord Chamberlain (at his office in St James's Palace) for a licence for the British premiere at the Birmingham Repertory Theatre, where it opened, directed by the BRT's leading director, H.K. Ayliff (1872–1949), on 9 October 1923. (The world premiere was in New York, 27 February 1922.) Securing a licence was the responsibility of the theatre management, not the author, and Bache Matthews, general manager of the BRT, had gone through the process many times. Shaw, however, was ready with advice when things got a little tricky. Having submitted the text of* Back to Methuselah *to the Lord Chamberlain early in May 1923, Matthews was informed in a letter dated 16 June 1923 (BCL, MS 978/2/1/11) that a licence would be issued provided that Matthews gave 'an undertaking' on three points: that the 'parody' of the Athanasian Creed (in Part 5 of the play) be removed; that the actors playing Burge and Lubin not be made up to resemble David Lloyd George and Herbert Asquith (both former prime ministers; see also notes to Letter 131); and that 'the usual conventionalities of dress of various other characters in the Play are observed' – by which was meant no nudity for Adam and Eve. Matthews – no doubt on Barry Jackson's advice – consulted Shaw. Shaw replied to Matthews at some length ('I object to the implication that I write passages that are unfit for public performances': the full letter is published in* Collected Letters, *III, 840–1), but sent the letter to Jackson for him to deal with. When the dust settled, however, Shaw accepted the Lord Chamberlain's requirements and the formal licence was issued on 20 July 1923.*

Dear Barry Jackson

I enclose a formal letter of which you had perhaps better send a copy (or the original) to St James's. The real point of it is that we must not proceed subject to 'an understanding' of any kind. The Censor must specify the passages he objects to; and we then yield to *force majeure*. This relieves us of all complicity in the outrage, and makes it impossible for an accusation of bad faith to be made against us if – as often happens – the cut makes matters worse from the Censor's point of view instead of better. Therefore he must make it himself.

But of course the more goodhumored we are, the better. It is important that you should be on the friendliest possible terms with the Department; and if you send on the letter I suggest that you do so not as expressing your own feelings, but as a document that may possibly interest the Lord C., and at all events make it clear that I am not mulish in the matter.

faithfully

G. Bernard Shaw

2 / To Barry Jackson   Ayot St Lawrence, Welwyn, Herts.
 From Charlotte F. Shaw   16th October 1923

[ALS]

The Shaws spent the last ten days of September 1923 on holiday in Malvern, then travelled to Birmingham on Sunday 30 September to stay with Jackson at his home in the suburb of Moseley. Shaw attended dress rehearsals of Back to Methuselah *on the Monday and the rest of that week, taking some time off for visits to a nearby cinema and to attend a local boxing match (Trewin,* Birmingham Repertory Theatre, *3). He also had to have a session with a Birmingham osteopath for treatment of damaged ribs caused by an accident in Ireland in August. Shaw and Charlotte attended all five parts of* Back to Methuselah, *which concluded on 12 October. The Shaws left Birmingham the next day. Among the critics who reviewed the BRT production was St John Ervine, who wrote in the* Observer *(14 October 1923) that he had 'never undergone an experience so moving and remarkable' as the BRT production of* Methuselah. *Ervine (1883–1971) was subsequently to write a major biography of Shaw,* Bernard Shaw: His Life, Work and Friends *(London: Constable, 1956)*. *The Shaws' regret – certainly Charlotte's, as she makes clear in this letter – at not being able to return to Birmingham was compounded by a disastrous (in Shaw's view) Oxford production of* Heartbreak House *in October (see Letter 3). They had gone to Oxford by way of Bath, where Shaw attended the Autumn Festival of the British Drama League, unveiling a plaque to Sheridan there on 26 October.*

Dear Barry Jackson

Here we are back again, up against the rough & tumble, and Malvern & Birmingham seem like a lovely, elusive dream. We are only beginning to realize what an amazing business it all was about Methuselah. It seems to me now it was probably the crown of G.B.S.'s career. And we owe it to you that it came just as it did. It was a *big thing*.

It was splendid of you to ask us to come down again, & to ask us so nicely as you did! We cant. Alas! Alas! We *cant*. G.B.S. has to go to Bath on the 25th, stay there till the 27th, & see Heartbreak House on his way back through Oxford. And that will exactly cut us out of the last cycle. Lady Keeble is going. Our accounts excited her so much she threw over everything else on the spot!

'Joan' was read to a few people on Sunday, & had a great reception. Two of the ladies had real hysterics over the end of the trial scene! I was amazed myself how it worked up. I had not heard it straight through before. I want you to hear it. It is a big job reading it, but G.B.S. is nearly himself again. What did you think of St John Ervine's Observer article? I told you he was all broken up when I was talking to him.

We are looking forward to The Immortal Hour.

Our remembrances.

Ever

C.F. Shaw

Lady Keeble, the actress Lillah McCarthy (1875–1960), married the Oxford biologist Frederick Keeble in 1920, after divorce ended her marriage to Harley Granville Barker (1877–1946) in 1918. Keeble was knighted in 1922. Shaw read *Saint Joan* at the Keebles' on Sunday 14 October, by then being **nearly himself again** after a fall on the rocks in Kerry, Ireland, in August. *Saint Joan* opened in New York on 28 December 1923 and in London on 26 March 1924. A revival of the Birmingham Repertory Theatre production of Rutland Boughton's (1878–1960) musical drama *The Immortal Hour* opened at the Regent Theatre in London on 14 November 1923 and ran for thirty-seven performances.

3 / To Barry Jackson

Ayot St Lawrence, Welwyn, Herts.
22nd October 1923

[ALS]

An interview with Shaw on 'the serial drama' appeared in the Observer *on 21 October 1923. Asked whether 'his Birmingham experience' with* Back to Methuselah *'suggests that the public can be educated to serial plays,' Shaw 'demanded, somewhat testily, why people reserved all that solicitude for the public.' The problem, he argued, was not the public, but the lack of people and companies such as Barry Jackson and the Birmingham Repertory Theatre: 'The production of "Methuselah" was a feat possible only to such a manager and such a company, and in such an atmosphere of enthusiastic artistic cooperation as he has created.'*

My dear Barry Jackson

Will you tell the photographers to send me a set of prints from their flashes, with the bills therefor. This is part of my regular commercial routine.

In last Sunday's Observer I took the chance they offered me of expatiating on the serial drama. I hope I did not bang the drum too loudly for your modest nerves. It is the penalty of doing things.

But for this Bath business and the fact that Saturday is the last night of Heartbreak House at the new playhouse in Oxford I might have looked in again on Methuselah, Archer, L.K., and yourself. You made our visit very easy and very jolly.

Bless you!

ever
G. Bernard Shaw

The **Bath business** was Shaw's attendance at the British Drama League (Letter 2). William **Archer** (1856–1924), influential drama critic and translator of Ibsen, championed the plays of Shaw and other new playwrights. **Laura Knight** (1877–1970), an artist best known for her circus and ballet paintings, was also a theatre enthusiast and friend of Barry Jackson. She met Shaw on one of her visits to Malvern, where she painted his portrait in 1933. It now hangs in the Hereford City Museum.

4 / To Barry Jackson   Ayot St Lawrence, Welwyn, Herts.
                                                    28th October 1923

[APCS]

Shaw saw Heartbreak House *at the Oxford Playhouse on 27 October 1923. It was directed by Reginald Denham, who recalled the occasion in his autobiography,* Stars in My Hair *(1958). In response to Shaw's presence the actors 'overplayed and overwaited for laughs, and the audience overlaughed out of politeness. The result was distinctly debilitating.' At the end of the performance Shaw spoke from the stage: "'Ladies and gentlemen," he said, "this has been one of the most depressing evenings I have spent in the theatre. I imagined I had written a quiet, thoughtful, semi-tragic play after the manner of Tchekov. From your empty-headed laughter, I appear to have written a bedroom farce. All that remains for me to do is to give the actors, and particularly the director, my most heavy curse.* Good night"' (quoted in Collected Letters, *III, 851–2).*

Just back from Bath. Saw H.H. in Oxford on the way, played as a farcical comedy, with appropriate cuts. Horrible. I was forced onto the stage by a fearful clamor at the end, and politely told them I should have committed suicide if there had been a weapon handy.

                                                    G.B.S.

5 / To Barry Jackson   Ayot St Lawrence, Welwyn, Herts.
                                                    9th November 1923

[APCS]

We shall expect you on Thursday the 15th to lunch at 1.30 at 10 Adelphi Terrace.

    Charlotte has had to return to bed with a relapse of her bronchial trouble; but she will be all right by the middle of next week.

                                                    G.B.S.

6 / To Barry Jackson   10 Adelphi Terrace WC2
                                                    21st December 1923

[ALS]

Shaw had been to see the Birmingham Repertory Theatre production of Rutland Boughton's Christmas musical drama Bethlehem, *directed by Jackson, at the Regent Theatre, London.*

Dear Barry Jackson

In justice to Chris, I feel bound to say that the dresses are thoroughly artistic – really color-schemed – and some of them beautiful. That confounded angel, who must be redressed, put me off the affair in the first part; but the three Kings were wonderful; and the dresses of Herod's bayaderes extraordinarily bold, right, and effective. Joseph & Mary, too, very good. But Chris should do the whole thing, scenes and all, to get the setting for her peculiar color sense. It fits the play somehow.

I am writing a line to Rutland as to the musical revision of that angel, who is the bad angel of the whole production. His peruke is the most dreadfully absurd thing.

Herod shouldn't look like a prizefighter: he should have terrific moustaches. His chucker-out has stolen his make-up.

I hope the public will rise to it. It has an anti-artistic character of a kind quite unknown in the London theatres, just as Methuselah had; and this is a matter of management as much as of material; so good luck to you.

We are off to Bournemouth (Boscombe Chine Hotel) tomorrow morning.

ever

G.B.S.

Chris[tina] Walshe designed the costumes for *Bethlehem*. Shaw's **line to Rutland** about the angel ('That angel is impossible') is published in Michael Hurd, *Rutland Boughton and the Glastonbury Festivals* (Oxford: Clarendon Press, 1993), 152.

7 / To Barry Jackson

10 Adelphi Terrace WC2

23rd January 1924

[TLS]

Following the success of Saint Joan *in New York, there was great public anticipation concerning the London premiere. Given his considerable satisfaction with* Back to Methuselah *in Birmingham, Shaw would have been delighted to have Jackson involved in the production of* Saint Joan. *Jackson's response to Shaw's invitation to approach Lewis Casson has been lost, but it is clear from Shaw's next letter to Jackson (Letter 8) that Jackson declined the opportunity, probably because, having decided to close down the Birmingham Repertory Theatre at the*

*end of the 1923–4 season (a decision subsequently reversed), he was ambivalent
about his future role in professional theatre.*

Dear Barry Jackson

I enclose an extract from a letter I have just received from Lewis Casson.
At present he has The New Theatre from Lady Wyndham (Mary Moore)
and her son Bronson Albery, on sharing terms, and subject to the possibility of Matheson Lang exercising a right to come back to it in July.
Grossmith, no doubt moved by the reports of the New York success, is
also sounding Casson about it with a view to a big production at His Majesty's. But Lady Wyndham belongs to the eighteen eighties, and Grossmith to the world of the stunt revue. Casson and Sybil Thorndike, both
as modern as can be, and very nice people at that, would be happier at
more congenial artistic moorings.

I need hardly say that I, too, should be much more at home with you
than with anyone else; so you may take me for granted if you feel disposed to discuss the matter with Casson. I should, in fact, have offered
you the play if it had not been clear that it must go to Sybil Thorndike as
the only possible Joan. As, after the New York success, Joan is as nearly a
cert (to the extent, at least, of not losing much money) as anything theatrical can be, I feel no delicacy about putting the suggestion before you
with my blessing; but of course if you ask me as a friend whether it is
wise to speculate in Joan or in anything connected with the British theatre I must reply, certainly not. But if you *will* do these things, well –
there it is.

Ever

G.B.S.

The **extract** from Casson's letter reads as follows (the clarifications in square brackets have
been added in handwriting by Shaw to the typed copy): 'Do you think it would be possible
to approach Barry Jackson about doing it [Saint Joan] with him at the Regent or elsewhere? What I have in mind is, if we succeeded in working successfully together, to make it
the opening play of a fairly permanent theatre for us, with a definite policy. I do not know
Barry Jackson personally, so perhaps if you approve of the idea, you might like sounding
[him] about it. Of course, it is no use saying anything that would disturb present relations
here [the New Theatre] until matters have gone further.' **Lewis Casson** (1875–1969),
actor and director, married in 1909 **Sybil Thorndike** (1882–1976), who played Joan in the
British premiere. **Lady Wyndham** (Mary Moore, 1869–1931) was actor-manager Charles
Wyndham's (1837–1919, knighted in 1902) leading lady. The widow of playwright James

Albery (1838–89), Mary Moore married Wyndham in 1912, continuing in theatre management after his death. **Bronson Albery** (1881–1971), Mary Moore's son from her first marriage, became a major London theatre manager. The Albery Theatre in London (formerly the New) is named after him. Actor-manager and playwright **Matheson Lang** (1879–1948) enjoyed a successful career in London and touring the Commonwealth. George **Grossmith** (1874–1935) was best known as a star of musical comedy.

8 / To Barry Jackson   10 Adelphi Terrace WC2
                                                        31st January 1924
[TLS]

Having run the Birmingham Repertory Theatre for a decade at considerable personal financial cost, Jackson became disillusioned by the lack of public support for the theatre. After a poorly attended run of Georg Kaiser's Gas *in November 1923 Jackson announced that the BRT would close after the season's final play,* Eden Phillpotts's comedy The Farmer's Wife, *in February 1924. Tangible expressions of public and civic support during the summer of 1924, however, persuaded Jackson to reopen the BRT in September 1924. In the meantime, he maintained his interest in London theatre with a revival of* Back to Methuselah *at the Court Theatre in February and* The Farmer's Wife *in March. He did not tour* Methuselah *to the provinces; a different production opened at the People's Theatre, Newcastle upon Tyne, on 13 October 1924 and ran (in three cycles) until 21 November 1924. Jackson returned to the Court with a series of productions (including another revival of* Methuselah*) in 1928.*

Dear Barry Jackson

Have you any views as to Methuselah in the provinces? I have just had an application from a crew of desperadoes who call themselves The People's Theatre of Newcastle-on-Tyne, and who keep steadily acting my plays and any others equally advanced without the slightest regard to their own chronic destitution or to the age, sex, color or culture of themselves as performers. But they pull it off somehow. They now want to attempt Methuselah; and before letting them loose on it I should like to know whether it has ever occurred to you to tour it. It is the last thing I should advise you to do; but I don't like to take any decisive step without letting you know in time.

Tomorrow (Friday) at 4.30, Charles Ricketts, Casson and Sybil Thorndike are coming to tea, and to discuss Ricketts' plans and sketches for Joan. If you care to look in, we shall regard it as a happy accident. Ricketts came into the business before there was any question of Casson changing his present arrangements at the New. I am under strong obligations to Ricketts, who in the old days at the Court Theatre did a magnificent Don Juan in Hell for me, and several other jobs for which he would never accept anything. Casson also remembers these times, as he was at the Court nearly all through. Now that Ricketts does this sort of thing professionally, though still not very eagerly, we naturally approached him first; and after some coaxing he has taken on the job.

I explain this, because if there had been any question of your taking on Joan I should not have committed you.

You ought to meet Sybil Thorndike anyhow. A good deal will depend at the Court on a strong woman for leading business; and it might be well to ascertain how far she is really accessible.

By the way, I did not realise at first that you were going to drop Birmingham. I thought you were going to keep it open with something musical, or with a company made up with your back numbers re-enlisted. Is the theatre now available for anyone else who would care to take up the running?

Ever

G. Bernard Shaw

Charles Ricketts (1866–1931) designed the costumes for Shaw's *Don Juan in Hell* at the Court Theatre, 4 June 1907, and for the New Theatre production of *Saint Joan*, 26 March 1924.

9 / To Barry Jackson   10 Adelphi Terrace WC2
                                    21st February 1924
[ALS]

My Dear Barry Jackson

I have been ringing you up all over the place, and cant get you anywhere. The Midland Hotel denies that you are staying there. The Regent is shutting up and thinks you are at the Court. I tried for you at the Court in the last interval, and learnt that you had just driven off in your car.

Charlotte has been expecting to see you every night, and fussing about your being ill in Birmingham, and imagining all sorts of things. Implying also that it is all my fault.

I have to start the Joan rehearsals on Monday with the awful job of reading the play. Being dead beat, I cannot face this and the subsequent month in London without snatching at least three days in the country; so I shall go down to Ayot St Lawrence tomorrow by the 11.30 from Kings + [King's Cross Station], and put off visiting As Far As Thought Can Reach to some later cycle, so that it may be truthfully said, if anyone asks, that the author is not in the house.

Would it be possible for you to lunch with us on Saturday. If you take the above train to Hatfield I will meet you there with a car. Or if you prefer to drive down all the way, I can instruct you as to the road. To communicate tomorrow ring us up here, Gerrard 331 until 10.50, or, after 12.30, Codicote 18 through Toll.

In great haste to catch the 11.50 clearance at the pillar box.

Ever

G.B.S.

PS If Saturday is impossible what about Sunday?

PPS Charlotte is sending you a letter to the Regent by this post.

As Far As Thought Can Reach is Part V of *Back to Methuselah*. The performance that Shaw chose to miss was at the Court on 22 February 1924.

10 / To Barry Jackson   Ayot St Lawrence, Welwyn, Herts.
    From Charlotte F. Shaw   16th March 1924

[ALS]

Dear Barry Jackson

Thank you for your letter. I have been really under the weather & very wretched all last week. I went up to London for a couple of nights, but coughed all the time!

I expect to be at Adelphi Terrace from Tuesday evening for the rest of this week. I cannot have lunches as I never know when G.B.S. will be in – but could you come to tea on Wednesday, Thursday or Friday? Do!

I am heartbroken at the muddle that has been made about the places for the first night of Joan. I cannot tell you about it in a letter, but it really is rather dreadful. I think if I had not been ill in bed down here I could have intervened in time; but I knew nothing about it till too late – & G.B.S. was so taken up with his rehearsing he never gave it a thought; and he is no good at that sort of thing anyhow! I will tell you when we meet.

About you we have not been so distressed because we always meant to ask you if you would come & see the play from our box on the 26th. Will you? I should have written about it before had I not been so ill – really *non compos*!

Hoping to see you Wednesday, Thursday or Friday.

Ever

C.F. Shaw

11 / To Barry Jackson   10 Adelphi Terrace WC2
                                         18th March 1924

[ACCS]

Despite the Shaws' concerns and efforts to have Jackson at the opening of Saint Joan, *he didn't attend, preferring to follow William Archer's advice that 'first performances were occasions to be avoided by sincere theatregoers.' He went instead to the second night, witnessing an 'unforgettable' performance by Sybil Thorndike in a 'noble' play. Jackson waited twelve years before producing (and directing)* Saint Joan *(at Malvern, 1936), with Wendy Hiller as Joan. (See Barry Jackson, 'My Memories of "Saint Joan," ' Radio Times, 22 September 1950.)*

I was so preoccupied with the production of Joan that I forgot to secure my tickets until they were all gone, and I was left waiting for rearrangements and returns and so forth. The enclosed did not become available until this morning. However, better late than never. It will save you from being shoved away into my very poky box at the back of the circle, where, however, you will perhaps look us up in the course of the evening.

G.B.S.

12 / To Barry Jackson   Ayot St Lawrence, Welwyn, Herts.
From Charlotte F. Shaw   1st April 1924

[ALS]

Dear Barry Jackson

We have arranged to spend a fortnight in Malvern at Easter – from the 14th to the 28th – & finish up with a Shakespear week at Stratford before coming back. Your offer of your house touched us very much, but we are going to be ungrateful enough not to allow it. G.B.S. wants the utter irresponsibility of a hotel, & a stationers shop & telegraph office round the corner! I want to escape for a moment from houses & servants & consultations with the housekeeper & having to consider everybody & everything. If you were not there as a guardian angel, as you were in Birmingham, I should be more anxious about your house & about your servants than about my own; & then, as the man in Pygmalion says, 'Goodbye to happiness'! Now that I have said this you could never feel free to go off for your holiday, or even to come & go as usual while we were there – & that would end in your hating us! So we will go to our old quarters at the Malvern Hotel & see as much of you as you can bear. G.B.S. urges that you will be saved trouble & thought by this, & will lose nothing but another opportunity for your kindness, which he regards as a suicidal quality – not to be indulged!

Please write at once & say that you forgive us – & even approve.

I do so want to know what you think of Joan.

Ever
C.F. Shaw

as the man in Pygmalion says: Doolittle, in Act II of *Pygmalion*, declining £10 from Higgins, says, 'Ten pounds is a lot of money: it makes a man feel prudent like; and then goodbye to happiness.'

13 / To Barry Jackson   Reid's Palace Hotel, Funchal, Madeira
28th January 1925

[ALS]

The Shaws spent Christmas 1924 in London. They sailed to Madeira on Boxing

Day, returning to England in mid-February. Both Shaw and Jackson were eager to develop their professional relationship after the success of Back to Methuselah, *but nothing had so far materialized. Jackson had not been involved with the British premiere of* Saint Joan, *and his interest in producing the first licensed British performance of* Mrs Warren's Profession *seems to have been inadvertently thwarted by Shaw's giving the rights to 'C.M.,' Charles Macdona (1860–1946), whose touring repertory company, the Macdona Players, had long served Shaw well, albeit with no great theatrical distinction.* Mrs Warren's Profession *had been performed privately by the Stage Society in London on 5 January 1902, but was not authorised by the Lord Chamberlain for public performance in England until Macdona's production at the Prince of Wales Theatre in Birmingham on 27 July 1925. The Birmingham location must have been especially irritating to Jackson, particularly since he had tried much earlier than Macdona to produce* Mrs Warren's Profession *in Birmingham (at the Rep, of course), but had been thwarted by the Lord Chamberlain's ban on the play. (Bache Matthews, general manager at the BRT, wrote to Shaw on 6 July 1921 to tell him of the Lord Chamberlain's refusal to lift the ban; the letter is in the BRT archives, BCL, MS 2129/ 4/1.) There is no record of Jackson's having given a rival private performance, Jackson perhaps finding Shaw's prediction of sparse attendance compelling – that is, Jackson (King Ludwig of Bavaria, Wagner's patron) in his office and Shaw (Wagner) in the stalls. Things went more smoothly, however, with Jackson's production of* Caesar and Cleopatra. *After a short run at the BRT, it transferred to the Kingsway Theatre in London on 21 April 1925. Both productions were directed by H.K. Ayliff and starred Cedric Hardwicke as Caesar and Gwen Ffrangcon-Davies as Cleopatra. The 'unpublished version' of* Caesar and Cleopatra *was that written by Shaw for Johnston Forbes-Robertson (1853–1937) for his farewell tour of 1912–13, first published in the French translation by Augustin Hamon* (César et Cléopâtre, 1926), *and first published in English in 1930* (Collected Edition).

My dear Barry Jackson

The steamer that brings our letters once a week is followed so quickly by the one that takes the replies that only the most perfunctory scribbles are possible.

I feel ridiculous about Mrs Warren. The issue of the licence to C.M.

was such a senseless caprice of pure luck – binding on me because C.M.'s luck on previous occasions has been so often the other way – that there is no sort of reason in my position; and I don't defend it. If you give a private performance, it will be a case of Ludwig in the manager's office and Wagner in the stalls; and it seems to me that if I encourage such an extravagance I shall presently have you walking into the Serpentine exclaiming 'I *will* be drowned; and nobody *shall* save me.' If Edna is such a thundering genius why not give her a contract for five years at £10 a week, and farm her out to C.M. at £200?

I love these magnificent gestures of yours; but they cost too much to make it decent to meet them with anything but remonstrances.

If theatre rents do not soon crash, you will finally have to build a theatre (with someone else's money, please); but meanwhile I think you are safe with a lease of the Kingsway (now chockfull of traditions) as you can always let it.

The F.W. is wonderful: it is the really Immortal Hour.

I want you to go to the Grand at Putney Bridge and tell me what on earth Trebitsch's play Jitta's Atonement, with Violet Vanbrugh as Jitta, is like. I gave them two or three rehearsals early in December to arrange the stage business and put them on the job roughly; but I remained in secret bewilderment about the whole unnatural business. Violet will probably give matinées of it in Birmingham on her tour if it does not crumble into dust when the curtain goes up; but to make sure I should like you to see it at Putney.

I note Caesar in Birmingham after Easter. Shall I leave it to Ayliff, or shall I come down for a day or two to amuse the company? They tell me that Joan is better at the Regent than it was at the New, which suggests that they got on better without me.

Apollodorus should be a brilliant spark: an Osric with ability. A budding London man would be best. Rufio must be a real heavy weight: a thick un. In my experience by far the hardest part to cast is the chap who cuts off Pompey's head (I forget his name), as he has to hold a big scene against Caesar in his cold, trim, bitter way.

By the way, do you know that there is an unpublished version of this play in which, instead of the published first scene, there is a tremendous prologue by the god Ra. But it needs a better actor than Caesar, and depreciates his Sphinx opening, which immediately follows, dreadfully.

We must talk it over when I return. We expect to sail on the 12th February, arriving at Southampton on the 15th.

Ever

G. Bernard Shaw

PS Sunderland would make a dashing Apollodorus and an irresistible Britannicus [Britannus]. And Margaret as Ftatateeta? – what!

Edna may have been a member of Jackson's company, either Edna Lester, who first appeared at the BRT in 1921, or Edna Randall, who first appeared in 1919. Neither achieved fame. The **Kingsway** Theatre opened on 9 December 1882 (as the Novelty). The first British production of Ibsen's *Doll's House* took place there (7 June 1889), as did the first London performance of Synge's *Playboy of the Western World* (10 June 1907). Jackson leased the Kingsway on several occasions, including for his celebrated modern-dress *Hamlet* in August 1925. Eden Phillpotts' comedy *The Farmer's Wife* (**F.W.**), premiered at the BRT on 11 November 1916. A new production opened at the Court Theatre in London on 11 March 1924 and ran for over 1300 performances, one of Jackson's few commercial successes. (For The *Immortal Hour* see notes to Letter 2.) *Jitta's Atonement* is Shaw's translation and adaptation of *Frau Gitta's Sühne*, by Shaw's German translator, Siegfried **Trebitsch** (1869–1956). It opened in Washington and New York in January 1923, and in London, at the Grand, Putney, on 26 January 1925 (sixteen performances), with **Violet Vanbrugh** (1867–1942) as Jitta. Scott **Sunderland** (1883–1952), one of Jackson's most reliable and versatile actors and a close friend, played Britannus, but the role of Ftatateeta went not to **Margaret** Chatwin (1881–1937) but to Florence Marriott Watson.

14 / To Barry Jackson   10 Adelphi Terrace WC2
From Charlotte F. Shaw   26th February 1925

[ALS]

Having established his credentials, as it were, with Shaw as director and producer, Jackson was now eager to seek Shaw's views on his playwriting ability. He had ventured into playwriting in a modest way with an occasional farce or children's play for the Pilgrim Players or at the BRT, and had collaborated with other playwrights, John Drinkwater and Basil Dean among them. But the play that he sent to the Shaws was his most ambitious undertaking yet: a translation and adaptation of La merveilleuse histoire du jeune Bernard de Menthon *by French playwright Henri Ghéon (1875–1944). Jackson's version of Ghéon's account of the Frenchman who renounced marriage (on the eve of his wedding) to combat the devil's harassment of pilgrims on their way to Rome was called* The Marvellous History of Saint Bernard. *It opened at the BRT on 16 May 1925 and in the following year at the Kingsway Theatre, London, 7 April 1926, directed by A.E.*

Filmer, with set and costume designs by Paul Shelving, and ran for seventy-six performances. Shaw might have been expected to react quickly to a play about a sainted Bernard, but it was Charlotte who gave the initial response.

Dear Barry

The play has just arrived & I have been dipping into it. It's *very nice*. I'll tell you what we think when we have both read it.

We are being drownded at Ayot. We came up yesterday through rivers! I believe this is going to be a second deluge to sweep this wicked world away. What a good thing!

Ever

C.F.S.

15 / To Barry Jackson   Ayot St Lawrence, Welwyn, Herts.
    From Charlotte F. Shaw   1st March 1925

[ALS]

Charlotte soon gave a more detailed response to Jackson's play.

Dear Barry

I promised to tell you what I thought of the play when I had read it. I like it much. It held, & interested & charmed me from start to finish, & I think it ought to come out delightfully, with your setting & production.

In reflecting about it one thing has come to me.

These – what I may call – middle-age ideas of monks & nuns & devils; celibacy & temptations & sacrifices, will strike most of your audiences as things of the past. 'So quaint & old-world' they will say: 'very religious & proper, of course, but nothing to do with us now.' Whereas, of course, it would be hard to find anything more modern, or more eternally young & instant than every bit of the story. The youthful pride & self-confidence, brought to smash by the instability & cowardice of life (Bonaventure): there, in Bernard, the apprehension of the Divine Sight; the struggle to keep sight of the gleam through the murkiness, vanity and good intentions of the world, the flesh, the devil; the half achieved, half missed communion with other humans in the like case. Then the moment of trial; the choosing of 'the better' rather than 'the dearer';

the victory; the confident certainty of fulfilment. Just the plain history of every soul (or spirit) that goes the Royal Road; the road of evolution; of the struggle-up.

Now it struck me that you are a little adapting the piece; not translating it literally. Suppose you could manage to get all this so clearly into the play in performance, that the human in the gallery, & the human in the stalls, would have to say 'That's me'; to realize that it is their own lives that are before them, their own story that is being told; not that of a monk & a nun far away in the 'middle ages'.

It would be a big thing.

Ever
C.F.S.

G.B.S. has not read it yet – but he will soon.

Bonaventure is a character in the play, a pilgrim.

16 / To Barry Jackson   10 Adelphi Terrace WC2
From Charlotte F. Shaw   5th March 1925

[ALS]

Charlotte, who had much enjoyed her visit to Jackson's Birmingham home during rehearsals of Back to Methuselah *in 1923, was delighted by the prospect of staying there again during the BRT rehearsals of* Caesar and Cleopatra.

Dear Barry

Of all things I should like to go & stay with you for the *Caesar* rehearsals, &, if you really don't think I shall be too much of a bother, I will most gladly go with G.B.S. He, of course, looks upon it as an engagement already – only he thought it was going to be in the middle of April, & is a bit surprized at the early date. However he will gladly keep it free – the 23rd to 29th March – that's right, isn't it.

Did I dream it, or did you say you had taken a flat in Chelsea where letters should be addressed?

Yours ever
C.F.S.

Because of his heavy involvement in London theatre, Jackson had indeed taken **a flat in Chelsea** (at 3 Chelsea Embankments).

17 / To Barry Jackson   Ayot St Lawrence, Welwyn, Herts.

                                                    10th March 1925

[ALS]

My dear Barry Jackson

Are you closing the Birmingham Rep. for the final rehearsals, and working at it night and day? If so, Tuesday–Friday, morning and evening,
would be enough for me to meddle with. But if, as I presume, you are
having business as usual, with one of the days cut short by a matinée,
and no evening rehearsals, I think I had better catch a breakfast car
train on Monday morning so as to attend the rehearsal on that day, leaving Charlotte to follow in the car with the luggage.

I had a faint intention of catching the Jitta matinée at Leicester on
the 21st, and placing myself within easy reach of Birmingham on the
Monday. I am prevented from catching her at Oxford as I intended. But
this is not important: I love not Leicester.

Just drop me a card to say how matters stand as to the rehearsals. I
shall be in London on Thursday.

I am assuming that you will be at Malvern for the week-end and will
not be at Moseley until the afternoon on Monday the 23rd.

Miriam Lewes has written in for Ftatateeta. I have told her that the
play is cast and that, anyhow, she is not ugly enough.

                                                    Ever

                                                    G.B.S.

The **Jitta matinée** was on Violet Vanbrugh's tour of *Jitta's Atonement*, discussed by Shaw in
his letter to Jackson, 28 January 1925 (Letter 13). Shaw did indeed see it in Leicester on 21
March (Weiss, 254). Jackson's Birmingham home was in the suburb of **Moseley**. **Miriam
Lewes** had shared the role of Hypatia in *Misalliance* at the Duke of York's in 1910, but
the role of **Ftatateeta** in Jackson's production of *Caesar and Cleopatra* at the BRT went to F.
Marriott-Watson.

18 / To Barry Jackson   10 Adelphi Terrace WC2

                                                    3rd April 1925

[APCS]

Caesar and Cleopatra *opened at the BRT on 28 March 1925 for a two-week run before transferring to the Kingsway Theatre in London on 21 April. The inclusion of the prologue (see Letter 13) made for a long evening – 'Here is another bottle of medicine from Mr Bernard Shaw, a big bottle, too, taking over four hours to imbibe' (Birmingham Evening Dispatch, 30 March 1925) – but despite Shaw's advice Jackson retained the prologue for the London production, though Shaw prepared an abridged version for him (Dan H. Laurence, Shaw: An Exhibit [Austin: University of Texas at Austin, 1977], no. 262). The prologue was spoken by Lewis Mannering in both the Birmingham and London productions. The Shaws had been at the Birmingham opening of Caesar and Cleopatra, returned to Ayot St Lawrence on 29 March, and were back in Birmingham (via Malvern) on 9 April (Thursday) for lunch with Jackson at the Queen's Hotel (rather than at Jackson's home on Wake Green Road).*

I should cut the prologue without a moment's hesitation. It is quite superfluous as a source of information to the audience when the first scene is played, and therefore comes in solely as a sort of overture to establish the atmosphere of the play. Unfortunately the achievement of this effect depends entirely on the power and impressiveness of the executant (say £200 a week). If we could get this, or afford it, then we might face 8 to 11.30. As it is, it is clearly better to cut the prologue and play from 8 to 11.15.

Charlotte suggests that instead of putting Wake Green to the bother of lunching us on Thursday we should lunch you at the Queen's. Let us have a line to Ayot St Lawrence, Welwyn, Herts, as to which would be the more convenient for you.

The Day bulletins seem satisfactory; but the doc. wont let him get up.

G.B.S.

Fred **Day** (1883–1959), who had not been well, was the Shaws' long-serving chauffeur, occasionally loaned to Jackson.

19 / To Barry Jackson   10 Adelphi Terrace WC2
    From Charlotte F. Shaw   14th May 1925

[ALS]

Relations between Shaw and his close friend and associate, playwright, actor, and director Harley Granville Barker, had been strained since Barker divorced actress Lillah McCarthy (to whom Shaw was also close) in 1917 and subsequently married Helen Huntington ('H.' in this letter) in July 1918. Among other things, Barker's new wife encouraged him to hyphenate his name and, somewhat more disconcertingly, discontinue his involvement in theatrical production, an involvement that had been so important to Shaw and other British and European playwrights, especially during Barker's co-management (with J.E. Vedrenne) of the Court Theatre, 1904–7. ('She hates me with a lethal malignity which seriously damages my health if I come near her,' Shaw wrote of Helen Huntington to fellow American Molly Tompkins a few years later [Collected Letters, IV, 227–8].) Barker continued, however, to write plays and to write and lecture about theatrical matters, culminating in his celebrated Prefaces to Shakespeare *(1927–46). On 13 May 1925 he gave the Annual Shakespeare Lecture of the British Academy at King's College London on the need for a 'dual guild' of 'scholars of the printed page' and 'scholars of the spoken word.' Shaw gave the vote of thanks, and, according to Charlotte (who was not present), also took the opportunity to offer some gratuitous advice to Barker. Jackson, however, had other things on his mind, principally the opening of his play* The Marvellous History of Saint Bernard *at the BRT on Saturday 16 May. It is not known how influential Jackson was in securing a venue for the London premiere of Sean O'Casey's* Juno and the Paycock, *but it opened at the Royalty Theatre on 16 November 1925. Jackson produced* Juno *at the BRT in 1945.*

Dear Barry

It was shocking luck about that luncheon, altogether everything went wrong & now G.B.S. is down with influenza! It seems like a judgment. He went to Granville-Barker's Shakespear lecture & was asked to move a vote of thanks. He did; & after a wonderful panegyric gave G.B. a most tremendous slating & ended with an appeal to him to leave off sulking in his tent, which seems to have made the audience move the roof off the place. I was not there, but everyone who was says it was one of his best efforts. Immediately after, he was smitten down by this. Wouldn't H. be pleased, if she knew!

Lady Lavery is going to write to you to beg you to go & lunch with her next Monday & meet Lennox Robinson. I gave her your address. We would have gone to the lunch had all been well. It is to try & devise means of doing Juno & the Paycock in London. Lennox is really nice & an old friend of ours. You would like him. Perfectly fresh & natural; no side or affectation. He is very seldom in London as he much prefers being in Ireland. I have wanted myself to bring you together. I don't think they want to get anything out of you; only your advice & experience. Lennox wrote very nicely about Caesar, didn't he. I thought it possible you might be coming up from Malvern on Monday. It was Elisabeth Bergner (the Berlin Joan) who gave us 'flu. She is a strange little creature, arched eyebrows, big eyes, full of nobility. G.B.S. says just like Joan was really. But Elisabeth is – well we will tell you about the visit. I think G.B.S. was rather unkind to her. But he is paid out now!

O dear Barry. I wish I was going to be at Malvern this week-end. How lucky you are!

Most warmest wishes for success on Saturday. I wish G.B.S. had been more use about Bernard.

Yours ever
C.F.S.

Theatrical patron **Lady Lavery** was also the wife of society portrait painter Sir John Lavery (1856–1941), who painted Shaw's portrait in 1925. Playwright **Lennox Robinson** (1886–1958) was long associated with Dublin's Abbey Theatre. Robinson described *Caesar and Cleopatra* (*Observer*, 3 May 1925) as 'a production which every lover of the theatre must see, a production which places us all deeply in Mr Barry Jackson's debt.' **Elisabeth Bergner** (1900–86), Austrian actress, played Joan in Berlin and Vienna in 1924.

20 / To Barry Jackson　　　　　　　　Spa Hotel, Strathpeffer [Scotland]
　　From Charlotte F. Shaw　　　　　　　　　26th September 1925

[ALS]

From mid-July to early October 1925 the Shaws toured Scotland, Shaw hoping to use the time to complete 'the book on Socialism,' The Intelligent Woman's Guide to Socialism and Capitalism, *started in 1924, but not finally published until June 1928. Jackson kept closely in touch with the Shaws while they were away, worrying on this occasion about the possibility of Charles Macdona getting the rights for* Heartbreak House, *a play that Jackson had produced at the BRT in 1923 and hoped to take to London. In fact, Jackson didn't do it in London until*

1932 (25 April 1932 at the Queen's Theatre), with Cedric Hardwicke as Shoto-ver and Edith Evans as Lady Utterword, directed by H.K. Ayliff. In the mean-time, however, he did another BRT production of Heartbreak House (1930) and two Malvern productions (1929, 1930). Some 'fuss' surrounded the London opening of Mrs Warren's Profession at the Regent Theatre on 28 September 1925, a sensitive issue for Jackson who had hoped to produce the play himself, only to be thwarted by Shaw's giving the rights to Macdona (Letter 13). Hence, perhaps, Jackson's particular caution about the rights to Heartbreak House and his care-ful solicitation of Charlotte's support.

Dear Barry

Thank you for your lovely long letter, & all its news. I made G.B.S. write off the *very same day* to Macdona about Heartbreak House, & snuff him out. But I believe there was really no danger at all, as the matter had been made perfectly clear to him before. Perhaps he was feeling his way.

How ridiculous, & *how* unpleasant, all this fuss about Mrs Warren. I can never get over my regret that you are not doing that play. It will need such careful handling! Perhaps you have seen it by now.

We are here because G.B.S. is trying to finish up the book on Social-ism he has been writing all the year. It is a very quiet & exceedingly com-fortable place, & he feels that the moment he gets back there will be piles of things to attend to & endless interruptions; whereas here, noth-ing – so he is going to try & stay until the book is ready for the printers. That may mean a few days only – it depends on what turns up to be added or deleted. The book is written: it is a matter of 'pulling together.' I will let you know as soon as we have any plans.

I am *longing* to see Hamlet.

I am sorry about Tess. I quite foresaw how it would be. I am sorry for Gwenny, too! I havnt liked her pictures in the part. They look too 'made up.'

Looking forward to meeting soon, & with love from us both.

Yours

C.F. Shaw

The BRT modern-dress **Hamlet**, directed by H.K. Ayliff, designed by Paul Shelving, had opened in Birmingham on 9 November 1925, and transferred to the Kingsway Theatre,

London, on 15 August 1925. A stage adaptation of Hardy's *Tess of the D'Urbervilles*, with Gwen Ffrangcon-Davies (**Gwenny**) as Tess opened to mixed reviews in Barnes on 7 September 1925, but ran for fifty-two performances when it transferred to the Garrick Theatre in the West End on 2 November 1925.

21 / To Barry Jackson   Ayot St Lawrence, Welwyn, Herts.

9th October 1927

[ALS]

In the two years that elapsed between this letter and the previous one (a gap caused by loss of the letters, not a cooling of relations), Jackson remained busy with Birmingham and London productions, including several Shaws – How He Lied to Her Husband, Caesar and Cleopatra, *and* The Philanderer *in the BRT 1925–6 season, and* The Devil's Disciple *the following season – and his own* Marvellous History of Saint Bernard *in London (Kingsway Theatre, April 1926). Shaw, in the meantime, celebrated his seventieth birthday, turned down a knighthood, and accepted the Nobel Prize. He published* Translations and Tomfooleries, *but completed no new plays. With Charlotte, he took two lengthy Italian holidays in Stresa in the summers of 1926 and 1927 (dallying both years with the young American actress Molly Tompkins). When the Shaws returned to England after their 1927 holiday they moved into a new London flat in Whitehall Court, Westminster, a move necessitated by the demolition of their previous flat in Adelphi Terrace. The move took its toll on Charlotte.*

My dear Barry

Charlotte is not at present responsible for her actions. The shock of coming back to a new flat, and seeing all her furniture arranged by somebody else, culminated yesterday in a return of Italian cholera (from which we both suffered in Stresa) and a retirement to bed, where she now lies. She is getting over it; but she is anxious about you, as she is not clear as to what is to happen about Chaliapin, and has misgivings as to what form her message may have taken in transmission.

Cochran, who had a jolly day with us on the Lago, promised a box for Thursday, as we refused Tuesday; but he may have forgotten all about it. If he has, what about going with you, which would be very agreeable for us? If he hasn't, and sends us a box as distinguished from a couple of seats in his own box, will you come with us. It was the prospect of your company that induced us to consider going at all.

Have you taken any steps? This is another way of asking need I take any? You have perhaps told Charlotte; but she is for the moment incapable of retaining clear impressions, and is apprehensive that you have not been properly attended to. I am not too lucid myself.

Our movements will be as usual: Charlotte up to town on Wednesday afternoon: I follow on Thursday. Our phone here is Codicote 18, through Toll. Our old London number is cancelled: you ring up Victoria 3160 (Whitehall Court); and they put you through to Flat 130.

I sleep amazingly there. It is at least 2 floors higher than the roof of Adelphi.

Tomorrow, if Charlotte is well enough, we go to Golders Green at 2.30 to cremate dear Jane Wells (Mrs H.G.). If C. is not well enough I shall go alone, though I bar funerals as a rule.

Ever
G.B.S.

The great Russian operatic bass Feodor **Chaliapin** (1873–1938) gave a series of concerts at the Albert Hall in October 1927, opening on Tuesday the 11th. The producer was Sir Charles B. **Cochran** (1872–1951). Both the Shaws attended the funeral of **Jane Wells** on October 10th.

22 / To Barry Jackson   4 Whitehall Court SW1
                                             28th January 1928

[APCS]

Jackson had taken the BRT's production of Back to Methuselah *to the Court Theatre in February 1924. He now planned another full (five parts) production at the Court for March 1928. As usual, he was eager to have Shaw's advice on casting, and, as usual, Shaw was eager to give it. After making some arrangements to have lunch in Cambridge with Jackson, Sydney Cockerell (director of the Fitzwilliam Museum), and Otto Kyllmann (a partner in Constable & Co., Shaw's publisher), Shaw plunged right into his advice.*

... Ozymandias doesn't matter a dump; but we can't let S.S. off the Elderly Gentleman; and I think it would be a mistake for him to give up Cain, in which he makes a flamboyant mark.

Gwen's delivery, by the way, is slipping into a mannerism which, though effective in curt dialogue, spoils the long speeches in the second scene of In The Beginning. She was really great in them before; and it would be a thousand pities if she lost her grip (as she did a little at the recent matinée) by ceasing to be classically articulate and dignified.

As to Edith, *good*. I was afraid we should have had to engage Mrs P.C. for the serpent, and trust to her being wedged into a barrel for protecting the others.

G.B.S.

Ozymandias was played by Brian Clarke, who also played Cain. **S.S.** (Scott Sunderland) played the Elderly Gentleman. In the 1923 BRT production Sunderland had played all three parts. **Gwen** Ffrangcon-Davies (1896–1992) played Eve, Amaryllis, and The Ghost of Eve, as she had in Birmingham in 1923. **Edith** Evans (1888–1976) was the Serpent at the Court and at BRT, a slim Edith Evans being much preferable, in Shaw's view, to the increasingly corpulent **Mrs P.C.** – Mrs Patrick Campbell (1865–1940), the original Eliza in *Pygmalion*, and one of Shaw's feistier correspondents (see *Bernard Shaw and Mrs Patrick Campbell: Their Correspondence*, ed. Alan Dent [London: Gollancz, 1952]).

23 / To Barry Jackson

Ayot St Lawrence, Welwyn, Herts.
13th February 1928

[TLS]

Jackson made what appears to have been his first visit to the Shaws' home in Ayot St Lawrence in February 1928. Shaw's letter to Jackson in anticipation of the visit gives a good idea of the kinds of things they must have talked about.

My dear Barry

You come by the No. 2 route as far as Ayot Green. Instead of turning to the left there you keep straight on the main road and down the hill to Welwyn. The new by-pass branches off to the right: you must avoid it, also the right hand turn as you enter the town. Just keep straight on until you bunt into the church at the fork at the other end of the main street. There you will find us or await us.

I have to bar appeals for money; so Mrs Andrae's net is spread for me in vain. I'll write something that she can read if she likes. It would be a pity not to follow up Cosi if it really made good at the box office, or indeed whether or no if the loss was not too discouraging.

I had a fancy that Eric could be coached to play the Bastard in King John effectively; but Hardwicke is the only man within your reach who would have a dog's chance as Macbeth. All's Well would have been a success; but when it comes to big Burbage parts it is no use putting coat-and-trousers men into them: you must have either a Burbage or one of Bridges Adams's cast-off heavy leads.

Mrs Bennett tells me that Lady Macduff is a wonder. So, by the way, is Rosalie Fuller: go and have a look at her in The Unknown Warrior, which you must see anyhow. Maurice Brown [*sic*], a good Shavian, is also a most remarkably useful actor.

Ever

G.B.S.

PS Note, by the way, that Welwyn Garden City is *not* Welwyn. They are not even on speaking terms.

Mrs **Andrae** is unidentified. Jackson had produced Mozart's *Così fan tutte* at the BRT in the summer of 1920. A production by Walter Johnston-Douglas opened at the Kingsway Theatre, London, on 23 March 1927, transferring to the Court on 18 April 1927. A year later, 29 May 1928, Johnston-Douglas mounted it again at the Court, where Jackson held the tenancy. *King John* was among Jackson's first productions at the BRT in 1913, directed by Arnold Pinchard, a Birmingham vicar, with Jackson playing the Bastard. *King John* was not done again at the Rep until directed there by a young Peter Brook (b. 1925) in 1945. Jackson's modern-dress *Macbeth*, directed by H.K. Ayliff, opened at the Court on 6 February 1928 with **Eric** Maturin (1883–1964) as Macbeth. Maturin couldn't handle the verse, and the production was deemed a failure, though **Mrs Bennett** (Dorothy Cheston, Arnold Bennett's partner, but not married to him) seems to have been impressed with the **Lady Macduff**, played by Chris Castor. Cedric Hardwicke (1893–1964) was not in *Macbeth*, but he was a stalwart of the BRT and appeared regularly in Shaw, including Magnus in the British premiere of *The Apple Cart* at Malvern in 1929. Hardwicke was knighted in 1934. A modern-dress *All's Well That Ends Well* was directed at the Rep by Ayliff in 1927 (Shaw was at the opening), but Jackson never did it in London. Richard **Burbage** (c 1568–1619) created many major Shakespearean roles. Walter **Bridges-Adams** (1889–1965) was director of the Stratford Memorial Theatre, 1919–34. Actress **Rosalinde Fuller** (1901–82) was appearing in Paul Raynal's *Unknown Warrior* (translated by Cecil Lewis from Raynal's *Le Tombeau sous l'Arc de Triomphe*) at the Little Theatre. **Maurice Browne** (1881–1955), born in England, founded the Chicago Little Theatre in 1912. He first appeared in London in 1927. Jackson leased the Queen's Theatre from him in September 1929 for a long run of *The Apple Cart*.

24 / To G. Bernard Shaw   8th June 1928

[Bishop, *Barry Jackson*, 7, extract; original not located]

The first letter in this collection from Jackson to Shaw strikes a pessimistic note about the economics of theatre, an issue that Jackson and Shaw discussed frequently. Jackson had already (in 1924, see Letter 8) temporarily closed the Birmingham Repertory Theatre, and now, after twenty-nine productions in London, saw little hope of making any money. Jackson's difficulties in London were compounded by the fact that he had no permanent theatrical base there, relying, as he puts it, on 'furnished apartments.'

I enclose a list of plays for which I have been responsible in London since 1918. Every production has lost money in varying sums from £10,000 downwards. The only plays which have paid their way are the two works of Eden Phillpotts and John Drinkwater's *Abraham Lincoln*, and it took me three months of solid loss to induce the public to come to one of these. Where are we who love the theatre, and are of sincere endeavour, situate? Is history going on repeating itself to the end of time, and is the Birmingham Repertory Theatre to go the way of the Horniman and Barker ventures?

The financial loss, as you see, has been no light burden to fall on the shoulders of one individual. But quite apart from this is the more important fact of the moral effect on the public and the members of my staff. Many of the latter who are with me for a transitory period perhaps care only for treasury night, but I refuse to believe they are in the majority.

The causes of our troubles are legion. To take a few: the theatre is absolutely permeated with purely financial interests; the new rich will not go to intelligent plays (one might include many of the older rich), and unfortunately we depend upon them for a part of our income, and when they do come, they are often a nuisance to everybody and themselves; the cheaper seats are so uncomfortable that I wonder anyone sits upon them; then we have the difficulties of advertising (which to-day appears to be the only method of inducing anyone to do anything); and the fact that in London we are living in furnished apartments, so to speak, with no roof of our own.

[Barry Jackson]

The **list of plays** mentioned by Jackson has not survived, but a full list would have started with Drinkwater's *Abraham Lincoln*, which opened at the Lyric in Hammersmith on 19 February 1919, and concluded with Luigi Pirandello's *Six Characters in Search of an Author*, which opened at the Globe on 28 May 1928. Jackson went on to produce another twenty-eight plays in London, concluding with Shaw's *Caesar and Cleopatra* at the Old Vic in July

1956. *Abraham Lincoln* ran for 467 performances, while the two plays by **Eden Phillpotts** (1862–1960), *The Farmer's Wife* (Court, 11 March 1924) and *Yellow Sands* (Haymarket 3 November 1926), ran for 1328 and 612 performances respectively. Annie **Horniman** (1860–1937) founded the Manchester Repertory Company in 1907. She closed it ten years later, having produced over 200 plays – half of them new works – but at considerable financial loss. Similarly, Harley Granville **Barker**'s programming at the Court Theatre, 1904–7, with J.E. Vedrenne, had been innovative (new plays by Shaw, for example), but financially unsuccessful.

25 / To Barry Jackson June 1928

[Bishop, *Barry Jackson*, 8–11; original not located]

Shaw's lengthy response to Jackson's account of his financial disappointments was not very encouraging. And Shaw's pessimism about the prospects for a National Shakespeare Theatre takes on a particular significance in the light of Jackson's appointment nearly twenty years later (Letter 142) as director of the Shakespeare Memorial Theatre in Stratford.

My dear Barry Jackson

In reply to your important letter of the 8th I have really nothing to say that you do not know already. Except that the situation has been worsened by an inflation of theatre rents and the rise in salaries and prices of all sorts through the war[,] it remains much as it has been throughout my experience, which began with Grein's Independent Theatre, the Stage Society, and Miss Horniman's start at the old Avenue Theatre in 1894, when *Arms and the Man* was produced by her. But none of these effected a lodgment as a going concern in London; and nothing that has any bearing on your present position happened until 1904, when Vedrenne and Barker started at the Court Theatre with the unrepeatable asset of a tame author (myself) carrying a reserve of unacted plays at the back of his current activities, and a beautiful young genius -- actor, author, and producer of exquisite taste [i.e., Barker] – as partner in the concern. There was no capital: the venture paid its way and yielded to the two partners, not always the thousand a year apiece they put themselves down for, but near enough to it to keep them going for a few years. But Barker was bent on a real repertory theatre (this was never realised) as distinguished from a short-run theatre; and both he and

Vedrenne wanted to launch out into a real West-End theatre. I believed in the fixed short-run system, and not in the nightly-change repertory system except as a remote development of the fixed short run; and I greatly doubted whether the enterprise would bear expansion; but I agreed that we could find out the limit only by going on until we were stopped.

Well, we went on until we were stopped; and the winding-up cost Barker every rap he had, and I had to disgorge a sum which may have been equal to all the royalties I had taken, or may not: I never made the calculation; but it was a substantial sum, anyhow.

On the basis of our experience Barker calculated that a self-supporting repertory theatre was impossible; but that with a theatre free of rent and rates he could do it. That meant a municipal theatre.

After that, Lord Howard de Walden backed Barker in a lordly way at the St James's and lost. He afterwards, at my request ('Will you put down £500 if I do the same?') backed him in a small way at the Little and Kingsway Theatres, and I did well out of it through the success of *The Great Adventure*. Finally came the war and Barker's retirement on his second marriage. Nothing occurred meanwhile to shake his calculation that highbrow theatre could not exist without an endowment sufficient to cover at least rent, rates, and taxes.

Then you took up the running, with, as it seems to me, virtually the same moral: that is to say, an enthusiast with an independent income could run a repertory theatre in a provincial city for no more (barring his own labour) than it would cost to run a steam yacht. My guess as to Miss Horniman is that her experience came to the same thing.

Now it is hardly possible for a private person to stand this racket without getting cold feet when the adventure has lost its first novelty and exhausted its possibilities of further novelty without any signs of becoming a big national institution. Also one gets tired of the discouragement of the critics, who soon become more generous in their recognition of last year's work, but invariably praise it only to show what a terrible falling off there is this year. My last play but one is always a masterpiece: my last play is always most unsatisfactory; and this holds good also of the manager's productions.

Every year almost, no matter what you deal in, the cost of selling the article becomes greater in proportion to the cost of producing it. Unless you shout, Buy, buy, buy from the walls and newspaper columns and railway stations louder than your competitors you are overlooked.

Nevertheless, I am not convinced that with capital enough a much nearer approach to solvency, and certainly a great saving of business worry in hiring theatres might not be achieved. The first thing to do is to give up once for all the snobbery of West-End box office and face the fact that good drama must live by the class that cannot afford more for an evening's entertainment than five shillings first class, half a crown second class, and a shilling third class. The rich people must be thrown over completely, not because they are less susceptible than the relatively poor to dramatic art, but because they can afford to pay for so many counter attractions both at home and in society, whereas the shilling and half-crown people have to choose between a theatre and a dull evening in a not too comfortable home. Even the present shilling galleries are better fun than the domestic alternative.

But low prices will not pay in small theatres. When the Bancrofts introduced the tiny theatre and the cup-and-saucer drama, they had to introduce ten-shilling stalls and abolish the pit, which until then came right up to the orchestra and was the heart of the house. By doing so they smashed your theatre and mine and produced the present impasse.

Therefore we need large theatres; and a large theatre in a central situation in London means a huge ground-rent, with a correspondingly high valuation at heavy rates. It may be therefore that a central theatre would be impossible without a free site and exemption from rates as an educational institution. But in the suburbs or in the provinces large theatres, moderate prices, and morning dress might make the manager's situation, if not eligible, at least bearable. Finally, the municipality might take it on if there had been sufficient propaganda of the municipal idea to make that step popular and possible – if only to enable the dole system to reach its historic climax in bread and circuses.

What to suggest is not so clear. The Old Vic has kept afloat with all sorts of odd scraps of endowment and sending the hat round, trading heavily on Shakespeare's sanctity, but making its money by Opera. Incidentally it is squeezing all the money that is to be got out of the public for Sadler's Wells, whilst the Stratford people are draining the Americans.

Neither of them has asked for a subsidy, though both would if they thought they had a chance of getting it. The question is, What are you to ask for or propose if you go beyond a mere statement of the situation?

Meanwhile, the old Shakespeare Memorial Theatre Committee is sitting helplessly on the £70,000 put down by Carl Meyer. They helped Archie Flower to finance Bridges Adams's Stratford Company with the interest; but now the Charity Commissioners will not allow them to do anything with either the principal or interest except build a National Shakespeare Theatre in London at a cost which will remain beyond their means until the £70,000 has accumulated at compound interest to half a million, the date of which event may be fixed roughly at 1970! The utter refusal of the British public to contribute anything to hasten the process, and the fact that practically the entire principal was put down by a German, makes the national part of the business such a hollow sham that one could very well call on the Charity Commissioners to make a new scheme. But if you ask me what scheme, I am stumped. Between private adventurers like yourself and State and municipal theatres it is not easy to find a *tertium quid*.

And then the films – the talking films and their future!

It is no use: I give up.

Ever,

G.B.S.

The **Independent Theatre** Society was founded as a private club in 1891 by J.T. **Grein** (1862–1935). Its first production was Ibsen's *Ghosts* on 13 March 1891, followed by *Widowers' Houses*, Shaw's first play, on 9 December 1892. The Independent Theatre was succeeded by the **Stage Society**, whose first production was Shaw's *You Never Can Tell* on 26 November 1899. The Stage Society also produced the premiere of Shaw's *Mrs Warren's Profession* (5 January 1902) and several other unlicensed plays. *Arms and the Man* had its premiere at the Avenue Theatre on 21 April 1894. **Lord Howard de Walden** was Harley Granville Barker's patron for a repertory season at the St James's Theatre in 1913–14. Arnold Bennett's comedy *The Great Adventure* (from his 1908 novel, *Buried Alive*) opened at the Kingsway Theatre on 25 March 1913 and ran for 674 performances. The **Bancrofts**, Squire (1841–1926) and his wife Marie (1839–1921), presented domestic ('**cup-and-saucer**') plays at the Prince of Wales's Theatre, particularly the plays of T.W. Robertson (*Society*, 1865, and *Caste*, 1867). The **Old Vic** was being managed in 1928 by Lilian Baylis, mainly on a repertoire of Shakespeare and opera. Baylis was also fund-raising for a new theatre on the site of the original **Sadler's Wells** Theatre, which eventually opened in 1931. She began fund-raising in 1926, just as the campaign began for a new Shakespeare Memorial Theatre in Stratford, the first, which opened in 1879, having burned down. At the same time, the **Shakespeare Memorial** National **Theatre Committee**, of which Shaw was a member, was campaigning for a theatre located in London, hoping to build on a generous 1909 donation by Anglo-German busi-

34

nessman **Carl Meyer**. Stratford interests, however, led by brewing magnate Archibald **Flower** and William **Bridges-Adams** (1889–1965), director of the Shakespeare Memorial Theatre from 1919 to 1934, wanted a new theatre in Stratford. Assisted by American donations, Stratford got their wish with the opening of the new Shakespeare Memorial Theatre (still in operation) in 1932. Funds from the Shakespeare Memorial National Theatre Committee eventually went to the National Theatre, founded in 1961 at the Old Vic (under Laurence Olivier) pending construction of the permanent site on the South Bank, which opened in 1976 – just six years later than Shaw's prediction.

26 / To Barry Jackson   4 Whitehall Court SW1
13th July 1928

[APCS]

A letter from Bridges Adams has this instant reminded [me] of my appointment at 87 Regent St 11 hours and 43 minutes ago.

I am flabbergasted.

All the morning I was up to my neck in telegrams to hotels, railway tickets, letters of credit, retrieving arrangements that had fallen through, and finally meeting Helen Wills (a siren!) at Lady Astor's lunch.

The appointment was in my diary staring me in the face, and I never became conscious of it.

I did not really matter; but the frightful thought occurs – perhaps YOU forgot it too.

Decidedly I am ageing. Our address from Monday will be Hotel des Roches Rouges, Agay, Var, France.

G.B.S.

Helen Wills (1905–98) was an American tennis player, the world leader in women's tennis in the 1920s and 1930s. Nancy **Astor** (1879–1964) was the first woman to sit in the British House of Commons. Shaw met her in 1926 and they remained close for the rest of his life.

27 / To Barry Jackson   Ayot St Lawrence, Welwyn, Herts.
14th November 1928

[ALS]

There are numerous accounts of the genesis of the Malvern Festival, including several by Barry Jackson himself. In one of these accounts (Drama: The Quarterly Review of Theatre, n.s. 20, Spring 1951: 29–31) Jackson expresses his admiration for the annual Shakespeare Festival at Stratford and the Three Choirs Festival at Hereford, Gloucester, and Worcester. Jackson had bought a home near Malvern, 'Blackhill,' and on one of Shaw's visits there in 1928 – at a time when, as earlier letters (24, 25) have shown, both Jackson and Shaw were disillusioned with the commercial theatre of London's West End – Jackson proposed a 'Festival of Drama' at Malvern. 'My proposition met with something more than the customary twinkling enthusiasm which has been of unfathomable help to innumerable adventurers. "I must write you a play," he immediately said' – and that play was The Apple Cart. *Jackson assumed from the beginning that the world premiere would take place at Malvern, but Shaw disappointed him by giving that privilege to the Teatr Polski in Warsaw, where* The Apple Cart *opened (in Polish) on 14 June 1929. Jackson had to be content with the English-language premiere, which opened the first Malvern Festival on 19 August 1929, with no objections from the censor (see Letter 33). Cedric Hardwicke (not George Arliss) played King Magnus.*

My dear Barry Jackson

Strictly between ourselves for the present, and because you ought to be the first to know, my suggestion of a new play for the Malvern Buhnenfestspiel may materialize. In fact I have actually written the equivalent of the first two acts of a five act play, though of course it will not be in acts of the old sort.

The snag in it is that we may have difficulty with the censor, as the hero (a good Arliss part, by the way) is a King – *the* King, at an undetermined future date beyond present lifetimes. But as he is a very clever King, and gets the better of his ministers, I doubt if the demurrage will be insuperable.

ever
G.B.S.

Bühnenfestspeil ('stage festival performance') was a term used by Richard Wagner for his *Ring* cycle of operas, performed over several days.

28 / To Barry Jackson   Ayot St Lawrence, Welwyn, Herts.
21st November 1928

[ALCS]

Shaw was an active partner from the beginning in planning the programs for the Malvern Festival, although Jackson did not always follow his advice. Despite

36

Shaw's enthusiasm for Harley Granville Barker's His Majesty, *for example, Jackson never produced it, at Malvern or anywhere else. It had opened in Brighton on 26 March 1927, but never achieved a London production. Nor was* Saint Joan *chosen for the inaugural Festival. The all-Shaw program consisted of* The Apple Cart, Back to Methuselah, Heartbreak House, *and* Caesar and Cleopatra.

My dear B.J.

Get Granville-Barker's new play 'His Majesty' just published by Sidgwick & Jackson. I have read 2 acts: it must be produced by somebody. If he has not arranged for a production at the Ambassadors or the like what about staging a grand come-back for him at the Malvern Festival. It happens that my play is also about a King. The coincidence would be interesting. Two new plays by the *ci devant* Damon & Pythias of the advanced drama, with St Joan & Caesar, would give Methuselah a rest. Think it over.

By the way, as to secrecy, use your discretion. I do not want the press to get it until I have carried it so far that its completion in time is fairly certain; but you cannot conveniently make your arrangements with your lips padlocked. Besides, complete secrecy is not possible. So treat it as *your* secret, and let it go if and when you think best.

G.B.S.

Shaw's nostalgic allusion to **Damon & Pythias,** models of loyal friendship and mutual support from fourth-century BC Syracuse, recalls his relationship with Barker before Barker's marriage to Helen Huntington (see headnote to Letter 19).

29 / To Barry Jackson   Ayot St Lawrence, Welwyn, Herts.
   From Charlotte F. Shaw   6th January 1929

[ALS]

Dear Barry

I didn't answer your letter before Christmas as you said you were going away at once. I hope you have had a happy, peaceful time – that you are much the better for it. I have been in a wild racket – but I am none the worse!

Now I have great news. The play is finished! I myself think that as a successor to St Joan it is as good as it could possibly be. A complete break away. Everything there is of a contrast! He is starting now to revise & cut it, & would rather read it to *you* when that is done – but he read it at Cliveden in its rough state, & it was an entire & overwhelming success – kept them in fits of laughter, & a little frightened at the same time. He tells me to say you can count on it, for even if he 'died tomorrow, it's fit to play as it is.'

So that's that.

Will you let me know directly you get back, because we will fix up a reading as soon as possible.

Renewed best wishes of all sorts for the New Year.

Ever

Charlotte F. Shaw

Cliveden was the home of Waldorf and Nancy Astor, where the Shaws were frequent guests.

30 / To Barry Jackson   Ayot St Lawrence, Welwyn, Herts.
[January 1929]

[TLS]

While Shaw took some pleasure in seeing himself as the Wagner of Malvern, he also, as he says in this letter, felt 'rather apologetic about being the only fish' in Jackson's 1929 Malvern basket. So he pushed Harley Granville Barker's His Majesty again, to no avail. Shaw was successful, however, in dissuading Jackson from including Man and Superman, a play never done at Malvern, though Jackson did eventually produce it in Birmingham in 1945, directed by Peter Brook, with Paul Scofield as Tanner. Shaw's caution about press announcements was perhaps reflected in one that appeared in the periodical Everyman on 31 January 1929: 'Mr Bernard Shaw has written a new play in one act. It is entitled "The Apple Tart," and will be produced at Mr Barry Jackson's Festival at Malvern round about next August. All we can say about it, at present, is that it has an appetising title.' Shaw sent a clipping of this to Jackson, commenting, 'Observe the happy change of title in the enclosed.'

My dear Barry

I should go slow about the announcements, doling them out in relays.

The announcement about Malvern-Bayreuth alone, without any details as to the programs, will provide a quite sensational lot of paragraphs to start with. The new play by me written ad hoc would produce a fresh crop. And the ball could be kept rolling kick by kick until all the cats were out of the bag.

In particular I deprecate your committing yourself on the subject of Man & Superman. Esmé Percy, the only man who knows the frightfully long part of Tanner at full length, has left Macdona to play Byron in a play of that name. He may not return. The only occasion on which I saw the complete performance was with a cast which was not up to your standard. To bring such a cast – especially the women – into immediate comparison with your proposed casts for Malvern would let the Festival down heavily. All Macdona's best young people are on his African and Far East tours. He believes his productions to be far superior to anything of the kind hitherto witnessed on earth, and would take on your proposal confidently. But whether the goods would satisfy you when delivered is another matter. Certainly they would not satisfy me if they were no better than the necessarily cheap articles with which he tours the provinces.

Suppose you leave out Man & Superman it is easy to give extra performances of any of the others. But I am rather apologetic about being the only fish in your basket. Remember that you are a full generation younger than I, and that even in Malvern it is not wise to worship the setting sun, especially on the east side of the hills. What about that play of Barker's? He would give you a very distinguished production of it and take it quite off the overloaded hands of Ayliff. As a matter of prestige, I don't think you ought to let another manager get it. It could not fail, even if it had not a very rowdy success. Just turn it over in your mind once again.

The first two acts of The Apple Cart are already at the printer's.

It is excellent policy to boost the local people. Their magnification will help the Festival and please them immensely.

I go up to town tomorrow as usual until Saturday.

ever

G.B.S.

Esmé Percy (1887–1957) toured extensively with the Macdona Players in the 1920s in several major Shaw roles. He played Tanner in the first production of the full *Man and Superman* in Edinburgh in 1915 and again in the first London production of the full text, which opened at the Regent Theatre on 23 October 1925. He played Byron in Alicia Ramsey's play of that name in Portsmouth in January 1929 and in a short run at the Lyric in London, where it opened on 22 January 1929.

31 / To Barry Jackson   Ayot St Lawrence, Welwyn, Herts.
                                                    10th February 1929

[TLU (c)]

The Apple Cart was first published in German, as Der Kaiser von Amerika, on 19 October 1929. The English text was first published (with Saint Joan) in the Collected Edition, volume 17, on 22 August 1930, and the first separate text in English appeared on 11 December 1930. The version referred to here by Shaw was a rough proof. On 3 October 1929 Shaw gave a rough proof copy of The Apple Cart to Jackson, inscribing it 'My dear Barry[,] Here is the play, which owes its existence entirely to you. By the way, though I took it as a matter of course, I was not insensible of the care you took of us – Charlotte and myself – at Malvern. For that and a thousand other kindnesses ten thousand thanks. G. Bernard Shaw[.] PS Bon voyage to Canada!' This copy is now in the archives of the Birmingham Repertory Theatre, Birmingham Central Library. For Jackson in Canada see headnote to Letter 47.

My dear Barry

The Apple Cart has arrived from the printer. Can you and Ayliff sacrifice next Tuesday to a reading down here? If you come by car, time yourself so as to arrive here round about 12, so that I can read the first act before lunch and the rest after. If by train, take the 11-30 from Kings Cross to Hatfield, where our car will meet you and take you on.

If you prefer reading-and-dinner at Whitehall Court we can, I think, arrange that for Friday. But it would be rather less gloomy down here.

If you drive down by the Hatfield route remember that the printed instructions above have been obsoleted by the new by-pass. In Barnet keep to the right of the church, and then take the St Albans road which turns out of the main street to the left. The by-pass turns to the right out of that, and lands you beyond Hatfield a little short of the Bull Inn. You can let the car rip on the new road.

I am duplicating this letter for Birmingham and Chelsea.

When is Jitta on? I think I must rush down and see a matinée.

                                                    ever
                                                    G.B.S.

Shaw's letter is typed below **printed instructions** headed 'FROM LONDON TO AYOT ST LAWRENCE BY ROAD.' Jackson never produced *Jitta* (*Jitta's Atonement*). Charles Macdona opened a four-week season of eight Shaw plays at the Embassy Theatre in London on 26 February 1929, but it did not include *Jitta's Atonement*.

32 / To Barry Jackson   Ayot St Lawrence, Welwyn, Herts.
    From Charlotte F. Shaw   [19th February 1929]

[ALS]

Dear Barry

GBS is very sorry he cant manage Thursday; he has an important engagement. But he wants you & Mr Ayliff to come at 6 on Friday to Whitehall Court. He will read the first act before dinner. Then you will both dine with us, round about 7.30 & he will read the rest after.

    Morning dress, I suggest, but whatever you prefer. GBS wont dress.

    Looking forward so much to this, & a chat.

Yours
C.F.S.

Shaw's diary indicates that he spent Thursday 21 February in bed at Whitehall Court, ill with influenza. His **important engagement** for that day, then, probably did not materialize.

33 / To Barry Jackson   4 Whitehall Court SW1
    6th April 1929

[ALS]

Shaw left England for a visit to Europe on 14 April 1929, not returning until 13 June. In the meantime he alerted Lord Cromer, the Lord Chamberlain, to the potentially sensitive subject matter – royalty and politics – of The Apple Cart. *The Lord Chamberlain, as official censor, normally looked askance on plays that commented on, or might be perceived as commenting on, British royalty or British politicians. In the case of* The Apple Cart, *however, there were no difficulties. It may have helped that Cromer, Jackson, and Shaw were colleagues on the Council of the Royal Academy of Dramatic Art (RADA), an organization that Shaw served loyally from 1911 to 1941 and to which he left a generous bequest. Jackson, on the other hand, though a member of the Council, was not very active.*

My dear Barry

The only copies left are this one and the one Owen Nares has. In sending you this one I am leaving myself destitute. I havn't even a copy to revise for the printer. Therefore you must retrieve one for me somewhere and somehow.

Charlotte's sister died yesterday morning. We shall be at the funeral in Shropshire on Monday. Our departure for Italy is now fixed for Sunday the 14th. Our address will be Hotel Brioni, Brioni Island, Istria, Italy. On the 16th we shall be at the Savoy Hotel, Trieste; but that is only to break the long journey and look round the town.

We shall be in London from Thursday morning until we start.

I have prepared Cromer for the worst. Don't forget that he is our colleague on the Council of the R.A.D.A., which you so scandalously neglect.

ever
G.B.S.

Owen Nares (1888–1943), actor and producer, was a serious contender for the part of Magnus in *The Apple Cart*, but the role eventually went to Cedric Hardwicke. **Charlotte's sister**, Mary (Sissie) Cholmondeley (wife of General Hugh Cholmondeley), died in London and was buried in Edstaston, Shropshire. There is a memorial window to her in the Edstaston Church.

34 / To G. Bernard Shaw

The Birmingham Repertory
Theatre Companies
34 Henrietta Street, London WC2
9th April 1929

[TLS]

Jackson's comment in this letter on the 'splendid people working on the [RADA] Committee' provoked a response from Shaw. He underlined Jackson's words, added 'Hideous sarcasm. Three is about the outside quorum. The place is really interesting in its way,' and returned the letter to Jackson on 11 April.

My dear G.B.S.

I called at the Lord Chamberlain's office this morning and deposited the remaining copy of the play [*The Apple Cart*], asking to have it returned to Mr Phillips at this office the earliest possible moment, and it shall then be sent back to you.

I deplore my dreadful neglect of the R.A.D.A., but I really do have to stop somewhere, and as there are such splendid people working on the Committee, I fear I should only be in the way. However, in future I will try to mend my ways.

I am so sorry you have had all this trouble just before embarking on your journey.

Yours,
Barry

Cyril **Phillips** (b. 1894) succeeded Bache Matthews as General Manager of the Birmingham Repertory Theatre.

35 / To Barry Jackson   Hotel Brioni, Brioni, Italy
                                           13th May 1929

[ALS]

Shaw's absence abroad did not, of course, deter him from continuing to comment on matters relating to the production (and publication) of The Apple Cart.

My dear Barry Jackson

A question has arisen of publishing the Apple Cart in August, simultaneously with the production at Malvern. Naturally, the publishers and the booksellers are eager to profit by the curiosity which the play has created.

Now after thinking it carefully over I am very decidedly of [the] opinion that however jolly this might be for the booksellers it would be very bad for the box office. The opposite view is tenable: it is argued that the people who read the play will be wild to see it acted. I don't believe it. What do you think? Would publication, in your opinion, satisfy the current curiosity or stimulate it – on balance? I say it would satisfy. But if you say it would stimulate, you need not fear to damage me, as I reap the harvest either way.

If you prefer to have the book kept back until the play has had its first fling in Malvern, Birmingham and London I shall applaud your sagacity, and comply all the more readily as I rather want to wait until I can add another play, and give the bookbuyers the usual good value for their money.

I gather from the Observer that O.N. [Owen Nares] did not smile on the part, and that it has gone to Cedric [Hardwicke]. On the whole, I think this is lucky. I am not sure that we could get the reserves of power needed to give full value to the part from anyone else within our reach; and I am sure that it is good policy, when you have so good a card in your hand as Cedric, to play him for all the parts are worth.

We have now been four weeks in this island, which is all that Caliban claims for it, and which, nevertheless, Prospero is glad to quit before it makes him incapable of moving. We sail on Wednesday (day after tomorrow – the 15th) for Dubrobnic (ci devant Ragusa), and when we have had enough of it we shall have a look at Spalato and its ruins of Adelphi Terrace, and cross the Adriatic to Venice, where we shall perhaps stay long enough to escape the election. As we cannot fix dates, all letters had better go to Miss Patch.

ever
G.B.S.

Charlotte sends affectionate messages.

The general **election** was held on 7 June 1929 (a week before the Shaws' return to England). Ramsay MacDonald led the Labour Party to victory over Stanley Baldwin's Conservatives. Blanche **Patch** (1879–1966) was Shaw's secretary from 1920 to his death.

36 / To Barry Jackson   Grand Hotel, Dubrovnik, Yugoslavia
    From Charlotte F. Shaw   21st May 1929

[ALS]

Dear Barry

It seems untold ages since I have heard anything of you. Far, far too long. How is all going with you. I do wonder.

We shall not go back before the election, but directly after, I think. We are deliberately staying away till then because it would be so difficult for G.B.S. to refuse the many requests to him to go to speak for people, & he really is not strong enough now to knock about in the rough & tumble of an election.

We have had only middling luck on our holiday. We went, as you know, to Brioni. It had many advantages: complete & entire rest: nothing to do & a great Island 3 miles by 1 mile to roam all over at our pleasure: wild, with lovely southern sea all round. But alas! it did not agree with us. It was the most relaxing & depressing place I ever was in. I used to wake every morning feeling suicidal, & we got so stiff & old from the damp – or something! We got so run down we couldn't summon up energy to get away!

However at last we escaped here, *Ragusa* – called in the Slav language Dubrovnik. A darling little place, where we are slowly getting younger again. We have done some marvellous drives over perpendicular mountains. I must leave these to tell you about later. The hedges are pomegranates – in *flower*! We found a really marvellous mausoleum by Meštrović. The people are nice – but back boneless.

How about Malvern. I feel it beginning to come near. I am looking forward to it quite out-of-the-way much.

Do you remember I asked if I could have a Box, (paying!!). You did not know at the time. Can I? Our friend T. E. Shaw (Col. Lawrence) is coming for part, possibly all, of the time as our guest. Can you give him a seat? Of course if I have a Box he will be there.

I know you will make it all right.

G.B.S. wrote from Brioni, but I don't know what he said, & am sure he would forget Lawrence!

We go to Venice next Monday (26th) & shall stay there a week or 10 days.

With love, ever
C.F. Shaw

Ivan **Meštrović** (1883-1935), Yugoslavian sculptor, designed two mausoleums near Dubrovnik, in the villages of Cavtat and Otavice. **T.E. Shaw** (1888–1935), Lawrence of Arabia, first met Shaw in 1922. He subsequently (1927) adopted Shaw's surname by deed poll. He is the model for Private Meek in *Too True to be Good.*

37 / To Barry Jackson   Ayot St Lawrence, Welwyn, Herts.
                                                              20th July 1929

[APCS]

After the Malvern production, The Apple Cart *moved to Birmingham for a short*

run and then, on 17 September 1929, it opened at the Queen's Theatre in Lon-
don's West End for a run of 285 performances. A production by Robert Loraine
(1876–1935) of Edwin Burke's comedy This Thing Called Love!, *in which*
Loraine also starred, closed at the Apollo Theatre on the day that Shaw wrote this
letter. Loraine had created the role of Don Juan in Don Juan in Hell *at the Court*
in 1907, but business prevailed over sentiment, neither Shaw nor Jackson want-
ing distractions from or competition for The Apple Cart, *so Loraine had to do*
without Arms and the Man.

Loraine came round to the O.V. this morning wanting Arms & the Man
as a stopgap at the Apollo, as frost prevails there in spite of the heat. Of
course I said that any anticipation of the Apple Cart at a West End house
would upset it. He found this so extraordinarily unreasonable that he
said he would ask you whether you really objected. So be prepared to
explain that a production by him would eclipse our little enterprise. Or
else offer to send him to Australia as Magnus. Of course what is the matter with his theatre is the heat, and a part not good enough for him.

G.B.S.

O.V. is the Old Vic, where Shaw was rehearsing plays, including *The Apple Cart,* in preparation for the August 19th opening of the Malvern Festival.

38 / To Barry Jackson   Ayot St Lawrence, Welwyn, Herts.
                                                        23rd July 1929
[APCS]

After writing to you I wrote to Robert in conclusive terms.

He is right, probably, in thinking that two apparently competing Shaw
seasons would help one another for once in a sensational way; but then
you would have to run both and find the two companies. Bogus competition is quite a good game sometimes; but real competition is ruinous.

I shall be up tomorrow (Wednesday) at the O.V.

G.B.S.

39 / To Barry Jackson   Ayot St Lawrence, Welwyn, Herts.

29th July 1929

[APCS]

*As the opening of the first Malvern Festival approached, Jackson continued to consult Shaw on many details, including the contents of the handsome souvenir programs provided to patrons of the Festival. The 1929 forty-page program (twelve pages of advertisements) contained a biography of Shaw (see Letter 40), information on Malvern, brief notes on the plays (*The Apple Cart, Back to Methuselah, Caesar and Cleopatra, *and* Heartbreak House*), and notes (with photographs) on the artists and the Malvern Theatre.*

Not nearly thick enough nor long enough. I have drafted a considerable expansion & sent it to Miss Patch to type and let me have it at the O.V. on Wednesday morning.

G.B.S.

I am not sure that the program should not have some exegetical notes to Methuselah. It will be a *very* important document & should have pictures &c galore.

40 / To Barry Jackson   4 Whitehall Court SW1

31st July 1929

[ALS]

The particular part of the Malvern souvenir program referred to by Shaw in this letter was a short biography of Shaw himself, published, as Shaw directed, with 'A.B.,' Alan Bland, as the designated author. Bland was publicity manager for Jackson, as well as occasional playwright and actor.

My dear Barry

I enclose the corrected copy for the program. It reads all right; but it must have a signature, as the personalities in it could not appear in a managerial manifesto which could be attributed to you. I have therefore signed it A.B. If Alan Bland objects, sack him, or put the initials of the office boy.

You must keep an iron hand on your press agents. The other day they wanted me to be photographed *at rehearsal.* They have now induced

Hardwicke, under protest, to write a thousand words entitled *G.B.S. rehearses The Apple Cart*, for publication. No doubt they have extracted *Barry Jackson Behind the Scenes* from Scott [Sunderland], *Ayliff Assuages Tantrums* from Phyllis Shand, and *Shelving Struggles with Stockings for Soubrettes* by 'Superwoman.'

Make them understand, by bodily violence if necessary, that they must not lift the smallest corner of the curtain – that it is worse than betraying the secrets of the confessional to give away the sacred intimacies of the holy of holies.

Poor Hardwicke's article is so nice that I enclose it for your perusal. Ask him to sign it and make me a present of it. It cannot be published until I am dead.

I had a horrid headache this morning, and was of next to no use.

Do not imagine that these things worry me: they are all in the day's work; and I have long since acquired the skin of a rhinoceros.

ever

G.B.S.

Cedric Hardwicke's account of the rehearsals for *The Apple Cart* appeared in his memoirs, *Let's Pretend: Recollections of a Lucky Actor,* published in 1932 (London: Grayson & Grayson), some years before Shaw's death. A slightly longer, but essentially the same, account appeared in *A Victorian in Orbit: The Irreverent Memoirs of Sir Cedric Hardwicke* (London: Methuen, 1961). Paul **Shelving** (1889–1968) was Barry Jackson's leading designer. His work was celebrated in an exhibition at the Birmingham City Museum and Art Gallery in 1986, accompanied by the publication of *Paul Shelving (1888–1968): Stage Designer,* edited by Tessa Sidey. **Phyllis Shand** (b. 1894) performed regularly in BRT productions and at Malvern (though not in *The Apple Cart*).

41 / To Barry Jackson   Ayot St Lawrence, Welwyn, Herts.
19th January 1930

[APCS]

The Apple Cart *was still running at the Queen's Theatre in the West End when this letter was written. The speech that Jackson (and, presumably, the BBC) had in mind is Magnus's in Act 1 when he defends his role as monarch as a bulwark against 'the squalor of the political arena in which we have to struggle with foolish factions in parliament and with ignorant voters in the constituencies.'*

I am quite against a broadcast of the King's long speech until the play is stone dead on the stage. Taken out of its context it would sound exactly like a page of Macaulay, and a dull one at that. The listeners-in would conclude that the whole play is like the speech, and would carefully abstain from buying tickets, to the great damage of both the tour and the London season. I have resisted urgent pressure to publish the play so as to keep the theatre the only avenue to its delights; and it would be idiotic to sanction a detrimental broadcast after refusing repeatedly to sanction what would be for me at least an immediately lucrative publication. I take it that you will not disagree.

I have been unable to go to the Scala, much as the operas interest me. But as to the enterprise, what are you going to do with a handful of students who start by asking 17/- instead of 1s/5d (tax included) for stalls?

G.B.S.

Shaw was familiar with the work of essayist and historian Thomas Babington **Macaulay** (1800–59) from as early as 1889 when he read his work in the *Edinburgh Review*. Carl Maria von Weber's *Der Freischütz* opened at the **Scala** Theatre in London on 14 January 1929, conducted by Sir Thomas Beecham, part of the Scala's 1929–30 London Opera Festival. The production drew upon members of the Oxford University Opera Club – hence Shaw's sardonic reference to high ticket prices.

42 / To Barry Jackson   Ayot St Lawrence, Welwyn, Herts.

2nd March 1930

[ALS]

The inaugural Malvern Festival had been an artistic (and social) success, and Jackson was prepared to fund a second season. The London run of The Apple Cart *closed in May 1930, so there was no problem in casting Cedric Hardwicke, Eileen Beldon (1901–85), and Edith Evans for the 1930 Malvern season. Edith Evans, however, was not in the 1930 Malvern company; Cedric Hardwicke and Eileen Beldon were, though neither appeared in the new production of* The Apple Cart. *The Shaw plays at Malvern in 1930 were* The Apple Cart, Heartbreak House, Candida, The Admirable Bashville, Widowers' Houses, The Dark Lady of the Sonnets, *and* Getting Married. *(In a letter of 24 April 1930 Shaw told Siegfried Trebitsch, 'I ought to write a new play to give it [the 1930 Malvern Festival] a genuine raison d'être; but I am afraid that is impossible in the time at my disposal' [Weiss, 314].) The 1930 season also included the first non-Shaw play at Malvern, Rudolf Besier's* The Barretts of Wimpole Street, *which went on to con-*

siderable success in London and New York. The proposed London revival of
Heartbreak House *did not take place until 1932 (25 April, Queen's Theatre).*
Shaw's reference at the end of this letter to Malvern's being 'the death of us' has,
no doubt, implications beyond the merely financial, but whereas Jackson always
lost money at Malvern, Shaw did quite well from royalties. His royalties' ledger
(kept among his business papers at the British Library of Political and Economic
Science) shows income of just over £270 from the inaugural Malvern Festival,
plus a further £143 from the two-week BRT run of The Apple Cart *immediately*
following the Festival.

My dear Barry

It did not occur to me until you were gone that if the Apple Cart over-
runs the Festival we can't do Heartbreak House at it. Without Cedric &
Eileen & Edith we should have to break the continuity of cast leading up
to a London revival; and we might have a fiasco (a press one) that would
make such a revival more difficult.

What devil tempted us to go to Malvern? It will be the death of us.

ever

G.B.S.

43 / To Barry Jackson   The Palace Hotel, Buxton, Derbyshire
2nd May 1930

[ALS]

It sounds as if a member of the audience at the London production of The Apple
Cart *had a problem hearing or understanding a key phrase in a speech by Mag-*
nus (Cedric Hardwicke) and wrote to Jackson, who passed on the question to
Shaw. The phrase occurs in a speech in Act 1: 'I should never have dreamt of
entering on a campaign of recrimination such as the Prime Minister suggested.
As he has reminded you, my own character is far too vulnerable. A king is not
allowed the luxury of a good character.' While Shaw was in London attending
rehearsals of a revival of Jitta's Atonement *at the Arts Theatre (where it opened*
on 30 April 1930, directed by Henry Oscar, with Violet Vanbrugh as Jitta), Char-
lotte became ill, much more seriously so than Shaw indicates in this letter (see Let-
ters 44 and 45).

Dear Barry

The lady mistook 'far too vulnerable' for 'far from vulnerable,' and put me to the trouble of writing to Cedric about it, as I have no copy of the A.C. left.

I came up to town for the final rehearsals of Jitta at the Arts Theatre; and what with Oscar trying to prevent Violet from acting (his school being the natural reserved force one) and I egging her on to bring the house down with every speech (my school being the ultra-stagey) we made a pretty mess of it. Nevertheless it will pass the evening if you are round that way and at a loss.

Meanwhile my back was no sooner turned than Charlotte collapsed with what – thanks to a nice young Irish doctor – she believes to be severe tonsilitis, but is in fact mild scarlatina. She is mending rapidly today, and will probably be able to return to town – or at least to Ayot – some time next week; but I cannot put a date to it and am for the moment on duty as a nurse.

So that's *my* news.

G.B.S.

44 / To Barry Jackson   The Palace Hotel, Buxton, Derbyshire
13th May 1930

[ALS]

This letter is written (in pencil) on the back of a letter to Shaw from H.K. Ayliff, dated 11 May 1930. Ayliff invited Shaw to Birmingham to see his production of Heartbreak House, *in which Ayliff came out of retirement as an actor to play Shotover. 'I hope you're coming to see us. The play goes beautifully in spite of obvious drawbacks. There was an ovation at the finish last night. I was a horrid mess on the first night, after my seven years retirement: but I'm enjoying myself now. I dare say I do a lot that will annoy you, but not being able to go in front & watch myself, I've had to trust the actor's instinct – a damned disloyal urge.'*

My dear Barry

Charlotte's illness, which was serious enough (at our ages) to keep us both in the shadow of death for nearly a week, put Heartbreak House clean out of my head; and now I have to go up to town on Wednesday afternoon and miss the Thursday matinée. I am assuming that there is not a matinée on Saturday; so I must contrive to go on Friday night or Saturday and sleep on the spot on my way down here.

Charlotte is now convalescent, though still so weak that she can do no more than sit up in her bedroom for an hour or two. But she is eating voraciously and evidently heading for a complete rally. To avoid a killing torrent of enquiries I am keeping it as quiet as possible; but it might have been a devil of a business away from home if, providentially, the hotel had not been a comfortable one with a first rate chef, and the doctor and the nurse ideal.

The prolonged stay here and the upset to my work has knocked the best chance of a new play on the head, I fear.

I should have written before; but it was better to wait until I had decisively good clinical news.

I am due to reach St Pancras tomorrow evening at 6.15, and shall dine alone at 7.30 unless by any chance you are in London and would care to ring up Miss Patch and tell her to order dinner for two.

ever
G.B.S.

Although there is no surviving correspondence on the subject, Jackson had, presumably, been hoping for **a new play** for the 1930 Malvern Festival. Jackson had to wait until 1932 for his next opportunity to present an English premiere of Shaw (*Too True to Be Good*; see Letter 50).

45 / To Barry Jackson   The Palace Hotel, Buxton, Derbyshire
   From Charlotte F. Shaw   [16th] May 1930

[ALS]

The roses, oh! the roses! They are so lovely & as fresh as if just cut.

Thank you, Barry.

I am slowly coming back to life. I nearly went. I hope I shall be able to repay G.B.S. even a little of what he has done for me.

I am so glad you have been with him & cheered him, these two evenings in London!

Ever
C.F.S.

46 / To Barry Jackson   [The Palace Hotel, Buxton, Derbyshire]
26th May 1930

[APCS]

On Wednesday we return to Ayot St Lawrence, and shall probably stay
there until the 5th, though if I can secure a ticket I *may* run up on Sunday for the Toscanini concert, as Albert Coates and Howard de Walden
urge – God knows why! – that my presence is indispensable. Anyhow I
am curious to hear T. conduct.

G.B.S.

Arturo **Toscanini** (1867–1957) conducted the Philharmonic Symphony Orchestra of New
York at the Royal Albert Hall on Sunday 1 June 1930. **Albert Coates** (1882–1953) was the
Russian-born composer and conductor friend of Shaw.

47 / To Barry Jackson   4 Whitehall Court SW1
25th October 1930

[APCS]

*Jackson ventured twice to Canada – on an autumn 1929 lecture tour (on which
he also gave readings from* The Apple Cart*) and in 1931–32 with the Barry
Jackson Company of Players (only one Shaw play –* The Dark Lady of the Sonnets *– was in the repertoire of six plays), but he did not take up Shaw's suggestion
to tour South Africa. Macdona was there in the winter of 1928–9.*

The Durban Repertory Co. wants the Apple Cart; but I think a tour of
South Africa with it might pay. Macdona seems to have come away with
some shekels. Would you care to extend your operations to the Dark
Continent?

Charlotte has bashed her ribs, and is staying in town this weekend. I
come up from Ayot on Tuesday to propose Einstein's health at the Ort
& Oze dinner.

Where are you?

G.B.S.

Shaw proposed the health of Albert **Einstein** (1879–1955) at a dinner given by the Joint
British Committee of **Ort and Oze** (organizations for the promotion of East European
Jews) at the Savoy Hotel on 28 October 1930.

48 / To Barry Jackson   4 Whitehall Court SW1
                                             17th November 1930

[ALS]

It was not Jackson's habit to participate in the dissolution (rather than the cre-
ation) of an activity or institution, but he did agree to remount the 1930 Mal-
vern production of Widowers' Houses *as a final production for the Stage Society.*
Directed by H.K. Ayliff, it opened at the Prince of Wales's Theatre on 22 March
1931 for just two performances. In the event, the 'corpse' of the Stage Society
stayed alive until 1939.

My dear Barry

My first effort to ring you this morning was unsuccessful: I was buzzed
off; and after the exchange had promised to get you and failed (I
believe they were trying the wrong number) I tried again, and was just
late: you had gone out.

What kept me out so late was the Stage Society. We have at last
decided to bury this living corpse at the end of the present season in
March; and for the last performance we want something that will sell
guest tickets enough to enable us to die solvent, and that will have a historic Stage Society flavor about it.

Gerald Bishop proposed the Malvern performance of Widowers'
Houses by the grace of Sir B.J. This was received with acclamations from
all; and every other suggestion was postponed until you were sounded
on the subject. I think it quite a good idea if the Barretts are still in
Wimpole St in March. We ought to try that show on a London audience:
there might be a revival in it. Its success in Berlin as Zinsen has been followed by a similar one in Brussels. The housing question is in the air.
The Stage Society show would be a good excuse for a non-committal
experiment; and the cast would be handy.

How do you feel about this?

                                             G.B.S.

Gerald Bishop may be a mistake for *George* Bishop (1886–1965), theatre critic for the
Observer and author of *Barry Jackson and the London Theatre* (London: Arthur Barker, 1933).
Barry Jackson had become **Sir B.J.** in June 1925 (*The Times*, 3 June 1925); Shaw had been
instrumental in advocating the knighthood. There was no **revival** of *Widowers' Houses* in
London until 2 February 1949, when Esmé Percy directed it at the Arts Theatre (23 perfor-

mances). **Zinsen** (*Usury*) was the title used for the Berlin production of *Widowers' Houses*. **The Barretts of Wimpole Street** opened at the Queen's Theatre on 23 September 1930 and ran until early January 1932 (530 performances).

49 / To Barry Jackson

4 Whitehall Court SW1
13th July [1931]

[ALS]

The two plays discussed by Shaw in the first three paragraphs of this letter have not been identified, but the letter is, nonetheless, a useful illustration of Shaw's interest in advising Jackson on programming for the Birmingham Repertory Theatre as well as for Malvern. Shaw left for Moscow (sans Charlotte) with a small tourist party (including the Astors) on 18 July and returned, as promised, in time to attend the third Malvern Festival in August. For the first time the Festival did not include a Shaw play. The film version of Shaw's How He Lied to Her Husband *was, however, shown as part of the 'First Malvern British Film Festival.' Jackson selected 'Five Centuries of English Drama' as the Festival theme, explaining in the program that the 1931 Festival should be regarded as 'the conscription of dramatists from every age to pay tribute to one who belongs equally to present and future.'*

My dear Barry

I think you had better read this play. I don't know the author or anything about him – Miss Dickens asked me what I thought of it. It is an old fashioned situation play without the old fashioned comic relief, and this omission makes the exposition drag a little. And the last act, of course, is helpless. But the catastrophe comes off all right; and the honest husband and his little whore of a wife make two very good acting parts.

The play is a safe and presentable article at all times, and therefore something to have by you for the B.R.T. So I send it for inspection. Please return it to Miss Dickens (address on copy) or negotiate with her if you care to secure an option on it.

There is a brother of Leslie Henson's who writes impossible plays of the sort you are kind to. He sent me one which he said Henrietta St had rejected, the action of which is carried on by a set of ghosts from the XVI century and by their modern descendants, the dramatic conflict being between the Church & the Reformation. There are two very good and well contracted men in it. I suggested that he should cut Pope Paul – offstage – out of it and other historical diversions, and send it in again. I think it would be worth your while to read it so as to know about the author; so tell them to let you see it if it comes in again.

It was heroic of you to translate and produce the Ghéon play, as it had not a dog's chance of paying either in money or (for you) prestige. Nevertheless I think it was worth doing. The allegory was very truthful: in fact it was so good that it made Ghéon careless about his characters; and it was on their thinness and flatness that he fell down. The fact that nobody but you would have done it is, I feel, one up to you, whereas if there had been nothing at all in it it would have been one down.

Do not tell anybody that I expect to depart for Moscow (Golden Arrow) on Saturday next the 18th, and to land at Harwich on Sunday the 2nd and have a hectic week before going to Malvern on the 9th.

ever
G.B.S.

Ethel **Dickens** (1864–1936), granddaughter of the novelist, owned a typewriting service, frequently used by Shaw. Actor **Leslie Henson's** (1891–1957) playwriting **brother** was Bertram Henson. **Henrietta St** (WC2, just west of Covent Garden) was the London home of the Birmingham Repertory Theatre Companies. The **Ghéon play** was Jackson's translation of Henri Ghéon's *La merveilleuse histoire du jeune Bernard de Menthon* (*The Marvellous History of Saint Bernard*), produced at the BRT on 16 May 1925.

50 / To Barry Jackson Ayot St Lawrence, Welwyn, Herts.
5th October 1932

[ALS]

There is a long gap in the extant Shaw/Jackson correspondence between the last letter and this one, which is a pity because there must have been considerable discussion between them about Too True to be Good, *which had its British premiere at the Malvern Festival on 6 August 1932, an event somewhat marred by the late arrival of the London critics, whose aircraft (chartered by Jackson) got lost and landed at Hereford rather than Malvern. The world premiere of* Too True *had been given by the New York Theatre Guild in Boston on 29 February 1932, followed by a production in Poland on 4 June 1932. A short run at the BRT followed the Malvern production, and the London production opened at the New*

Theatre on 13 September 1932. Despite the strong cast (Cedric Hardwicke, Donald Wolfit, Ralph Richardson), it closed after forty-seven performances, prompting Shaw's diatribe to Jackson about the economics of the West End theatre. As it turned out, he was also unduly sanguine about the success of Caesar and Cleopatra; *it closed three days after this letter to Jackson after only twenty-one performances at the Old Vic (19–24 September) and Sadler's Wells (3–8 October).*

My dear Barry

I'm sorry; but we must face the facts. People won't pay 13/- to be told to their faces that they are inefficient fertilizers. We should have started boldly at the Euston, or the Chelsea Palace, or the Streatham, or at one of these new big theatres at which you can control the prices. Caesar, they tell me, is filling the Old Vic and Sadler's Wells. It was the west end stall prices that broke the revival of Heartbreak, and that is now breaking Too True. Mine is a proletarian audience in the sense that I attract only a percentage of any class; and the proletariat is the only class big enough to make the percentage remunerative.

I grieve for those poor things who have worked so hard and hopefully and got only five weeks in London out of it. I hope you have not dropped too much over it.

I suppose the New wont let you turn it into a 5/- house.

What's happening in the provinces?

Charlotte welcomes the wane of my popularity. It is what she bargained for when she married me.

Look in if you can in the course of the next few days.

I bought a new car yesterday just to defy the returns.

ever
G.B.S.

51 / To Barry Jackson   4 Whitehall Court SW1
                                                 19th April 1933

[APCS]

The Shaws set out on a world cruise (from Monaco) on 16 December 1932 and arrived back in England (Southampton) on 19 April 1933. One of the first people Shaw wrote to when he got home was Barry Jackson. Shaw had written two plays on his cruise: Village Wooing *and* On the Rocks, *and even before he had finished he had wanted Jackson to have an exclusive progress report: 'Tell Barry Jackson – but no one else,' he wrote to Blanche Patch in February, 'that my efforts to write resulted in nothing at first but a very trivial comedietta in three scenes for two people which only Edith Evans could make tolerable; but I am now well into a more considerable political play, rather in* The Apple Cart *line, but contemporary. But I cannot hold out much hope of its being any use except to fill up the* Too True *volume into bulk for money' (Blanche Patch,* Thirty Years with G.B.S. *[London: Gollancz, 1951], 74). Shaw subsequently offered* Village Wooing *to Jackson for the 1933 Malvern Festival, but* On the Rocks *went to Jackson's rival Charles Macdona (see Letter 52). Jackson chose not to do* Village Wooing, *so the 1933 Festival theatre program was again Shaw-less (except for Shaw's personal presence). Jackson never did produce* Village Wooing, *but* On the Rocks *was included in the 1936 program at Malvern. Both plays were published in a volume with* Too True to Be Good *by Constable in February 1934.*

(Just home)

All I have brought back with me is an endless mess of shorthand out of which I may possibly be able to put up enough stuff to fill up a volume beginning with Too True with an impossibly long political play and an impossibly short trifle for two performers in 3 scenes. May I take it that you can quite well – or even better – do without me for this year at Malvern?

This is only a provisional reply: I am too tired to write another word before tumbling into bed in a heap. More when we meet.

G.B.S.

I have had a bulletin from Elgar about you which seems satisfactory.

Sir Edward **Elgar** (1857–1934), the English composer, settled in Malvern in 1891 and became a close friend of Shaw and Jackson.

52 / To Barry Jackson   4 Whitehall Court SW1
                                              28th April 1933
[TLS]

Shaw's decisions about producers for his plays had frustrated, perhaps even annoyed, Jackson in the past – when Shaw gave a Polish company the world pre-

miere of The Apple Cart *in 1929 (Letters 27, 101), for example, and when he allowed Charles Macdona to present the first public performance in England of* Mrs Warren's Profession *in 1925 (Letter 13). And now Shaw told Jackson that Macdona was getting* On the Rocks. *Macdona opened it – at the Winter Garden, not the Prince's, Theatre – on 25 November 1933, but Shaw's confidence in Macdona was only partially justified;* On the Rocks *ran for only a modest seventy-three performances. The consolation prize for Jackson was* Village Wooing *for Malvern, but in the absence of Edith Evans (who was about to begin a long London engagement – see Letter 53) Jackson decided against it. In an interview published in the* Daily Express *on 26 July 1933 (his seventy-seventh birthday) Shaw explained that he had given* On the Rocks *to Macdona because he 'has been keeping the pot boiling all over the country for years.' In addition to these professional disappointments, Jackson had not been well. The answer to Shaw's implied question in the final paragraph of this letter is that Jackson was at his home in Malvern recovering from an appendix operation (see Letter 53).*

My dear Barry,

I told you that I had brought back from the ship two plays: one of them being a sort of comedietta for two performers lasting just an hour. Two scenes, the first of which is only a front cloth suggesting the deck of a liner, and the other a solid village shop. But the two performers would have to be Edith Evans and somebody of the calibre of Thesiger or Hardwicke. I have not read the stuff since it has been typed; but Charlotte has, and she thinks it presentable. It occurs to me that you may have in your Malvern program a short bill that would bear filling up, and that you may also have Edith in the company. If so, this piece (called Village Wooing) might come in handy and get my name, for what it is now worth, into the posters.

This is purely for information and in case.

The political play, which is not finished though it is already an enormous outsize, is no use for a West End theatre on the old lines. I cannot afford another fiasco like Too True and Heartbreak; nor can you. Your expenses are too high for my drawing powers. Macdona is taking the Prince's Theatre, which he declares will hold £1700 a week at prices from one and tuppence to five shillings. He swears he can get stars at present for sixpence a cluster just as he has got the theatre for nothing but a share. At these prices my play would have some chance of escaping being classed as a failure (which is the really damaging thing: the money doesn't matter so much); and if Macdona really gets going on the new footing I had better let him do his worst, especially if his revival of Too True, now staggering through the provinces, comes to anything. He has for years contended that I owe him a new play; and this may be an opportunity to give him one; for I never did fit into the West End half guinea stall game, and am more impossible than ever now that the stalls and salaries and expenses and rents have soared into millionaire land. If I offer the play to you, you will feel bound to produce it, and thereby hasten the ruin which awaits every West End management sooner or later, no matter how glorious. I wish I could induce you to turn your back on London altogether before the ground landlords absorb all your fortune. Irving had to take to the road, destitute, after all the triumphs of the Lyceum. Barry Sullivan, who left London indignantly because he lost £800 in three months, died worth £100,000.

Anyhow, think this over.

The news about Macdona is strictly confidential. It is probably in all the papers by this time. As he proposes to open in May with Diplomacy and Gerald du Maurier, he is making no pretence of ultra-modernity.

I have not settled anything as yet, and have held back to avoid worrying you when you are laid up; but as you must settle your Malvern program right away the suggestion as to A Village Wooing will be too late if I wait any longer; and I cannot help seeing that the alternative of Macdona for the other play may be a relief to you, in spite of your natural desire to kill anyone who comes after your authors.

This letter will at least elicit some news of you. We don't know how convalescent you are, or whether you are in London or Malvern.

Ever

G. Bernard Shaw

Ernest **Thesiger** (1879–1961) was a regular at Malvern. He created the role of Charles II in *In Good King Charles's Golden Days* at Malvern in 1939. Henry **Irving** (1838–1905) assumed management of the Lyceum Theatre in 1878 and gave it up in 1899, following a disastrous fire at the theatre. It was said of Irish actor **Barry Sullivan** (1821–91) that 'Well indeed must he have so ordered his way of life that ... he could bequeath legacies amounting to considerably over £25,000' (R.M. Sillard, *Barry Sullivan and His Contemporaries* [London: Unwin, 1901], II, 238). **Diplomacy**, adapted from Victorien Sardou's *Dora* by B.C. Stephenson and

Clement Scott, opened at the Prince's Theatre on 27 May 1933, produced by Charles Macdona, directed by English actor-manager **Gerald du Maurier** (1871–1934).

53 / To G. Bernard Shaw

Blackhill, Malvern
30th April 1933

[ADS]

My dear G.B.S.

From a welter of disappointment a scheme is being evolved which will ease my burden in the West End by 50% without lessening the standard of presentation. It was with this scheme in mind that I suggested an autumn production of your new work [*On the Rocks*] but as you say this is now in Macdona's hands there is no more to be said. You need have no fear of my venturing into the press. Edith is on the point of going into a new play at the St James so her future is in the air for a couple of months at least. There is always a remote chance of a dead failure in which case it might be possible to include her in some matinées at Malvern: this suggestion can only be discussed when we know whether she is at liberty.

An appendix was the final straw which laid me low after a year of one disaster after another and the theatrical disasters were not as you imagine restricted to the West End. The public would not have 'Too True' in the provinces. Doctors and what is more patently common sense, warn me that rest is essential so for a few weeks I am lying bone idle at Blackhill.

B.

The **new play** was Emlyn Williams's *The Late Christopher Bean*, which opened at the St James's Theatre on 16 May 1933. Starring Edith Evans and Cedric Hardwicke, it ran until 21 July 1934 (487 performances).

54 / To Barry Jackson
From Charlotte F. Shaw

Ayot St Lawrence, Welwyn, Herts.
27th November 1933

[APCS]

Jackson wasn't at the opening of On the Rocks, *but Shaw, of course, was, and so was Charlotte.*

Dear Barry

I was touched by your telegram – & cheered. I practically got out of my bed to go to the show on Saturday night & though I had to stand 10 minutes in the street after, waiting for Nancy's [Astor] car, it did me no harm! Also G.B.S. though very tired seems perfectly *well.* No reaction so far.

It was a most curious experience. That great audience seemed somehow electric. They took all the points – it seemed – before they were made. Of course it was a 'GBS' audience – all his friends, no doubt, together – probably the whole Fabian Society! – but the effect was amazing!

We *may* stay down here this week for rest. We send our loves & hope to see you soon.

Yours
Charlotte

55 / To G. Bernard Shaw [no address]
1st December 1933

[TLU (c)]

Although no doubt disappointed that he had not had On the Rocks *for Malvern, Jackson was warm in the play's and the production's praise.*

My dear G.B.S.

I thoroughly enjoyed my evening on the rocks. It would be possible to find things to criticise as usual, but why bother? I went for entertainment, and I got it in full measure, so there is no more to be said.

The very solid table helps one to settle down the moment the curtain goes up; a momentary glance proves that like the hands of the P.M.'s clock it is never going to be moved during the evening, or in fact during the next six months, and consequently the text holds one's entire attention from the word 'go.'

The cast and Lewis Casson's work were admirable, and little Walter Hudd's performance quite astonishing. The audience was in a constant ripple of mirth, and a man near by appeared to be on the verge of apo-

62

plexy during the scene between Brollikin and the P.M. All that remains is for the people to roll up in hordes, which I trust they will do.

Yours,
[Barry Jackson]

I suggest that in the distant future Charlotte bags that table for White-hall Court!

Lewis **Casson** directed *On the Rocks* and also played the part of Sir Jafna Pandranath. Walter **Hudd** (1898–1963) played Sir Broadfoot Basham.

56 / To G. Bernard Shaw [no address]
5th December 1933
[TLU (c)]

The only Shaw world premiere produced by Jackson was The Inca of Perusalem, *directed by H.K. Ayliff at the Birmingham Repertory Theatre on 7 October 1916 (seven performances).*

Dear G.B.S.

As you have no doubt gathered in the course of our friendship, I intensely dislike asking you for signatures, but I should be very grateful if you would add your name to those on the enclosed programme, – the only proof that I did once have the pleasure of being responsible for the first performance of one of your plays: a rather sad memento, but there it is!

Yours,
[Barry Jackson]

57 / To G. Bernard Shaw [no address]
11th January 1934
[TLU (c)]

Dear G.B.S.

I really think that 'You never can Tell' will be the best play to include at

Malvern this year. Have I your permission to go ahead with this, with the customary fees in force?

Yours,
[Barry Jackson]

You Never Can Tell, the only Shaw play in the 1934 Malvern Festival season, opened there on 27 July 1934, directed by Herbert Prentice. Shaw's **customary fees** were 15% of gross when receipts exceeded £300; 10% for receipts between £100 and £300; 7½% for receipts between £50 and £100; and 5% for receipts below £50. Shaw's royalties ledger (British Library of Political and Economic Science) shows that he received £82.16s.11d. for five performances of *You Never Can Tell.*

58 / To Barry Jackson

4 Whitehall Court SW1
11th January 1934

[ALS]

The Shaws left England on 8 February 1934 for a trip to New Zealand, returning to England on 17 May 1934.

My dear Barry

I enclose a formal license lest I die in New Zealand.

Sean O'Casey and his wife are coming to lunch here at 1.30 on Saturday. If by a happy chance you are in town will you join us then? As he is unquestionably a genius you ought on public grounds to be on speaking terms with him.

Besides, we havn't seen you for ever so long.

G.B.S.

59 / To G. Bernard Shaw

[no address]
12th January 1934

[TLU (c)]

The 1934 Malvern Festival program was in the relatively early stages of planning in January 1934. Jackson's final program ran from 23 July to 18 August, and consisted of an eclectic mix of plays. In addition to those mentioned in this letter, it included the medieval Interlude of Youth *and Irish playwright Denis Johnston's* The Moon in the Yellow River. *The Drinkwater play was the premiere of* A Man's House. *Among the 1934 company was Errol Flynn, who appeared in five plays (though not* You Never Can Tell*).*

My dear G.B.S.

Very many thanks for the Malvern permission. The programme will now consist of 'You never can Tell,' a new play called 'Mutiny' by David Stewart – an author who has not had a real hearing; Marlowe's 'Faustus,' a new play by John Drinkwater, and Ghéon's 'Saint Bernard.' I am sure the audience will think that you are the protagonist of the last.

It is very kind of you to ask me in to-morrow morning. I met O'Casey some years ago, and he very kindly sent me his fine play 'The Silver Tassie,' but I was unable to help him with the production.

I had tea with Edward on Tuesday, when I found him in considerable pain, for which there appears to be no relief: at all events the medicos seem unable to discover any soothing. It is a very good thing that he is now under his own roof, and away from what appeared to me an unusually gloomy nursing home.

Yours,

[Barry Jackson]

P.S. I am broadcasting to New Zealand on February 22nd. Will you be there then?

According to **O'Casey**, Jackson had told him (in 1928) that *The Silver Tassie* 'was an impossible play for me. I dare not put it on – an English audience couldn't stand it' (Sean O'Casey, *Autobiographies* [London: Macmillan, 1963], II, 272). Sir **Edward** Elgar died in February 1934. He had been among Shaw's Malvern Festival companions every summer since 1929. No record has been found of Jackson's **broadcasting** to New Zealand. The Shaws did not in any event arrive in New Zealand until 15 March.

60 / To Barry Jackson   4 Whitehall Court SW1
8th June 1934

[TLS]

Among the many important issues raised in this letter, which begins with comments on the 1934 Malvern Festival program, two stand out: Shaw's 'new plays' and Jackson's 'chucking the Rep.' Shaw had written Village Wooing *and* On the Rocks *on his 1933 world cruise, and the 1934 cruise to New Zealand produced* The Simpleton of the Unexpected Isles *and* The Millionairess. *Neither play was ready even for a 'try-out' in the BRT's 1934–5 season, but in the summer of 1935 Jackson presented the British premiere of Simpleton at Malvern (the world premiere was in New York on 18 February 1935). The Millionairess was at Malvern in 1937, after earlier productions in Vienna, Melbourne, and the British premiere in the unlikely surroundings of Bexhill-on-Sea, Sussex, on 17 November 1936. All was not so well, however, at the Birmingham Repertory Theatre. Once before, in 1923 (Letter 8), Jackson had decided to close the Rep because of lack of public support. According to some accounts (e.g., Trewin, Birmingham Repertory Theatre, 112), Jackson had put £100,000 of his own money into the Rep since its opening in 1913, and at the end of the 1933–4 season he again decided he had had enough. By June, however – and despite the failure of a fundraising campaign (an appeal for £20,000 raised only £3,000) – Jackson had changed his mind and the 1934–5 season went ahead. But on 1 January 1935 ownership and management of the Birmingham Repertory Theatre was transferred to a board of trustees (with Jackson still very much in the picture as governing director) in order to relieve Jackson of financial responsibility for the theatre.*

My dear Barry

You need not worry about Irene: she would have played Dolly off the stage and been quite wrong for Mrs Clandon. The play is a difficult one to cast because you have not only to get the separate parts right but the family right, which complicates the problem. The slightest touch of the soubrette in Mrs Clandon would be fatal: she must be a cold intellectual humorless dame of the British Empire – not dear Mrs Cadbury. Can you let me have a list of the company? Also the producer; for Ayliff writes that he is at a loose end and wants to get in at Stratford.

I take it that the first week is to begin with Drinkwater and end with me; but as you have seven plays on hand this does not mean that I could have the whole week for my finishing touch to the production. The pressing question for me is whether I shall have to be in Malvern before the 23rd. Remember, I am in the dark about everything so far; and with three productions on hand – Androcles and the Burghers for Regent's Park and Village Wooing for the Little, I must look ahead with some precision.

As to Birmingham Repertory I have promised to hold up On the Rocks for Macdona in the big towns for awhile on the chance of his being able to get up a tour; and as he has an infatuate affection for the play I feel that it would be inhuman to hand it over to his proud and prosperous rival so soon after the shipwreck at the Winter Garden. Better revive Too True if you still have the scenery. A try-out of one of the new plays would not be impossible if I could get them ready; but that will take a bit of doing, as I have just had to re-write the second act of the first of them; and heaven knows how much I may have to do to the rest. Besides, the first one involves some special scenery and expensive costumes (some [Paul] Shelving in fact) and the second is a star play, no use without Edith Evans or somebody of her weight.

I do not wonder at your chucking the Rep: I know what it is to have to write a 2000 word feuilleton every week: it is like being knocked down by the sail of the windmill and then being continually knocked down again by the next one when you stagger to your feet. Having to find a new play every week must be worse. But why did you go back on your decision?

Have you ever seen Katharine Cornell act? She is touring with the Barretts and Candida, in which she made an immense New York success a few years ago. It still keeps alive. I should say that a K.C. advent in London is inevitable, and that unless she opens her mouth very wide indeed there is money in it for a London manager. I am interested because Candida has never come to her own in London; and wherever she has come to her own she has had a success. I am not suggesting that you should stray from your course for a speculation of this kind; but if you get tired of virtue and feel that you must do something foolish, think of Katharine.

I have been to Bradford. I saw the Barker-Lillah production of Iphigenia there years ago. I can't go down on the 14th, as I have only that week to produce V.W. and must stick hard at it every day. Many thanks for the invitation, and also for your enquiries at the hotel.

Charlotte is up and getting about a little again; but it will take her a few days more to recover completely.

I am sitting to Epstein for a bust!

In a flurry – with one thing and another.

G.B.S.

Irene Vanbrugh (1872–1949) was the sister of Violet Vanbrugh. She created the role of Gwendolen Fairfax in Wilde's *The Importance of Being Earnest* (St James's Theatre, 14 February 1895). The role of **Dolly** in the 1934 Malvern production of *You Never Can Tell* was played by Curigwen Lewis; Margaret Chatwin (d. 1937) played Mrs Clandon. The director was Herbert Prentice. **Mrs Cadbury** is a reference to the Birmingham-based chocolate manufacturing family. The **seven plays** at Malvern were Drinkwater's *A Man's House*, *The Interlude of Youth*, Marlowe's *Doctor Faustus*, Jackson's adaptation of Ghéon's *La merveilleuse histoire du jeune Bernard de Menthon*, Denis Johnston's *The Moon in the Yellow River*, David Stewart's *Mutiny*, and Shaw's *You Never Can Tell*. Shaw's play on the **Burghers** of Calais, *The Six of Calais*, received its world premiere in the Open Air Theatre in Regent's Park, London, on 17 July 1934 on a bill with **Androcles** and the Lion. *Village Wooing* opened at the Little Theatre, London, on 19 June 1934, directed by Shaw himself; it ran for thirty-three performances. The **shipwreck at the Winter Garden** was the disappointingly short run of Charles Macdona's production of *On the Rocks* at the Winter Garden Theatre (see Letter 52). The American actress **Katharine Cornell** (1893–1974) played **Candida** in New York in 1924, and in 1934 was touring the United States in *Candida* and as Elizabeth in Besier's *Barretts of Wimpole Street*. She made her London debut as Jo in Louisa M. Alcott's *Little Women* in 1919. **Lillah** McCarthy performed Iphigenia, directed by Harley Granville **Barker** in Gilbert Murray's translation of Euripides' *Iphigenia in Tauris* at the Little Theatre, London, in 1912, and subsequently on tour. When Charlotte saw a photograph of the bust of Shaw by British sculptor Jacob **Epstein** (1880–1959) she 'absolutely refused to see it or to have it in her house on any terms'; Shaw thought' it made him look like 'an Australian Bushman' (*Collected Letters*, IV, 486).

61 / To Barry Jackson   Malvern Hotel, Malvern
                                             9th September 1934
[ALS]

The Shaws, as usual, were in Malvern in August and early September for the Festival. The 'enclosed revise' mentioned by Shaw in this letter was probably an early proof of The Simpleton of the Unexpected Isles.

My dear Barry,

Just look through the enclosed revise. There is practically no change in the first three sheets; but from page 49 onward there are cuts and changes which alter the close very considerably.

I wish you'd read it to me in this state.

We have to tea with the Brights this afternoon; so I shall leave this with you on the way thither, and look in again on the way back, between 5.30 and 6. This – unless you have visitors – will give you time to glance through the corrections.

                                             G.B.S.

Shaw had first encountered R. Golding **Bright** at the premiere of *Arms and the Man* in 1894 when Bright, alone among an enthusiastic audience, hissed Shaw when he took a curtain call, prompting Shaw's famous response, 'My dear fellow, I quite agree with you, but what are we two against so many?' (*Collected Letters*, I, 433). Bright went on to a successful career as a literary agent.

62 / To Barry Jackson   Ayot St Lawrence, Welwyn, Herts.
From Charlotte F. Shaw   30th October 1934

[ALS]

Jackson became a willing recipient of Shavian acorns from the garden at Ayot St Lawrence (see Letters 65 and 68). Many were planted in the garden of his Malvern home.

Dear Barry

G.B.S. was delighted to hear the acorns are planted for the trees here are *raining* them down & he says he can send you two more sacks full at once if you can do with them.

Glad to hear you are coming up – we have missed you! By the greatest bad luck we are tied up for luncheon both on Thursday & Friday – both rather boresome engagements! But *do* come to dinner one of those two days. What is Scott [Sunderland] doing?

Trebitsch has been over & stayed nearly 2 weeks! We nearly died of him. He is getting very old – & pathetic! But the state of Austria & Germany really doesn't bear thinking of!

See you soon.

                             Yours
                             Charlotte

We have taken to growing oaks in wine glasses now – Miss Patch's incitement!

Shaw's diary does not show a particular **luncheon engagement** for Thursday 1 November, though he had meetings at unspecified times with the Society of Arts and the Fabian Society. On Friday 2 November he lunched with Sir Robert Hadfield at 22 Carlton House Terrace.

63 / To G. Bernard Shaw   [no address]
                                         3rd November 1934

[TLU (c)]

Shaw's plea in The Dark Lady of the Sonnets *for a publicly supported national theatre was, as Jackson suggests in this letter, particularly germane to the situation in Birmingham now that the Repertory Theatre was owned and managed – through a board of trustees – by the City of Birmingham (see Letter 60).* The Dark Lady *ran at the BRT (in a double bill with John Drinkwater's* A Man's House*) in November 1934.* On the Rocks *was produced in Bournemouth by the Croydon Repertory Theatre in October–November 1934 (see also Letter 64), but not at the BRT or Malvern until the 1936 season.*

My dear G.B.S.

After discussion at Birmingham, it has been decided that 'The Dark Lady of the Sonnets' will fill the bill better than 'Village Wooing'; the former gives no difficulty as regards setting, and its moral should prove efficacious in plugging the fact that the theatre is now dependent on the citizens at Birmingham. I take it that there are no difficulties in the way of giving the play?

I see, by the way, that 'On the Rocks' is billed for Bournemouth. Does this mean that Macdona does not want to do it in the provinces? I really think we ought to consider it seriously for Malvern.

Yours,

[Barry Jackson]

P.S. The date of production of 'The Dark Lady' is not yet fixed, but it will either be at the end of this month or the beginning of next.

64 / To Barry Jackson   Ayot St Lawrence, Welwyn, Herts.
                                            5th November 1934

[APCS: HRC]

Bournemouth is nothing – not Macdona – repertory or amateur I suppose. The only difficulty is the gigantic length of the leading part: you would have to get Hannen for it, as he knows it.

The Dark Lady is available.

I shall be in town tomorrow at Whitehall from 11 to 12.30. I am coming up to be installed in the Livery as a member of a City Company: the Stationers and Newspaper Makers!!!!!

G.B.S.

70

Nicholas **Hannen** (1881–1972) played Sir Arthur Chavender in the premiere of *On the Rocks* at the Winter Garden Theatre, London, 25 November 1933. In the BRT and Malvern productions the role was played by Stephen Murray (1912–83), a BRT stalwart.

65 / To Barry Jackson   Ayot St Lawrence, Welwyn, Herts.
[10th] November 1934

[APCU]

To stress the importance of the subject matter of this message, Shaw wrote it in red ink.

The

Celebrated

St Lawrence Acorn

6 lbs

Each acorn guaranteed to produce timber enough for a 50,000 ton steel battleship within 200 years.

If it fails to do so its price will be returned in full.

[G.B.S.]

66 / To G. Bernard Shaw   [no address]
10th December 1934

[TLU (c)]

All of the plays at the inaugural Malvern Festival in 1929 were by Shaw, and all but one of the eight plays produced at the 1930 Festival were by Shaw. Since then there had been a decline in Shaw productions: none in 1931, one of seven in 1932, none in 1933, and one of seven in 1934. The next season, however, was to have a heavier Shavian content: Misalliance *(from the BRT's 1934–5 season),* Fanny's First Play, *and the British premiere of* The Simpleton of the Unexpected Isles *(the 'new play' referred to by Jackson in this letter). Shaw's illness was rather more serious than the influenza that Jackson refers to (see Letter 67).*

My dear G.B.S.

First of all, I do hope sincerely that your health is better, and that you have completely shaken off the effects of influenza.

I was in Birmingham last week, discussing plays with Prentice, and with your sanction, we are proposing to do 'MISALLIANCE' there some time in the Spring. I think this would be a very much better choice for Malvern than 'Arms and the Man'; Prentice knows the play well, and assures me that under his direction it was very successful at Northampton. This, with 'Fanny's first Play' and the new play, would be a very good bill to form the back-bone at Malvern.

I hope you have not forgotten that you promised me a copy of the new play; in fact, I should like two, for one must go to the Lord Chamberlain for licence – and the sooner this is done, the better.

Yours,

[Barry Jackson]

Herbert **Prentice** (1890–1963) directed for Jackson in Birmingham and at Malvern, including the three Shaw plays at Malvern in 1935. He directed *Misalliance* at the **Northampton** Repertory Theatre in October 1930.

67 / To Barry Jackson

Ayot St Lawrence, Welwyn, Herts.
13th December 1934

[APCS]

Now aged seventy-eight, and still pursuing a heavy and hectic schedule, Shaw suffered a heart attack on 24 November 1934: 'I just dropped down dead in the middle of a telephone conversation; and it is the greatest pity on earth that I revived like Lazarus. I was literally tired to death: hadnt even a Sunday off for months and months; and I slept for three days on end' (letter to Henry Salt, Collected Letters, IV, 391–2). The dates of the Shaws' cruise (to Africa) were subsequently altered; they sailed from Tilbury on 21 March 1935, returning on 10 June 1935. Misalliance opened in Birmingham on 9 March 1935.

The difficulty about Misalliance is the casting. The sort of Falstaffian comedian for Tarleton hardly exists on the English stage: a modernist Roy Byford is what is needed. The acrobat has to be brilliant and beautiful and holy; and Tarleton's daughter needs a demoniacal drive. In fact, a star cast; for the play underplayed is not popular. Ask Prentice how he proposes to cast it. Our final decision must depend on the try-out in Birmingham, which please defer until after our return from our cruise on the 1st April.

I am not yet out of the wood in point of health. I am still so tired that a two mile walk, however slow, brings me to the verge of my existence. You see, I actually died on the 24th Nov. My revival was a mere piece of officiousness on the part of Nature.

G.B.S.

After several years with provincial touring companies, **Roy Byford** (1873–1939) established himself in London and Stratford in Falstaffian-like roles.

68 / To Barry Jackson   4 Whitehall Court SW1
                                            15th December 1934
[ALS]

Here are two copies of The Simp.

The latest expert says that unless acorns are flavored with red lead the mice will devour them.

G.B.S.

69 / To Barry Jackson   Ayot St Lawrence, Welwyn, Herts.
                                            20th December 1934
[ALS]

This letter provides further evidence of the close artistic relationship between Jackson and Shaw, particularly in planning the Malvern program. Shaw, as usual, was generous with his knowledge and advice, but on this occasion Jackson didn't accept any of it. His final selection of plays for the 1935 program supplemented the four he had already chosen with Pinero's Trelawny of the 'Wells' *and Reginald Arkell's* 1066 And All That, *which had been a big success in Birmingham and London. Shaw's advice also encompassed Jackson's relationship with his company. In the absence of Jackson's letter to Shaw that prompted this reply, it is unclear what problems Jackson had encountered with his revival of Rudolf Besier's* Barretts of Wimpole Street, *which ran at the Piccadilly Theatre in Lon-*

*don from 22 January to 9 March 1935 and transferred to Birmingham on 26
October 1935, with Scott Sunderland as Robert Browning, Gwen Ffrangcon-
Davies as Elizabeth, and Wilfrid Lawson as Elizabeth's father. The play had created some controversy at its Malvern premiere in 1930 when grandchildren of
Edward Barrett, Elizabeth's father, publicly complained about Besier's negative
portrayal of him, including some dark suggestions of incest. Whatever the problem, Shaw's advice was unequivocal.*

My dear Barry

If your dates are fixed my suggestion that Misalliance should wait for
our return is a wash-out. I can give it a final coat of varnish for Malvern
if it needs one. So let not my postcards trouble you; and go ahead as best
you can.

As both Elizabeth Barrett and her father are – granted any sort of
physical suitability – absolutely actorproof, I should reply BARRY JACK-
SON RESENTS and will do as he damn well pleases. All Barrett salaries
down to £10.

I am all for catching them young. The children of the R.A.D.A. give a
quality that the hardened professionals cannot touch. They have of
course to be coached in the mechanical tricks; but unless they are hope-
lessly overweighted or incompetently directed they get everything that
is good in amateur acting and enough of what is good in professional-
ism. There must have been a good deal of that charm about the Pilgrim
Players; and I have always thought it a pity that the West End could not
preserve it, and hadnt even the sense to want to preserve it.

Volpone is a filthy cruel play, like all Jonson's, and curiously unreadable; but on the stage it has a terrific vitality that forbids one to bury it.

You say you want, in addition to Simpleton, Fanny, Misalliance &
Volpone, two eighteenth century plays and *one modern*. Dash it all, am I
so old that the Simpleton ranks as an antique? You mean a XIX century
play don't you? If so, Pinero's death, sidetracked by the Marina marriage, should be marked by a Malvern revival. Either Sweet Lavender or
The Money Spinner would be a good choice. As S.L. has had several
revivals I favor The Money Spinner, which is undeservedly forgotten.
Baron Croodle is a capital character part. His description of water as a
doglike and revolting beverage will ensure a good notice in The Morning Advertiser (if it still exists).

As to XVIII century plays, there was one called The Wonder: a Woman Keeps a Secret, which Barry Sullivan kept alive as a rest play from his heavy parts. Was Mrs Centlivre the author? Then there was The Jealous Wife (? Colman) and Tobin's The Honeymoon. Heavier stuff was Sheridan's Rollo, in which Kemble carried the baby across the bridge. Like St Christopher he found the load astoundingly heavy. The bridge creaked; and the infant whispered in a deep bass 'Go easy, you B.J., or we shall be in the cellar.' The property man handed Kemble a dwarf made up as a baby.

Was Tom Thumb popular enough to suggest Carey's Chrononhotonthologos? Or Bombastes Furioso? I am, however, very doubtful of old burlesques.

I must go to bed. If Charlotte were not in London I should not be let write letters after dinner. I am still tired, relapsing every second day, but gaining a very little on the week.

G.B.S.

The **Pilgrim Players**, founded by Jackson in 1907, were the precursor to the Birmingham Repertory Theatre. Ben **Jonson**'s (1572–1637) *Volpone* was first performed in 1605 or 1606. Sir Arthur Wing **Pinero** (b. 1855) died on 23 November 1934. His comedies *The Money Spinner* and *Sweet Lavender* had premiered in 1880 and 1888 respectively. On 29 November 1934 the Duke of Kent (fourth son of George V) had married Princess **Marina** of Greece. The *Morning Advertiser* was published by the Society of Licensed Victuallers; the issue for 20 December 1934 (the date of this letter) carried front-page advertisements (on either side of the paper's title) for two brands of whisky. Susannah Centlivre's *The Wonder: A Woman Keeps a Secret* opened on 27 April 1714; George **Colman** the Elder's *The Jealous Wife* on 12 February 1761; John **Tobin's** *The Honey Moon* on 31 January 1805; and R.B. **Sheridan's** *Pizarro* (in which John Philip Kemble [1757–1823] played **Rolla** – Shaw's 'Rollo' is a mistake – a commander in the army of the King of Quito during the Spanish conquest of Peru) on 24 May 1799, all at Drury Lane Theatre. Henry Fielding's (1707–54) burlesque *Tom Thumb the Great* premiered at the Little Theatre in the Haymarket on 24 April 1730 and was included in the 1932 Malvern Festival program. The Haymarket also gave the premiere of Henry **Carey's** burlesque *The Tragedy of Chrononhotonthologos* (22 February 1734) and W.B. Barnes's burlesque *Bombastes Furioso* (7 August 1810).

70 / To Barry Jackson

4 Whitehall Court, SW1
13th March 1935

[APCS]

In preparation for the Malvern production of The Simpleton of the Unexpected Isles, *Shaw sent Jackson photographs and reviews from the world premiere in New*

York (New York Theatre Guild, 18 February 1935). A combination of miscasting and misdirecting caused the production to flop: it lasted for only forty performances. Among the critical 'gems' mentioned by Shaw was the oft-quoted comment by Percy Hammond in the New York Herald-Tribune*: 'like a dignified monkey, [Shaw] climbs a tree and pelts us with edifying coconuts.' Simpleton opened in Warsaw in a translation by Floryan Sobieniowski (1881–1964) on 15 March 1935, but Charles Cochran's interest came to nothing.*

American flashlights to hand, also the press notices: a torrent of abuse. We must reprint a string of gems from it for the critics at Malvern.

The dresses are frightfully wrong: the four [Indian deities] are simply nude cabaret dancers. The Guild did its very best, with pejorative results. The business is only the subscribers: no public.

Come in and look at the pictures next time you are passing.

Cochran wants to take it on and just shew em! Sobieniowski produces in Warsaw on Friday after being held up by a flu epidemic.

G.B.S.

71 / To Barry Jackson   Marine Hotel, Durban, Natal
4th May 1935

[TLS]

Jackson had been disappointed that his production of The Apple Cart *at the 1929 Malvern Festival had not been a world premiere (see Letter 27), and as the planning for the 1935 Festival evolved (Letter 69) there still seemed no prospect for Jackson of such a coup. But only a few weeks before the 1935 Festival was scheduled to open (29 July), Shaw gave Jackson the opportunity to present the world premiere of* The Millionairess, *a play that he had drafted on his 1934 cruise to New Zealand (Letter 60). Shaw's offer precipitated a flurry of activity (Letters 72–74), but in the end – perhaps because of difficulties with Edith Evans, despite initial enthusiasm – Jackson again was disappointed. The world premiere of* The Millionairess *was in Vienna (in German) on 4 January 1936; it didn't reach Malvern until the 1937 Festival.*

My dear Barry

From Mombasa, which is within six days of London by Air Mail, I sent to Miss Patch on the 15th April, the full revision and extension of The Millionairess. It is quite unlike The Simpleton and very like Volpone and The Alchemist, except, of course, that the characters are ultra-modern. It is, however, a star play in respect of its dependence on a single actress with a very heavy part and a termagant personality: either Edith Evans or the young woman in Love On the Dole, whose name I forget.

If the fate of The Simpleton is too discouraging, a sensational change of plans is always a good advertisement; and it is all the same to me whether The Simpleton or The Millionairess goes up at Malvern, provided you can get your star. I have seen in the Jewish paper some quotations from notices of The Simpleton in Germany which are comparatively favourable. I do not know what happened finally in New York: before I left I saw only the first fortnight's returns, according to which absolutely nobody but the Guild Subscribers entered the theatre. I presume it has gone on the subscription for the few weeks and then been taken off. However, Miss Patch will tell you what has actually happened. She mentioned in her last letter something about using the New York flashlights for the Press preliminaries to Malvern. I deprecate this, as they will put much public expectation on a false scent completely. Prola, trying to look like a Javanese dancer, and succeeding in looking like what she really was: a middle aged female posing as a sinuous slinking odalisque, would kill any play, even in a photograph.

We are at present in Durban, recovering from the effects of our voyage, which was bearable, though frightfully cold in the Mediterranean and hot in the Indian Ocean, until we came to Portuguese East Africa, where the wharves were being torn up by pneumatic drills and the metal trays of the cranes loaded with copper in bars, night and day. The din was indescribable, and we left the ship hoping never to see her again.

Instead of sailing round the Cape as we intended we shall probably travel to Cape Town by rail or air, and pick up the 'Winchester Castle' there; but this will not affect our return on the 15th June.

There have been moments in the tropics when I would have given my life for a day at Malvern; but here the climate is ideal and the amenities of the town extraordinary.

Charlotte sends affectionate messages,

> Always,
> G. Bernard Shaw

The **young woman** in *Love on the Dole* was Wendy Hiller (b. 1912), making her London debut in the play by Ronald Gow and Walter Greenwood at the Garrick Theatre, London, on 30 January 1935. The **Jewish paper** is the *Jewish Chronicle*. The part of **Prola** in *The Simpleton of the Unexpected Isles* was played – badly, by all accounts – by the Russian actress Alla Nazimova (1879–1945). It had been declined, to Shaw's chagrin, by Mrs Patrick Campbell.

72 / To G. Bernard Shaw

3 Clifford Street W1
[29th May 1935]

[TEL (tr)]

PROPOSE OMITTING FANNY AND GIVING BOTH SIMPLETON AND MILLIONAIRESS AT MALVERN. EDITH EVANS ENTHUSIASTIC. PRODUCER MILLIONAIRESS ATHOLE STEWART BEST POSSIBLE FOR EDITH. BARRY.

Athole Stewart (1879–1940) was a prominent director who had worked previously with Jackson (see Letter 73).

73 / To G. Bernard Shaw

[no address]
29th May 1935

[TLU(c)]

My dear G.B.S.

On reading 'The Millionairess,' my first impulse was to do it at Malvern in place of 'The Simpleton.' A few hours later, however, the latter play being more or less on the stocks, it seemed too good an opportunity for publicity not to do both. I interviewed Edith Evans, who was in a strange mood and rather averse, but I left a copy of the play with her in order to give opportunity for closer study, and now – after nearly a week's interval – she is enthusiastic.

The question of a possible producer arose, and I can think of no one better suited both as far as the play is concerned and Edith herself, than Athole Stewart, who seems to know exactly how to manage her. They worked together for me in 'Evensong' with extremely good results. As I explained in the cable, the inclusion of two new plays will cause 'Fanny' to disappear. 'The Millionairess' will be rehearsed in London as a separate entity, while the remainder of the programme will be rehearsed in Birmingham.

I am unable to see any further than the Malvern Festival at present, as theatrical worries these last months have almost proved my undoing, and I have a feeling that if I last out till the end of August without a rest it is just as much as I can stand.

The Lawrence tragedy was ghastly. Why do such things happen!

Yours,

[Barry Jackson]

P.S. If by any chance 'The Millionairess' turns into a real success here, it might be worth while your holding the play for New York. Edith has quite a reputation there, but so far has had no first class vehicle for her particular talent. I have always had a feeling that The Apple Cart would have stood a much better chance with an English company.

Evensong, by Edward Knoblock and Beverley Nichols (adapted from Nichols's novel), had run at the Queen's Theatre, London, for 213 performances, 30 June 1932–31 December 1932 and had also toured. The **Lawrence tragedy** was the death of T.E. Lawrence (Shaw) on 19 May 1935 following a fall from his motorbike (a gift from the Shaws) on 14 May 1935.

74 / To Barry Jackson   S.S. Winchester Castle
30th May 1935

[TEL]

CONCENTRATE ON MILLIONAIRESS. CUT OUT SIMPLETON COMBINATION. EXTRAVAGANT AND UNCASTABLE AT MALVERN.

[G.B.S.]

75 / To Barry Jackson   4 Whitehall Court SW1
21st June 1935

[ACCS]

Here's a Tarleton – just 12 hours too late.
Gertrude Kingston says he has a voice like thunder.

G.B.S.

Included with the card is a résumé and photograph of the actor Alfred Wild, who had had extensive experience in the classical and modern repertory, including a previous **Tarleton** in *Misalliance* and a Jack Tanner in *Man and Superman*. **Gertrude Kingston** (1866–1937) was a prominent actress-manager and playwright who built the Little Theatre in London in 1910 and ran it successfully as a repertory house.

76 / To Barry Jackson

Ayot St Lawrence, Welwyn, Herts.
23rd June 1935

[APCS]

With just over a month to go before the opening night of The Simpleton of the Unexpected Isles *at the Malvern Festival, the play had not been cast. As always, Shaw was full of suggestions, but none of the individuals mentioned here appeared in the production.*

B. struck me as a good man for unfantastic characters – men of the world and so forth – but no use for clerical angels. Wee Georgie would be much nearer the mark: he'd be IT, in fact. Failing him, [Ernest] Thesiger could do it by a *tour de force*. Of course he would be cast for the Judgment angel if a good Hammingtap were available; but as matters stand we cannot do better than Ernest for the parson and Scott [Sunderland] for the angel. Utilities, however utile, would be futile.

I suppose there isnt another Georgie about. A youthful H.G. Wells would be ideal. Cedric [Hardwicke] could do it.

Stephen Haggard is a bit of a genius; but he may not think the job worth his while. Laughton would be tremendous in spite of his bulk, which could be attributed to nitrogen. He'd carry the play. Why not ask him?

G.B.S.

B. is probably Matthew Boulton (b. 1890), who was a member of the Malvern company in 1929 and who also appeared in several BRT productions. **Wee Georgie** (George Wood, 1897–1979) was a star of the English music halls. **H.G. Wells** (1866–1946) would have been amused (and probably appalled) by Shaw's vision of him as a clerical angel. When Wells read the volume containing *Simpleton, The Six of Calais*, and *The Millionairess*, he felt, he told Shaw, 'the same mixture of irritation & admiration that has been my normal response to you for years. How you go on! God grant me in spite of my drinking & meat-eating & whoring the same vitality' (*Bernard Shaw and H.G. Wells*, ed. J. Percy Smith [Toronto: University of Toronto Press, 1995], 181). **Stephen Haggard** (1911–43), prominent on the London stage in the 1930s, died on active service in the Middle East. Charles **Laughton** (1899–1962), stage and screen star, was prominent on the London stage in the 1930s, and then concentrated on his film career. However, he both acted in (the Devil) and directed *Don Juan in Hell* in 1951 and *Major Barbara* (Undershaft) in 1956, both in New York.

77 / To G. Bernard Shaw   [no address]
                                                         22nd November 1935

[TLU (c)]

*Perhaps because the Shaws were undertaking another cruise (destined to be their
last), this time to the Pacific, Jackson got into detailed discussions with Shaw
about the 1936 Malvern Festival before Shaw and Charlotte sailed from
Southampton in the New Year (22 January 1936; they returned on 6 April 1936).
Plans for the Festival evolved, of course, over the next several months, but of the six
plays mentioned here by Jackson all but one* (The Silent Woman) *were in the final
program. Two others* – Lady Precious Stream, *by S. I. Hsiung, and* The Brontës
of Haworth Parsonage, *by John Davison – were added later, and a Joan had still
to be found.* Lady Precious Stream, The Clandestine Marriage, Jane Eyre, *and*
On the Rocks *all appeared in the BRT 1935–6 season prior to Malvern.*

Dear G.B.S.

I think it would be rather a good move, if you will agree, to do 'On the
Rocks' at Malvern, so that the programme would stand like this:–

'ST. JOAN'
'PYGMALION'
'ON THE ROCKS'

(one of the two last to be given in Birmingham during their Spring season)

'THE CLANDESTINE MARRIAGE'
'THE SILENT WOMAN'

(this is now in Prentice's hands, and if he thinks he can do anything
with it, I feel we might venture upon it, despite its mutilation)

'JANE EYRE'

This latter is to be given at Birmingham early in the Spring, and I am
debating whether to include it in the Malvern programme or not. One
of its great assets is the fact that a version of 'Pride and Prejudice' by the

same author (Miss Helen Jerome) has aroused a frenzy of excitement in New York, and I learn this morning that there is a paragraph in the New York Times stating that I have accepted 'Jane Eyre' for production at Malvern. I imagine this statement emanated from the authoress herself, who I gather lives in the States, and who is a constant visitor to the Festival. Thus, a new play from her pen is ensured of very good publicity on the other side of the Atlantic.

Yours,

[Barry Jackson]

The Clandestine Marriage, by George Colman the Elder and David Garrick, opened at Drury Lane Theatre on 20 February 1766. Ben Jonson's *Epicoene; or, The Silent Woman* (1609) was dropped from Jackson's immediate plans, but was included in the BRT's 1946–7 season, directed by Willard Stoker. *Jane Eyre,* by actress, playwright, and screenwriter **Helen Jerome** (1883–1958), after successful Birmingham and Malvern productions transferred to the West End and ran for 299 performances at the Queen's and Aldwych theatres in 1936–7, directed by Athole Stewart. Helen Jerome's adaptation of *Pride and Prejudice* opened at the National Theatre in Washington, DC on 22 October 1935, transferring to the Music Box, New York, on 5 November 1935, a production described by *New York Times* critic Brooks Atkinson as 'shimmering with satire' (6 November 1935).

78 / To G. Bernard Shaw

[no address]

16th December 1935

[TLU (c)]

My dear G.B.S.

I went to see a performance of 'The Trojan Women' yesterday, with the intention of trying to discover the feelings of the audience towards Greek drama. I frankly do not believe that the play had the slightest appeal, except to those who have some knowledge of the conditions existing in the period when it was written. In imagination at least, the modern woman would not object in the smallest degree to a cruise with the conquerors; and the murder of the child is too horrible for modern audiences. The words of the Chorus, as usual, did not matter in the least. I think we must look elsewhere for something to fill the bill at Malvern.

Flora Robson's name has just cropped up again as a possible for

'Joan.' Is there any chance of you seeing her at the Playhouse this week in her Mary Tudor play, in which I am told she is extremely good?

Yours,

[Barry Jackson]

The production of *The Trojan Women* seen by Jackson on 15 December (a Sunday) has not been located. **Flora Robson** (1902–84), rapidly building her reputation as a major actress in the 1930s, played the title role in Wilfrid Grantham's *Mary Tudor*, which opened at the Playhouse in London on 12 December 1935 and ran for 143 performances.

79 / To Barry Jackson

Ayot St Lawrence, Welwyn, Herts.
17th December 1935

[APCS]

The T.W. [*Trojan Women*] is a monstrosity without a colossal Hecuba and a fascinating and very aristocratic Helen. But the Bacchae is right on the nail with Pentheus made up as Mussolini. I still think its magical beauty could be brought out sufficiently to make it more attractive, and certainly more classy than any alternative I can think of.

We might go to Flora on Friday.

G.B.S.

80 / To G. Bernard Shaw

[no address]
27th December 1935

[TLU (c)]

Shaw had brought Wendy Hiller to Jackson's attention earlier in 1935 (Letter 71). Apparently, he now thought Jackson should consider her for Joan for the 1936 Malvern production. Jackson wanted a bigger name, but Hiller was eventually selected, not just for Joan, but also for Eliza in Pygmalion. *In the event, Shaw was not impressed with her (*Collected Letters, *IV, 437), but she went on to a memorable stage and film career.*

Dear G.B.S.

All I can find out about Wendy Hiller is that she has been very seriously ill. I thought I would make no direct enquiries as to the likelihood of her appearing at Malvern without consulting you as to the possibility of finding anyone else whose name is known to the public. Though lothe [*sic*] to admit it, I am convinced this fact helps to draw audiences. The proposed list of plays for Malvern now stands thus: –

'ST. JOAN'
'THE CLANDESTINE MARRIAGE' (Garrick & Colman)
'PYGMALION'
'THE BRONTES OF HAWORTH PARSONAGE' (John Davison)
'ON THE ROCKS'
'JANE EYRE' (Helen Jerome)

Those marked with a cross will be produced at Birmingham in the Spring, and strengthened where necessary for Malvern.

Yours,

[Barry Jackson]

The plays **marked with a cross** (but only on the copy sent to Shaw, which has not survived) were *Saint Joan, The Clandestine Marriage, On the Rocks*, and *Jane Eyre* – at least, these were the ones produced in Birmingham.

81 / To Barry Jackson   Ayot St Lawrence, Welwyn, Herts.
28th December 1935

[APCS]

Shaw had previously raised concerns about the role of Chavender in On the Rocks *(Letter 64)*.

We are not coming up to town until next week on Thursday as usual.

If you are going to put on The Rocks at the Repertory who is to play Chavender? He is on the stage practically all through; and without a first rate man the play is unbearable. As Hannen knows the part and likes it he would, I daresay, come to Malvern on easy terms; but that's no use for the Rep. I am all for the novices if they can be found; but can they?

We must know something more about that illness before we commit ourselves to W.H. [Wendy Hiller]. Have you seen the Haydon film girl whom they are proposing for the Pygmalion film? I am promised a couple of reels of her at some private theatre by Pascal.

The change to mild rain has left us in the lowest spirits.

G.B.S.

Julie **Haydon** (b. 1910) acted in films in the 1930s before going on to a major stage career, including the original Laura in Tennessee Williams's *Glass Menagerie*. Wendy Hiller got the role of Eliza in the 1938 film version of ***Pygmalion***, produced by Gabriel **Pascal** (1894–1954), directed by Anthony Asquith and Leslie Howard (who also played Higgins). For Shaw's long relationship with Pascal, see Valerie Pascal, *The Disciple and His Devil* (New York: McGraw-Hill, 1970) and Bernard Dukore, ed., *Bernard Shaw and Gabriel Pascal* (Toronto: University of Toronto Press, 1996).

82 / To Barry Jackson   [s.s. *Arandora Star*]
                                                   10th February 1936
[APCS]

The picture on this postcard is of Shaw being interviewed, surrounded by the press and cameramen, on board ship in Miami. The 'two big jobs' were the preface to Great Expectations *(New York: Limited Editions Club, 1937) and 'Morris as I Knew Him,' published as an introduction to May Morris,* William Morris: Artist, Writer, Socialist *(Oxford: Blackwell, 1936). Of greater interest, at least from Jackson's point of view, was the 'new play.' This was* Geneva, *destined to be the first Shaw world premiere at Malvern, but not until the 1938 Festival, the first Malvern Festival not run by Jackson.*

1936 – My escape from publicity at Miami.

I have finished two big jobs: a great Dickens preface and a Morris preface.

Tomorrow I intend to begin a new play in the [Panama] Canal without the faintest notion of what it is about.

We had one frightful day off the Spanish coast. I missed two meals for the first time in this century. Except for this the weather has been perfect. The heat here in the Caribbean is infernal; but we shall be in the Pacific tomorrow night.

Love from Charlotte.

G.B.S.

83 / To Barry Jackson   4 Whitehall Court SW1
                                                      17th April 1936
[APCS]

Discussion between Jackson and Shaw about the casting of Joan for the Malvern production had been going on since at least early December 1935, and there was still no resolution. Sybil Thorndike had created the part magnificently for British audiences in March 1924 and was still Shaw's first choice, but she was unavailable (see Letter 84). Others were under active consideration, with more to come (Letter 85). The other worry about the Malvern Saint Joan was the potential impact on American visitors from the success of Katharine Cornell's Joan, which had opened at the Martin Beck Theatre in New York on 9 March. Brooks Atkinson spoke of the 'incandescence' of Cornell's performance (New York Times, 10 March 1936).

I should choose Sybil without a moment's hesitation if she is available. She is the only one who has the right sort of steel in her; she knows the part; and her figure is brilliantly presentable.

J.F.R. is, I was told, booked for a tour in Canada as Peter Pan.

F.R. would of course put up a good show; but she is not a bit *manly*.

M.N. means nothing to me.

I am not sure that the huge success of Katharine Cornell's Joan may not damage the American booking; but I have nothing to substitute but Geneva, my latest, which is very topical just now, but much more political than even On the Rocks. It's cheap: 3 easy scenes and 8 salaries.

G.B.S.

J.F.R. (Jean Forbes-Robertson, 1905–62), daughter of actor-manager Johnston Forbes-Robertson, was prominent in London theatre as Peter Pan in Christmas productions of J.M. Barrie's play from 1927 to 1934. Thereafter she played several leads in Shakespeare and Ibsen. She spent the summer of 1936 in Brighton (playing Shaw's Joan) and Dublin (playing Yeats's Deirdre), not in Canada. Jackson had mentioned Flora Robson (**F.R.**) as a possible Joan in December (Letter 78). **M.N.** may be Marie Ney (b. 1895), who was acting at the New Theatre in London in April 1936 (and went on to several major Shakespearean roles) or Moya Nugent (1901–54), who toured with Noël Coward and Gertrude Lawrence in 1935 in Coward's *Tonight at 7.30*.

84 /To G. Bernard Shaw [no address]
29th April 1936

[TLU (c)]

My dear G.B.S.

I have had a letter from Sybil Thorndike, in which she says that she would be delighted to do 'Joan' for us at Malvern, but that she is under contract to Gilbert Miller for a play which he is producing towards the end of May. She suggests that it might be possible to induce him to allow her to appear at Malvern for the 'Joan' performances. All this sounds very pleasant, but what on earth is going to happen to rehearsals! I think it would be most dangerous suddenly to shoot a Joan on to the stage who is entirely strange to the company. Such things have happened in bygone days, but I doubt if the result was satisfactory. I gather Lewis Casson is due back in the middle of June, just about the time we start rehearsing. I will look in at 4 Whitehall Court to-morrow morning for a few minutes.

Yours sincerely,

[Barry Jackson]

Sybil Thorndike opened in Edward Chodorov's *Kind Lady* at the Lyric Theatre on 11 June 1936. The play ran there for only eleven performances, but it then went on tour. The producer was **Gilbert Miller** (1884–1969).

85 / To G. Bernard Shaw
[no address]
6th May 1936

[TLU (c)]

My dear G.B.S.

We seem to be once more at a complete standstill in regard to a 'St Joan.' Jean Forbes-Robertson sticks out for a figure which is beyond what I can offer.

Sophie Stewart: This lady played in 'The Fair Maid of the West' at Malvern, and may or may not have made some impression upon you in the leading part of 'Bess Bridges.' She is Scotch, and has recently played 'Celia' in the Bergner 'As you like it' film.

Catherine Lacey: I mentioned her to you the other day. She played leads at Stratford last year.

Lucie Mannheim: Made a great name for herself in a play at the Criterion recently. She is probably a Jewess: I do not know how good her English is.

Dorothy Holmes-Gore
Margaretta Scott
Fabia Drake

The last three may be just names to you, and quite unsuitable. It would be advisable, I think, to have someone who has not played the part before, in preference to Holmes Gore.

Freda Gaye: Although this lady has been with me, I know very little about her, but [Cyril] Phillips assures me that she is very capable, and if you care to have a look at her, I am sure this could be arranged via Miss Leverton at this office.

Something may still come of Sybil Thorndike, but rehearsals and the production of her new play are pretty stiff difficulties. I go to Birmingham to-morrow and return to town next Tuesday. As a reminder, I put in Leonora Corbett's name, but as she has never done any big work, I have fears.

Yours,
[Barry Jackson]

Ena Burrill: From Armstrong at Liverpool has made a little name for herself in London.

Sophie **Stewart** (1908–77) was in Thomas Heywood's *Fair Maid of the West* (1610) at Malvern in 1933; she played Celia opposite Elisabeth **Bergner's** Rosalind in the 1936 film of *As You Like It*, directed by Paul Czinner (with Laurence Olivier as Orlando – his first film Shakespeare). **Catherine Lacey** (1904–79) had attracted attention at Stratford in several lead roles in the 1935 season. **Lucie Mannheim** (1905–76) was in Hubert Griffith's *Nina*, which opened at the **Criterion** on 17 September 1935 and ran for 183 performances. **Dorothy Holmes-Gore** (1896–1977) played several major Shavian roles, including Joan, in the 1920s and 1930s. **Margaretta Scott** (b. 1912) spent the summer of 1936 playing Rosalind at the Open Air Theatre in Regent's Park. **Fabia Drake** (1904–90) opened at the Arts Theatre on 19 April 1936 in *Indian Summer* by Aimée and Philip Stuart. **Freda Gaye** (1907–86) was a regular in the BRT company. **Leonora Corbett** (1908–60), who had impressed Shaw as The Patient in *Too True to be Good* at Malvern in 1932, opened in *Dusty Ermine*, a comedy by Neil Grant, at the Comedy Theatre on 6 March 1936 (225 performances). And **Ena Burrill** (b. 1908) worked with William **Armstrong** (1882–1952), director of the Liverpool Repertory Theatre, 1923–44, in the early 1930s before moving back to London in 1935.

86 / To Charlotte F. Shaw

[no address]
6th May 1936

[TLU (c)]

Charlotte wrote to Jackson on 5 May 1936 to invite him to spend some time with her and Shaw at Glyndebourne later in May. In the event, the Shaws couldn't get tickets until late June, when they saw five Mozart operas there.

My dear Charlotte

I should dearly like to have joined you in the visit to Glyndebourne, but I am now working hard to get the Malvern casting all settled so that I can get away for a holiday abroad in June before the strenuous doings at Malvern commence. I did not do anything about tickets for this reason. I have absolutely no advice to give you as to where you can stay in comfort; there is a Hotel in Ashdown Forest – of which I know nothing except that some friends of mine who like quiet go there from time to time.

I have to go to Birmingham to-morrow, and shall not be back till the beginning of next week, so I fear a meeting is impossible. I am still worried to death about the casting of 'Joan,' as Jean Forbes-Robertson asks too large a figure, though there is a possibility that she may climb down; I shall certainly not climb up!

Yours,
[Barry Jackson]

P.S. Since writing the above I hear the Ashdown Forest Hotel has gone all to pieces, but the Country House Hotel, Crowborough, is very clean and pleasant. One of the great things in its favour is that it has no licence, which means no rowdies, and if one requires a little whiskey, it is quite easy to take a bottle in.

87 / To Barry Jackson   4 Whitehall Court SW1
                               7th May 1936
[ALS]

My dear Barry

I should say Leonora, unhesitatingly. She is my second string for The Millionairess.

G.B.S.

88 / To Barry Jackson   Royal Automobile Club
                              9th May 1936
[TEL]

WHY NOT TRY ELISABETH BERGNER. SHAW

89 / To G. Bernard Shaw   [no address]
                                              12th May 1936

[TLU (c)]

My dear G.B.S.

My best thanks for your wire, but as I gather Leonora Corbett saw you on Saturday, she will no doubt have told you that she had been approached. She is coming to this office to-morrow morning (Wednesday) to see if we can come to terms. The Bergner suggestion was most interesting. It had occurred to me, but I dismissed it as impracticable, particularly as I did not wish you to have a recurrence of influenza. Your watch is safely with me in London, and I will leave it with Miss Patch to-morrow.

                                              Yours,
                                              [Barry Jackson]

90 / To Barry Jackson   4 Whitehall Court SW1
                                              22nd May 1936

[ALS]

The complications in choosing a Joan for Malvern seemed to multiply. Leonora Corbett thought she had an agreement with Jackson. Shaw persuaded her that this was not so, but at the same time softened the blow by giving her some hope that she would get Epifania in The Millionairess. *On the same day that he wrote this letter to Jackson, however, Shaw also wrote to Edith Evans – his first choice for Epifania (unknown to Corbett) – telling her, as he told Jackson, that Corbett was 'raging to play' the part and urging Evans to do* The Millionairess *as soon as possible in the potentially profitable West End ('I must make some money out of* The Millionairess*') and not, as she preferred, in repertory at the Old Vic (Collected Letters, IV, 432). In the meantime, Shaw also approved a production of* Saint Joan *in Brighton with Jean Forbes-Robertson as Joan; it ran for eight performances in the week of 11–18 July. Jackson had already rejected her for Malvern because she was too expensive (Letter 85), but Shaw seemed to hope that she might bring her price down if she got some income from Brighton as well. Some years later, in an article in the* Radio Times *(22 September 1950), Jackson recalled the difficulties in finding a suitable Joan, but explained it then as simply a matter of Wendy Hiller's* *being in New York at the time: '[M]essages flew to and fro across the Atlantic, and after seemingly interminable periods of waiting [we] eventually clinched the matter.'*

My dear Barry

Leonora swooped in yesterday morning, tempestuous and delightful. She insisted that she had a gentleman's agreement, with rehearsal dates and salary all fixed, and that she had told everybody that she was going to play.

I agreed that we were utter swine to throw her over, and led the conversation on to The Millionairess, which she is raging to play. My word, Barry, that young woman has a head on her as well as a pretty face!

She is not a cornstalker: she is Shropshire thoroughbred of nine (or was it 90) generations. I assured her that she was not peasant enough to play Joan, but that she might still have to do it if Wendy's conditions were impossible. She said Wendy would play it for nothing.

It ended in hopes for The Millionairess and an understanding that you are not to receive a solicitor's letter.

This morning a letter came from the Brighton theatre demanding a license for a fortnight of St Joan with Jean Forbes Robertson!!! I said yes.

She plays there for 10% on the receipts: say £30 or £40 a week. I have a great mind to run down and see what she can do with the part. After learning it and getting her little salary there she might be disposed to throw in Malvern cheap.

Leonora said that there were to be only four rehearsals of St Joan. What are our artistic consciences coming to? What will Wendy say?

G.B.S.

Jackson may well have told Leonora Corbett that there would be only **four rehearsals** of *Saint Joan*, but according to Wendy Hiller there were six (Holly Hill, 'Saint Joan's Voices: Actresses on Shaw's Maid,' *SHAW: The Annual of Bernard Shaw Studies* 6 [1986], 132).

91 / To Barry Jackson   Ayot St Lawrence, Welwyn, Herts.

31st May 1936

[APCS]

It looks as if an agreement had been reached with Wendy Hiller by the end of May to play Joan at Malvern, though Jean Forbes-Robertson ('Zillah' – one of the two wives of Lamech in Genesis 4) still entertained some hopes of displacing her. Shaw didn't live long enough to see The Millionairess *in the West End. A planned 1940 production (with Edith Evans as Epifania) at the Globe Theatre was cancelled when the theatre was bombed. Edith Evans did, however, play Epifania on a pre-London tour that year. The first West End production was at the New Theatre, 27 June 1952.*

I had a gay morning with, in succession, Zillah and Earth.

Zillah looks to me as if, like her father, she could throw the heavy stuff. She is anxious to come to Malvern on the chance of Wendy losing her voice or being a motor casualty. And she would be a tremendous understudy (or principal) for Aloysia.

Nothing is concluded about The Mill[ionaire]ss but I said I would not mind starting at the O.V. if I were guaranteed a West End production thereafter at Xmas or thereabouts.

The Photopress took three historic pictures of you sketching at St Pauls, Covent Garden. I have secured prints and ordered a double set to be sent to Blackhill.

G.B.S.

'Earth' has not been identified. **Aloysia** Brollikins in *On the Rocks* at Malvern in 1936 was played by Elspeth March.

92 / To Barry Jackson

Ayot St Lawrence, Welwyn, Herts.
21st September [1936]

[ALS]

The 1936 Malvern Festival ran from 25 July to 22 August and featured, among other productions (see Letter 77), five performances each of Saint Joan, On the Rocks, *and* Pygmalion. *The Festival also coincided with Shaw's eightieth birthday (26 July), about which, to Shaw's chagrin, there was much fanfare. The 1936 Festival also saw the opening of the Lanchester Marionette Theatre, for which Shaw subsequently wrote* Shakes versus Shav, *first performed, in Malvern, on 9 August 1949 (see Letter 179). It was, then, a more than usually hectic Festival for the Shaws, and Shaw was glad to take a post-Festival holiday in September in North Wales 'to shake off maddening Malvern before returning home,' as he told Edith Evans* (Collected Letters, *IV, 442*).

My dear Barry

We came from Port Meirion with unnatural velocity, stopping for the night at Norbury House in Droitwich for £5 worth of luxury. There we came upon the panting Brocky, who entertained us with an account of her stupendous adventures as a mother left penniless with four sons. Mussolini & Hitler, Riza Khan and Kemal Ataturk faded into weaklings by comparison. She kept us interested until her heart gave out and she went back to her doggie.

This morning I suddenly got a violent bellyache and was sick unto death. At the last moment I changed my mind, and am now nearly normal.

As to The Millionairess I have let several of the Number Two towns have a go at it; but as Edith [Evans] is pretty certain to want a star tour, or perhaps even a Number One try-out, I must hold up Birmingham for her. I have not had a potboiler since The Apple Cart; and as all my debentures and mortgages were paid off during the slump and my investments in crematoria have not yet fructified I am banking a little on The Millionairess to make me a millionaire. So it musnt go into stock in the Number Ones until it is squeezed dry by the star. And then it wont be any use. But suppose Jane Eyre fails!

Charlotte acknowledges chocolates and wishes she could share them with you on the hills. The Port M. climate has produced paroxysms of despair and transports of enjoyment from tide to tide. A crazy place.

G.B.S.

The **panting Brocky** has not been identified. **Riza Khan** (1877–1944) and **Kemal Ataturk** (1881–1938) were lesser-known dictators, in Iran and Turkey respectively, than their Italian and German contemporaries Benito **Mussolini** (1883–1945) and Adolf **Hitler** (1889–1945).

93 / To Barry Jackson   Ayot St Lawrence, Welwyn, Herts.
                                                              26th October 1936
[APCU]

SQUIRREL'S JOY

Best Ayot Windfalls warranted Unplucked.

[G.B.S.]

94 / To Barry Jackson   Ayot St Lawrence, Welwyn, Herts.

9th November 1936

[APCU]

BEST

BULLDOG AFTERMATHS

UNEQUALLED FOR

TENACITY

Warranted as having held on to the tree until dislodged by 80 miles an hour hurricane.

The season's lumbago pick.

[G.B.S.]

95 / To Barry Jackson   4 Whitehall Court SW1

20th April 1937

[TLS]

Jackson was, as usual, eager to have Shaw's advice in planning the next Malvern Festival. The 1937 program was a mixed bag: two sixteenth-century plays, Susanna *and* Gammer Gurton's Needle; *Henry Fielding's burlesque* Tom Thumb the Great; *Sheridan's* School for Scandal; *a new play,* Return to Sanity, *by Gerald Wynne Rushton and Thomas South Mack, from the BRT's 1936–7 season; and two Shaws,* The Millionairess *(with Elspeth March as Epifania) and* The Apple Cart. *It appears from Shaw's letter that at this stage of the planning Jackson had in mind only excerpts from* The Apple Cart, *but in light of the abdication of Edward VIII on 11 December 1936, a full production was a timely choice. The 1937 Malvern Festival was the last one organized by Jackson. His successor, Roy Limbert (1893–1954), took over in rancorous circumstances, as described in subsequent correspondence between Jackson and Shaw (Letters 101, 102, 166, 175, for example).*

My dear Barry

I don't understand what you mean by an orgy of Victorian plays. So far there isnt one in the whole program. Brassbound is horribly Victorian.

For that reason I strongly deprecate its resurrection unless we could get Phyllis N.T. to play it as a curiosity. She alone could raise Lady Cicely from her Victorian grave.

The king's long speech from The Apple Cart would be a very dull sermon without the context. Instead, I suggest the scene between Magnus and Boanerges at the beginning. It always goes well, and is complete in itself. The irruption of the American is also detachable, but too long.

I think the other play by me must be a new one. The Millionairess is obvious and easy. Whether Miss March could do it I cannot guess. If she could, she is entitled to her chance. If not, I should feel safe with Leonora Corbett, who would satisfy Limbert's craving for London stars; but she might not care to tackle it unless she had the reversion of the London production, which I cannot offer her, as C.B.C.–E.E. is still supposed to be on.

I think I now know how to finish Geneva; but as the play will be less suitable for Malvern than On the Rocks (which, by the way, is still available and certainly more eligible than Brassbound) I shall not recommend it. It will be devoted to a complete explosion of 'This commandment I give unto you.'

We start on Monday for Sidmouth, and shall be here until then. If you care to bring Palmer along to lunch any day, name it. The Sidmouth address is the Victoria Hotel, Sidmouth, Devon.

G.B.S.

Phyllis N.T. [Neilson-Terry] (1892–1977) played Candida at the 1930 Malvern Festival. The anticipated Charles Cochran–Edith Evans (**C.B.C.–E.E.**) London production of *The Millionairess* did not materialize (see Letter 98). *Geneva* received its world premiere at the 1938 Malvern Festival. Critic and playwright John **Palmer** (1885–1944) was also the author of a book of particular interest to Shaw, *The Censor and the Theatres* (London: Unwin, 1912).

96 / To Barry Jackson   Victoria Hotel, Sidmouth
                                                                  16th May 1937
[ALS]

It is not clear which 'lady' earned the dubious distinction of 'funking' the part of Epifania in The Millionairess, *but in the end Jackson took Shaw's advice and cast Elspeth March.*

My dear Barry

I suspect the lady of funking the part, or, like Katharine Cornell (to whom, by the way, I did not offer it), of finding it too unamiable. The truth is, it is an essentially tragic part: Leonora [Corbett] is too gay for it, though we should jump at her if she were available. The least sense of humor, or relaxation of any sort, would be fatal – Jane Bacon found out how to do it.

Failing these two – or Sybil Thorndike! – I see no fair excuse for not giving Elspeth her chance as one of the family. Birmingham ought to be a stepping stone to Malvern (the threshold of London) when there is no decisively brighter star available. Of course there are lots of old uns who would be glad of the chance; but our business is to discover the ripening young. So you had better cast Elspeth for it and get it off your mind. I am not sure that the Egyptian doctor, who ought to have three hats and an Assyrian beard, is not the more difficult problem. If Sybil played it [Epifania], Casson's peremptory manner would fit the part perfectly.

We have got through the coronation here quite quietly: a lot of bunting flapping all over the place, and a display of fireworks: nothing more: no unusual traffic.

Our telephone number is Sidmouth 11. Anytime you feel like having a breath of very mild sea air, ring us up. We know nobody here except the Ervines, who are at Sexton, just round the coast corner. Exeter cathedral is half an hour's drive. You can't possibly be inopportune.

We have to leave on the 1st of June, and shall stay with the Webbs at Passfield for a few days on our way back.

I have hardly had an hour to spare for Geneva; but it would be useless anyhow, as it would be improvident to waste a second new play on one season.

G.B.S.

Jane Bacon (1895–1956) played Epifania in the premiere of *The Millionairess* at Bexhill-on-Sea on 17 November 1936. The **coronation** of George VI took place on 12 May 1937. St John **Ervine** married Leonora Mary Davis in 1911; she died in 1965. Shaw's friendship with the **Webbs**, Sidney (1859–1947) and Beatrice (1858–1943), fellow Fabians, went back to the 1880s. The Webbs had a country home in **Passfield**, a small Hampshire village.

96

97 / To Barry Jackson   4 Whitehall Court SW1
15th July 1937

[APCS]

The 1937 Malvern Festival ran from 26 July to 21 August. As usual, Shaw attended rehearsals whenever he could. He was particularly concerned this year about The Millionairess, *Malvern being its first major production in England. He had already given the director, Herbert Prentice, detailed advice on how Elspeth March should perform Epifania – 'She is exotic and essentially tragic all through' – and what the character should look like – 'very white make-up and plenty of dark under the eyes' (Collected Letters, IV, 470). The Shaws drove to Malvern from Birmingham on Sunday 18 July; Shaw rehearsed* The Millionairess *on the Monday evening, returning to his hotel at 11:30.*

Do not bother about the Monday rehearsal being late. I shall be dog tired all the morning after the journey down, but will buck up in the evening and be quite equal to a rehearsal after dinner.

G.B.S.

98 / To Barry Jackson   4 Whitehall Court SW1
19th August 1937

[ALS]

The Shaws left Malvern before the end of the 1937 Festival for a six-week holiday in Sidmouth, Devon. Jackson did not 'look in' since he had made plans to visit Russia (Letter 99).

My dear Barry

On Sunday we go down to Sidmouth, Hotel Victoria as before. Look in whenever you feel so disposed. We *must* stay until our people's holidays are over. How much longer we *shall* stay depends on how we feel about it.

Cochran has cabled Edith definitely that he wont do The Millionairess, as he considers that the honor and glory of it have been rubbed off by Bexhill and Malvern. So Edith, keen and probably destitute after three months holiday, is crying what offers?

Czinner was here today. The St Joan film is to be a British one, made by London Films (Korda). I had made up my mind to bring Czinner round to this and throw over Hollywood. But he had come to propose it himself; so we parted with effusive rejoicings. Liesl is at Cortina.

Charlotte sends her love.

G.B.S.

The enclosed may interest you. You ought to try a serious play by Fielding some day. Not that I ever read one!

Shaw's **people** were his domestic staff in London and Ayot St Lawrence. Paul **Czinner** (1890–1972), husband of Elisabeth Bergner, the 1924 Berlin and Vienna Joan (see Letter 19), had hoped to direct a film version of *Saint Joan* with Bergner as Joan, but the plans for the project fell through. Hungarian-born Alexander **Korda** (1893–1956), a major figure in the British film industry, was to have been the producer. A film version of *Saint Joan* was not made until 1957, directed by Otto Preminger, adapted by Graham Greene, and starring Jean Seberg as Joan. **Liesl** was the nickname of Elisabeth Bergner. The **Fielding** enclosure has not survived, but Fielding was, of course, on Jackson's mind because of the current Malvern production of *Tom Thumb the Great*.

99 / To Barry Jackson

Victoria Hotel, Sidmouth
23rd August 1937

[APCS]

Immediately following the close of the 1937 Malvern Festival, Jackson left for a vacation in Russia. Shaw had been there in the summer of 1931, and reported to Charlotte (who stayed in England) on 27 July 1931 that he had 'visited a flaming collection of Gauguins and Van Goghs' in Moscow (Collected Letters, IV, 254). Jackson was also interested, of course, in Russian theatre, and he attended, among other events, the Soviet Theatre Festival in Moscow, 11–15 September, where he saw a production of The Apple Cart.

There is an extraordinary quality about the heat of a Russian summer that will wipe away all Malvern's tears, not to mention the interest of the Bolsky novelties. Be sure not to miss the Gauguins and Van Goghs in Moscow; they have a gallery practically all to themselves.

Bon voyage!

G.B.S.

Moscow's Pushkin Museum of Fine Arts houses major collections of the paintings of Paul **Gauguin** (1848–1903) and Vincent **Van Gogh** (1853–90).

100 / To Barry Jackson   4 Whitehall Court SW1

18th November 1937

[APCU]

Fearful Outrage

at

Ayot Saint Lawrence

by

A Pheasant

The entire windfall from Shaw's Oak, consisting of 1400 prime acorns destined for Blackhill was consumed by this voracious bird at a single meal.

It Still Lives.

[G.B.S.]

101 / To Barry Jackson   4 Whitehall Court SW1

10th March 1939

[TLS]

In the long period between Shaw's whimsical note about his acorns and this rather more serious letter, Jackson had been fêted during the twenty-fifth anniversary celebrations of the Birmingham Repertory Theatre (in February 1938), but had also seen the 1938 Malvern Festival succeed without his involvement or support. It was especially galling to him that his successor at Malvern, Roy Limbert, was given a Shaw world premiere, Geneva, *which ran for four performances from 1 August, directed by H.K. Ayliff, designed by Paul Shelving, with a cast that included Ernest Thesiger (Sir Orpheus Midlander) and Donald Wolfit (The Judge).* Geneva *subsequently transferred to the West End, where it achieved a run of 237 performances. The letter from Jackson to Shaw that prompted the following reply has not survived, which is unfortunate because it sounds as if Jackson dispensed with some of his usual reserve and expressed to Shaw a deep sense of griev-*

ance about Shaw's continuing commitment to the Malvern Festival after Jackson's departure. Jackson was clearly also still smarting – some ten years after the event – about Shaw's decision to give Warsaw, not Malvern, the world premiere of The Apple Cart. *It didn't help that Shaw had written another new play for Limbert's Malvern,* In Good King Charles's Golden Days, *which had its world premiere at the Festival on 12 August 1939.*

My dear Barry

I also left the theatre after Methuselah and could make no further discoveries. Sykes (Karsavina's son) was the best value. The oracle surprised me at the rehearsals, as she seemed the merest beginner at the first, and turned up quite competent at the second. The Napoleon has the making of a useful heavy in him.

Your question as to what I do with my managers is one which you ought to be able to answer; for you have been the best of them. But all managers are idiots (in the original Greek sense) in respect of the jealous sense of property they acquire in their authors if they produce more than one of his plays.

When I discussed The Man of Destiny with Irving he took it for granted that he should have the exclusive world rights. I said 'Have you any serious intention of performing the play in the Sandwich Islands?' (As a matter of fact he had no intention of performing the play at all; but he wanted to prevent anyone else performing it). A manager who toured my plays for years and years and years seriously put it to me that I ought to leave all my dramatic copyrights to his daughters in my will.

Before the war the German managers begged me to let them have my plays before they were produced in England, because Reuters always reported the London production as a failure, and forced them to put off production abroad for months until the evil report was forgotten. I accordingly adopted this practice, and from Pygmalion onward inclusive, took care to let the continent in first. The reports of these productions were ordinary news and always favorable, acting as useful preliminary pars for English productions.

In the meantime my field of operations had extended from China to Peru.

Now get a map of Europe large enough to make Worcestershire perceptible on it, and stick a pin into the Malvern Hills. Then contemplate Poland, and stick a pin into Warsaw. Compare the two. Reflect on their relative histories, their magnitudes, the parts they have played in the development of Christian civilization, and anything else that may occur to you.

Following my usual course, I gave Malvern the advertisement of a production at the National Theatre in Warsaw, and incidentally postponed the death from starvation of the devoted Sobieniowski, who still lives. It never occurred to me that this incident in my routine could be regarded as a blow in the face to you. But you immediately went stark raving mad over it; and though you magnanimously continued on speaking terms I was thenceforth a friend who had callously betrayed you. That is what managers are like. I had put Poland before Malvern and robbed you of what Limbert calls and clings to as 'the world première.' Charlotte was distressed, but was consoled when she found that it made no difference to me, and only made you kinder in forgiving what you were unable to forget.

Meanwhile you were building up the Malvern Festival, and made me its Shakespear, mulberry tree and all. Last year you dropped it, and threw your authors into the arms of whoever would carry on. This of course you had a perfect right to do; but you again fell a victim to managerial idiocy, and resented the conduct of the authors in doing their best to save the Festival instead of suicidally doing their utmost to smash it. Well, they saved it – for a year at least, and thereby saved you from the position of having failed in your biggest enterprize. If L. cannot carry on now (he says he is not sure that he can) the success of the Festival will be yours and the failure his. But now that you have forcibly made him my manager I hope he will not fail. And anyhow you must not hate me for the situation you have yourself created. Of course the situation has been created by circumstances for all of us. But if you regard me as an impishly capricious despot taking advantage of your being the victim of circumstances you get into an injured frame of mind which is wildly off the mark. We both, as money men, have more elbow room for caprice than most people; but I was for so long with no elbow room at all that I had the notion that I could please myself completely knocked out of me. Compared with me you are touchy; and this makes it harder for you than for me to deal with antipathetics. I can deal with anybody. Even apart from the money question, I was not a street corner Socialist for twelve years for nothing.

Now, if it amuses you, you can tell me your view of your view of (the repetition is intentional) these matters. In that case you can let yourself rip with even less consideration for my feelings than I have shewn for yours. Or you can lay low and say nuffin, which will save you the trouble of writing a long letter like this one.

G. Bernard Shaw

Let us know when you are in town again. You were considerably missed yesterday.

It is not clear what production of *Back to Methuselah* Shaw is referring to. There were no productions of the play in either Birmingham or London in 1939. Shaw did, however, attend a public performance by RADA students at the Apollo Theatre on 3 March, and it may be this occasion that he is referring to. As a RADA director, Jackson would probably have been there as well. The **Oracle** and **Napoleon** appear in Part IV of *Methuselah*. Tamara **Karsavina** (1885–1978) was a leading dancer with the Ballets Russes. She had a son, but his name was not **Sykes**. Cecil Sykes is, however, a character in *Getting Married*. Shaw's understanding of the **original Greek sense** of **idiot** perhaps refers to its meaning of 'private person' (OED) with the implication of managerial consideration of playwrights as personal rather than public assets (*idios*: own, private). Lengthy negotiations with Henry Irving for a production of *The Man of Destiny*, starring Irving and Ellen Terry, broke down in May 1897. The **manager** who toured Shaw's plays 'for years and years and years' was very probably Charles Macdona. *Pygmalion* premiered in Vienna (16 October 1913), and several of Shaw's subsequent plays – but by no means all – similarly premiered in Europe. The occasion on which Jackson was **considerably missed** was a lunch party on Thursday 9 March attended by Cecil Lewis – founding member of the BBC and film director – and others.

102 / To G. Bernard Shaw

[no address]
13th March 1939

[TLU (c)]

Jackson's almost-immediate response reflected on the hard lot of theatrical managers and the ingratitude of playwrights. In light of Jackson's later leadership of the Shakespeare Memorial Theatre, his pin's selection of Stratford was portentous.

My dear G.B.S.

I cannot resist your invitation to tread on the tail of your coat. My lack of skill with the sword must be apparent but it exceeds my skill with the mightier weapon, and endeavour to make out a case may prove clumsy and unconvincing.

There are varieties of theatrical managers; unlike authors they are not cast from one mould. The majority begin with some unreasoned urge for the real theatre, but this rapidly evaporates before the stronger urge for pounds, shillings and pence; preferably the former. The metamorphosis is not limited to managers; it may frequently be noted in others who start their career with an ideal. The original daemon is expelled neck and crop and a singularly unpleasant devil takes his place.

Through circumstances over which I had no control my daemon has been able to go his way with a loose rein. In consequence I should have imagined that those drawing some sort of income from the stage would have argued in this wise:– Here is a harebrained individual who only materialises once in many generations; let us be thankful he has happened in ours; let us exert every power to avoid awakening him from his dreams; although he is doing things for us to-day he may be able to accomplish even more to-morrow and as we are always wealthier through his sleep walkings it behoves us to be wary how we tread.

Not a bit of it. Clogs and the big drum became fashionable at once. Here are some of the echoes. During my first interview with John Drinkwater directly after I had planted him in London with 'Lincoln,' I was asked to go out of the room so that he might have a chat with a West End manager about his next play; after keeping 'The Farmer's Wife' running for months at considerable loss in order to force it into success, the author reviled me because I would not *produce* two more of his plays immediately, under threat of handing them to other managements hungry to share in the spoils of a writer in fashion; one year I suggested a revival of 'The Immortal Hour,' a production which has invariably cost me a great amount of money, but Rutland [Boughton] would only agree on condition that I guaranteed seasons in Manchester and other towns as 'a few odd performances at Malvern were of no use to him.' There have been many kindred experiences. I was not trusted.

As they have no concern in the present argument (if it is an argument) audiences, artists and other managers may be left out though all, in endeavour to exorcise my daemon, have left their indelible mark on a nature that is somewhat bewildered by the ingratitude and selfishness of a world realised only late in life.

All these people, to whom I hope I have been of service, are by their nature inarticulate to the public so far as I am concerned. But you let fly in the Press with a plaint that you cannot find a manager with a hundred thousand pence to introduce you to the public.

As you put me into a class with other managers, I must put you in a class with other authors – which brings us to Malvern.

The preliminary notices of 'The Apple Cart' and, if I remember it rightly, 'The Simpleton,' were not exactly encouraging even though they came from overseas. Their first production at Malvern would undoubtedly have added far more to the prestige of the Festival than gossip columns in the Press which are rapidly being found out and, unless I am mistaken, some of the plays have had their first production in this country. Has 'Geneva' reached Berlin?

In regard to this Festival adventure, I earnestly beg you to realise that the intense work and heavy expenditure from which any 'manager' would have died long before the curtain went up, were not inspired by sense of personal aggrandisement. My sincere and only wish was to make the thing into something lasting and worthwhile for authors, artists and audience. After struggling for nine years against irritating obstacles I could not carry the strain any longer, to the indecently obvious delight of some who had taken considerable toll. Even a beneficent Dictator should carry a human[e?] killer. The fact that I am not to blame for the Festival's lingering death is rather poor consolation if I have to live next door to the putrefying corpse. The most sinister method of making unhappiness is to strike through an intermediary and when the Festival breathes its last – a catastrophe at which you hint – one of my dreams will have a rude awakening. Sebastian in Heaven must envy the number of arrows flicked into my daemon, but when his end does come I shall count myself lucky in having outlets for surplus energy rather more selfish and less brutal than the theatre.

You say I am touchy; the word may be correct but I should rather be inclined to say over-sensitive. I am only too conscious that this failing (according to general standards) has proved detrimental to my work but I would be no other and indeed, only wish it were more general. The attending drawbacks are more than counterbalanced by a keen desire to be happy with my friends, among whom Charlotte and yourself have high place.

I return to London to-morrow, when I look forward to seeing you both.

[Barry Jackson]

P.S. I made the experiment of the map and the pin, but the pin stuck into Stratford which, so far as the theatre is concerned, has played far greater part in history than anything that ever came out of Poland.

For Jackson's earlier involvement with *Abraham Lincoln*, *The Farmer's Wife*, and *The Immortal Hour* see Letters 24, 13, and 2 respectively.

103 / To Barry Jackson   Ayot St Lawrence, Welwyn, Herts.
16th April 1939

[ALS]

The relationship between the Malvern Festival and the local community contin-
ued to generate controversy after Jackson's departure following the 1937 season.
Since Shaw's plays were still a principal feature of the Festival, he continued to
take an active interest in its affairs, and frequently urged a reluctant Jackson to
participate as well. Shaw's letter to the Malvern Gazette *(15 April 1939) praised*
both Jackson and Roy Limbert, Jackson's successor, but urged full disclosure from
both of them so that informed decisions about the future of the Festival could be
made. In a letter to the Gazette *on 1 April 1939 George E. Wharmby, 'a Malvern*
householder,' argued that 'the Festival is the milk in the cocoanut to Malvern,
and so must NOT be impaired.' Limbert replied on 8 April to the effect that he
had 'taken the entire burden [of the Festival] on my shoulders,' that he had lost
money in 1938, and couldn't guarantee a Festival for 1939, particularly since
'the international situation is an ever present worry.' The controversy continued
– with no involvement from Jackson – but a public appeal for funds brought in
£1000 and the 1939 Festival went ahead, opening on 7 August.

My dear Barry

I have made a jumping-off place for you in The Malvern Gazette, where one Wharmby, a local ratepayer with his knife into Limbert, has started a correspondence about continuing the Festival.

Have you any general view as to the conditions on which the Festival could be permanently instituted, leaving out, of course, all the Wharmby-Limbert squabbling? At the end of the Vedrenne-Barker experiment Granville-Barker was able to say definitely that with a rent free and rate free theatre he could go on. What do you say?

If you could state some conclusions as the result of your experience you could take the floor with magnetic effect, and make it clear that you are a true Malvern worthy and do not desire the destruction of the place (though you apparently do).

Nothing in the way of office jobs by Bache & Bishop can really do the work of an account of your experience by you in the first person.

In great haste – the village post.

G.B.S.

Bache Matthews wrote *A History of the Birmingham Repertory Theatre* (London: Chatto & Windus, 1924). G.W. Bishop wrote *Barry Jackson and the London Theatre* (London: Arthur Barker, 1933).

104 / To Barry Jackson   Ayot St Lawrence, Welwyn, Herts.
                                            17th April 1939

[ALS]

My Dear Barry

Be not hornier than Miss Horniman.

Of course we are doing all we can to save the festival. Do you suppose we are all as mad about it as you are? It is your big achievement; and to wreck it now would be suicide for you, for us, and for the biggest limb of the theatre in England.

It is no use writing to me about what the festival costs. I have no illusions about it. Write to the Gazette now that the ball is at your feet, and tell Malvern what running the affair really means. It will cost you nothing but a little good humor, and put you in the middle of the picture again. I have prepared the entrance of the star.

You are behaving like a nursery governess who wants to drown her charges when they outgrow her care.

Wake up, wake up, wake up. If you want to quarrel, quarrel with me; but don't on your life quarrel with Malvern.

G.B.S.

105 / To Barry Jackson   4 Whitehall Court, SW1
                                            19th April 1939

[ALS]

Shaw thought silence about the Malvern situation was a mistake. Jackson didn't.

He remained very much aloof from the 'melée' that provided the Malvern Gazette with impassioned copy for weeks.

My dear Barry

Of course you must not enter into any sort of controversy: who ever suggested such a mistake? You must *planer au dessus de la melée.*

You now say that there is no solid reason for the discontinuance. Then why did you discontinue it?

If you found the conditions impossible you should state the conditions on which it would be possible: a subvention, a new theatre fully equipped like Stratford, freedom from entertainment tax, one-man management, anything you darn please.

I think silence is a mistake unless you wish to disappear from the scene and become a forgotten pioneer.

There! I shall plague you no more.

G.B.S.

106 / To Barry Jackson Ayot St Lawrence, Welwyn, Herts.

1st August 1939

[ALS]

Jackson had visited Canada twice before, in 1929 and 1931–2 (see Letter 47), and had sought financial backing from the British Council for another tour, but was turned down. Maurice Colbourne (1894–1970) had partnered Barry Jones (1893–1981) on several Canadian tours, beginning in 1928–9, always with an emphasis on Shaw. The British Council supported Colbourne for another tour in 1939 (see Letter 107), for which Shaw gave him North American rights for Geneva, which received its North American premiere in Toronto on 30 October 1939.

My dear Barry

This in great haste.

Colbourne wants to tour Canada with Geneva. He declares that the British Council will back him.

I cannot understand the B.C. turning you down and taking up Colbourne. Was there any point on which you could not satisfy them? Colbourne says he is going west as well as east.

Bridges Adams is pressing me to give Geneva to Colbourne. But Malcolm Morley was beforehand with him. I have heard nothing from him and am completely bothered.

However, what I want to know is whether, in view of the alleged change of front – or possible change of front – by the B.C. you are still finally off Canada and I may conclude that you are out of the question.

Of course if not, you ought to do Geneva.

Send me a yes or no wire to Whitehall when you get this.

G.B.S.

Actor, manager, director, and theatre historian **Malcolm Morley** (1890–1966) served for one season (1941–2) as manager of the Birmingham Repertory Theatre.

107 / To Barry Jackson   4 Whitehall Court SW1
                                                              4th August 1939
[APCS]

Bridges tells me that the Council had no money when they told you so.

Then they got a little: only half enough to see you through but just enough for Colbourne.

Colbourne was an old Stratford hand under Bridges, whom he had primed with a rosy account of a former tour in Canada; so Bridges backed him generously.

It came to this: that the B.C. would give him its little all if he could get Geneva.

So, having ascertained that you and Morley had left the field, I have given the tour to Colbourne. This is all that can be committed to a postcard. Many thanks for your prompt reply.

G.B.S.

108 / To Barry Jackson   Hotel Esplanade, Frinton, Essex
                                                         9th September 1939
[ALS]

Britain declared war on Germany on 3 September 1939 and promptly closed all theatres and cinemas, a decision that Shaw attacked as 'a masterstroke of unimaginative stupidity' in a letter to The Times *on 5 September 1939. He argued that entertainment for troops on leave was essential and 'We have hundreds of thousands of evacuated children to be kept out of mischief and traffic dangers.' More theatres and cinemas should, therefore, be built, and 'actors, variety artists, musicians, and entertainers of all sorts should be exempted from every form of service except their own all-important professional one.' Several other theatre professionals – though not Jackson – used the correspondence columns of The Times to protest the government's decision, and theatres and cinemas were allowed to reopen on 20 September.*

My dear Barry

This dastardly funk in which the new jacks-in-office have madly closed the theatres and ordered the total abolition of light will soon pass, especially if you follow up my attack in The Times with all the authority of your prestige and title.

The theatres will soon be crammed with soldiers on leave and their girls; and leases will be changing hands at extravagant profit rentals. '1066 and all that' will revive fatter than ever.

But we must make a big ballyhoo about it.

I am writing to Kenneth Barnes protesting against the senseless closing of the School.

Do not dream of wasting your time as a melancholy inefficient copper brooding on imaginary wrongs. Write a superior Byng [sic] Boys for Birmingham. That will take your mind off the war. I am writing a Major Barbara film which is very successful in keeping me very usefully occupied.

Charlotte has had a horrible bout of lumbago, and cannot write to you or to anybody for the next day or two.

Your life and career have been very exceptionally fortunate. If you commit suicide out of sheer misanthropy the Recording Angel will tell you so in plain terms.

Buck up, damn you.

G. Bernard Shaw

Kenneth Barnes (1878–1957) was principal of RADA from 1909 to 1955. Shaw wrote to him on 9 September (*Collected Letters*, IV, 536–7) urging him to reopen the school: 'We kept going last time [First World War] with only eight male students and a crowd of girls.' George Grossmith's popular musical review *The **Bing Boys** Are Here* opened at the Alhambra, London, on 19 April 1916, starring George Robey and Violet Loraine. The film version of **Major Barbara**, directed by Gabriel Pascal, and starring Wendy Hiller (Barbara), Rex Harrison (Cusins), and Robert Morley (Undershaft), was released in London on 7 April 1941.

109 / To Barry Jackson

Hotel Esplanade, Frinton, Essex
24th September 1939

[APCS]

In the early weeks of the war, Shaw advocated the pursuit of peace with Germany, believing that Stalin (with whom Hitler had concluded a pact in August 1939) would exert pressure on Hitler to agree. Shaw argued his case in 'Uncommon Sense about the War,' an article published in the New York periodical Journal-American *on 6 October 1939 and in the* New Statesman *the following day: 'Our business now is to make peace with him [Hitler] and with all the world instead of making more mischief and ruining our people in the process.' In a letter to the 23 September issue of the* New Statesman *Wilfred Wellock had similarly argued that 'prudence no less than wisdom demands an early ending of hostilities' and that '[i]t still lies within the power of Britain to lead the way to a classless and stateless society via the path of freedom and democracy.'*

What on earth is P. thinking of? Does he suppose that the Brass Hat's work is more nationally important than yours? Fetch him back and let him plough half an acre. You will then, as a farmer, have unlimited petrol.

Anyhow, the war is now sheer nonsense, thanks to Stalin; and it will be over when that dawns on Downing St.

Get the current New Statesman and read a masterly letter from one Wellock, whom I don't know. Very important.

G.B.S.

Cyril Phillips (**P.**) was Jackson's general manager, who, it seems, was contemplating enlisting for active service.

110 / To Barry Jackson

Ayot St Lawrence, Welwyn, Herts.
9th June 1940

[APCS]

By December 1939 Shaw had given up hope of an early peace and had concluded that there was little alternative to striving for a military victory over Germany.

He agreed, therefore, to give a radio talk on the need to fight Hitler. The script, however, was not quite the patriotic exhortation that the BBC had, presumably, expected. There was rather more praise of Hitler than the BBC could tolerate: 'Mr Hitler did wonders for his country by his National Socialism ...,' ' nine-tenths of what Mr Hitler says is true ...,' 'his mind is a twentieth-century mind ... that of our governing class is mentally in the reign of Edward the Third, six centuries out of date;' and rather more criticism of the British government than seemed appropriate: 'Mr Hitler did not begin this war: we did,' 'nobody seems to know exactly what we are fighting for ...' The talk was suppressed by the government's Minister of Information, Alfred Duff Cooper. (An account of the episode and the script of the talk are given by the BBC producer who commissioned the talk, Anthony Weymouth [pseudonym of Ivo G. Cobb] in his Journal of the War Years and One Year Later *[Worcester: Littlebury, 1948].)*

I am to broadcast to the Empire on the short wave next Friday at 4 in the afternoon. It may amuse you to listen in. They *may* put a record on the Home Service too; but that is not settled yet.

How are you? Pipe up after Friday.

G.B.S.

111 / To Bernard Shaw   Malvern

14th June [1940]

[TLU: BL]

Running a theatre under wartime conditions was difficult, and as the war progressed would become still more difficult, and then impossible, at least for a while (see Letter 114). BRT programs in 1940 advised patrons that they would be 'informed at once from the Stage' in the event of an air-raid warning, and that anyone who chose to leave the theatre 'may do so,' but 'the performance will continue' and audience members 'are advised in their own interests to remain in the building.' Audiences were also advised to 'CARRY YOUR GAS MASK WITH YOU AT ALL TIMES.' Despite the difficulties, Jackson did his best to retain not just a repertoire at the Birmingham Repertory Theatre, but a repertoire with some artistic integrity. Thus it was that the 1939–40 season at the BRT included work by Shaw (Getting Married), *Sheridan, Ibsen, Coward, Anatole France, Aldous Huxley, Lady Gregory, and Maxwell Anderson. And in the early summer of 1940 he produced* In the Beginning, *Part I of* Back to Methuselah, *albeit with an inexperienced cast and minimal technical and administrative support. The ellipses in this letter are Jackson's.*

My dear G.B.S.

Part I comes out admirably. The young people have shown great keenness intelligence and give a performance that is, at least, worthy of the theatre's reputation. Eve, to the eye, is remote from your ideal in the physical sense; she is one of the modern willowy type, extremely beautiful, and with a pleasant voice: having range of tone she manages the old Eve with entire conviction. Her name is Rachel Gurney and she is a daughter of Irene Scharer though I trace no particle of 'the chosen.' Adam fills the bill but is not quite so good. He seems to be the most difficult of the characters, having changes of mood without links to build them on. The Serpent gets through her difficult (through immobility) lecture as convincingly as possible: both she and I found it no easy task to steer clear of monotony in the attempt to de-humanise. The heat wave adds to her difficulties. Cain is entirely after your own heart. Such audiences as we have had, the worst in numbers this season, express unstinted delight. Sitting among them on two occasions I came to the foregone conclusion that at least 99% have not the least idea of what you are talking about. The 'secret' proved too much for one elderly spinster on Tuesday and she became almost hysterical.

I think a spot of good news would bring people back into the theatre but at the moment there does not appear to be much hope. In addition to this all important factor our local commercial theatres have presented, throughout the winter, an unending procession of star evacuees from the West End mopping up any possible drama public. Now I gather that the money allocated to help for the theatre during war time is to be devoted to the formation of a touring company ... no doubt to be recruited from the West End ... how this ephemeral organisation is to help those of us who struggle year in and year out passes my comprehension. However, if it succeeds in making money for the theatre managers, who do not care two hoots who occupies their stages so long as their share of the loot is worth having, honour will be satisfied. We shall struggle on. At present we are working with one electrician, one carpenter and a very small but enthusiastic staff of girl volunteers. The actors do the scene shifting ... I should say those that are left, for the only one who stays 'put,' and that not for long I fear, is a Jew refugee from Berlin or Vienna. We are already receiving anonymous post-cards asking if we are aware that he is an enemy alien! He walks in fear and trepidation and though I dare not suggest it, cannot refrain from a feeling that he would be happier in the Isle of Man.

Via the Red X at Geneva I hear those Meyer people in Copenhagen are alive and well. A pity Miss Meyer will not be permitted to get photos of the place under the Nazis.

That poor gentle soul, de Smet, got to Paris after fleeing from Ghent, unhappily breaking a shoulder and a hip bone on the way. I imagine he left under orders as he was an officer of some sort.

The frenzied madness of present events has been intensified by the wonderful Spring; Nature around here has been in splendid fettle. The bitter contrast makes life poignant. My trees still show signs of the winter's ravage and we are very short of birds – quite noticeably so. Hardly a friendly robin to be seen and the flocks of starlings that in old days used to come and rid the oaks of caterpillars seem to have vanished. As the serpent says, there is hope for the gaunt and broken branches are showing little green shoots and the feathered folk rearing families in every possible nook and corner.

The cancellation of the Broadcast was a disappointment ... from the point of view of effort it may be as well for there is no denying that such talks are a heavy strain on the energy. I had intended having a tea party with you as the top of the bill. Perhaps you will be on the air later on. Be sure to let Miss Patch send me a card as B.B.C. programmes seem all higgledy piggledy.

Best love to Charlotte and yourself.

Barry

Why is it that the amateur typist is so often just one letter too soon?

Rachel Gurney (dates unknown) joined the BRT company in 1939 and went on to a successful acting career in the provinces, the West End, and in North America. Her mother, Irene Scharer (d. 1971), was a well-known concert pianist. Adam was played by Russell Walters, the Serpent by Elizabeth Vaughan, and Cain by Clement McCallin. The Meyer people have not been identified. As an enthusiastic painter himself, Jackson would have taken particular interest in the circumstances of Gustave de Smet (1877–1943), the Belgian expressionist artist.

112 / To Barry Jackson   Ayot St Lawrence, Welwyn, Herts.
                                               , 18th September 1940

[APCS]

In September 1940 heavy German bombing raids began on London, spreading that autumn to other cities in England, including Birmingham. Jackson was relatively safe in Malvern, the Shaws (including Blanche Patch) less so in Ayot (see Letters 114, 117, and 139). The Birmingham Repertory Theatre remained unscathed – at least for a time (see Letter 114).

Do you want any acorns? There are miraculous millions here.

We get no news of Birmingham here, only vague sentences about the Midlands and no casualties – or only a few.

We assume that no news from Blackhill is good news; but a postcard to confirm would be appreciated.

Charlotte has had another tumble and damaged her knee so that she can't get about or go up to London, which is a blessing slightly disguised just at present and gives me an excuse for skulking.

Miss Patch has taken hasty refuge with us, and is in difficulties because she had to leave most of her wardrobe behind; so we shall have to go back to the front line for a few hours anyhow.

Has the Rep. escaped?

                                               G.B.S.

113 / To Barry Jackson   Ayot St Lawrence, Welwyn, Herts.
                                           17th October 1940

[TLS]

It was difficult enough during the war to keep theatres open at all, so the prospect of introducing Sunday performances was remote. This did not stop Jackson and Shaw debating the issue – and Charlotte joined in as well (Letter 114). Though Shaw the playwright stood to gain financially by regular Sunday performances, he looked at it as well from the actors' point of view and remained opposed unless actors were guaranteed a day off along the lines of the French 'relâche' (Monday closure; Shaw gets his French accents mixed up).

My dear Barry

Sunday performances, like matinées, are very nice for the public, for the manager, for the author, and in the long run for the landlord of the theatre. But what about the actors? Before matinées were invented they gave six performances a week for their salaries. Now they give eight; but they still have a six-day week. Sundays would impose a seven-day week on them when other workers are agitating for a five-day week, and Friday to Tuesday off has long been common for heads of firms and professional men (barring doctors and parsons). When Bourchier called meetings to establish Sunday performances and asked me to speak at them, I told the actors that I, as an author, was enthusiastically in favor, as I should gain handsomely by them without lifting a finger, but that if I were an actor I should fight them to the last extremity. You as a manager are in the same position. You cannot honestly advise the players to support the movement unless their six-day-week is maintained by the French relâche [*sic*], or else the running plays are barred on Sundays, and replaced by entertainment given by otherwise unemployed actors. Of these alternatives the relâche is much the least troublesome and workable. Some of the repertory theatres now close on Mondays; and it would be far more in the general movement if this were made compulsory for all theatres and for the dramatic section of the wireless, making Monday a fast day dramatically, which would be no great hardship for the public, who could go to the pictures as at present.

Much as you hate actors I do not see how you can advocate a seven day week for them without coming to loggerheads with Equity. And that is not advisable. So do not commit yourself. Just explain the difficulties; and say that a change without safeguards is out of the question.

I should begin by saying that in big populations a general holiday is impossible, because as the holiday makers must be entertained there must be a body of persons working to entertain them. Thus if Sunday is to be an off day for industry, it must be a hardworking day for the clergy and the actors. But clergymen and actors need a day of rest like other people; therefore it is not enough to open the theatres on Sundays: we must close them some other day. We cannot have one without the other; and that is why no reasonable person can give a flat yes or no to the question 'Are you in favor of Sunday opening or are you not?'

Now I think you have your brief as far as I can help you to it.

If you can make any use of them I can send you enough acorns to cover Blackhill with oaks. As I have sown millions in former years without results (the squirrels, like resurrection men, dig them up and eat them) I now drop them into a hole made by my walking stick; but I fill it up with basic slag. I cannot imagine even the most morbid squirrel liking b.s. as a relish.

I wonder will the film kill your revival of Pygmalion. So far it seems to have the opposite effect.

Barbara is on the verge of completion.

Plenty of bombs here, as we are near enough to London for Jerry to hit us in the firm belief that he is demolishing the Bank of England.

G. Bernard Shaw

Theatre manager Arthur **Bourchier** (1863–1927) was also an actor (and playwright) and married actress Violet Vanbrugh in 1894. The Actors' **Equity** Association, a trade union for professional actors, was founded in 1929. **Resurrection men** were Victorian corpse thieves, though they stole for financial rather than gastronomic satisfaction. The **film** version of *Pygmalion* had been released in 1938 (see Letter 81); Jackson's production of the play was running in Birmingham (see Letter 114). The film version of *Major Barbara* was released in 1941 (see Letter 108).

114 / To Barry Jackson   Ayot St Lawrence, Welwyn, Herts.
   From Charlotte F. Shaw   30th October 1940

[ALS]

While Shaw had plenty to occupy him at Ayot St Lawrence during the early years of the war, Charlotte found life there tedious, despite the danger of stray German bombs. One way of dealing with the tedium was to write to friends, including Jackson. Jackson's 'new tragedy' was the loss of some thirty years' worth of sets, properties, and costumes, destroyed by enemy bombing on Birmingham on 24 October. The storage building was located near, but not adjacent to, the Repertory Theatre; the theatre itself was, however, also damaged by incendiary bombs. Despite the difficulties, Jackson kept the theatre running with a series of matinee performances (including Pygmalion*) until 14 December, when dwindling audiences caused him to shut down. The theatre reopened in December 1941.*

Dear Barry

I am so grieved about this new tragedy – your poor theatre & costumes – how astonishing it should have happened just when that Broadcast was going on. How sorry I am! What is going to become of us all! Here we have bombs all around us, & enemy planes overhead, & I feel quite ashamed of being intact – & even rather well!

I have been so interested in your correspondence with G.B.S. about the Sunday openings of theatre. I am definitely for it & G.B.S. obstinately against it – at least he has been – but I think he is coming round. Your last letter about it was most excellent & I could see it really made an impression on him.

We live the most dull life here it is possible to imagine. Seeing no one but the most countrified country neighbors – doing the same dull things every dull day! I am so ashamed of myself for I *cannot* settle down to any piece of work that would be worth doing. I suppose it is my nerves which have never got straight since that breakdown I had. But when, suddenly, you hear over your head – night or day – an enemy plane & know 'Next moment may be my last' – it *is* rather unsettling! That happens to us constantly – I hope that [it] is better at Blackhill, but in Birmingham it must be as bad as London – where we *don't* go!

How I wish I could pop down on Blackhill, & have tea with you all – now this very minute!

Anyway my love goes.

                                                    C.F.S.

The **Broadcast** was a program called 'Everybody's Scrapbook' on BBC radio, Thursday 24 October, 9:35–10:15pm. It included a segment on the life of Edward Elgar, whose music was frequently performed at the Malvern Festival. Jackson's **last letter** on Sunday performances – like his other letters on the subject – has been lost.

115 / To Barry Jackson   Ayot St Lawrence, Welwyn, Herts.
    From Charlotte F. Shaw   [30th?] October 1940

[APCS]

Bombs were a worry for the Shaws, and so was food – or the lack of it. Malvern is only about twenty-five miles from Gloucester, so perhaps Charlotte thought Jackson had better access to the area's cheese. And she no doubt recalled that his family had been in the grocery business.

In my letter of yesterday I quite forgot to ask you if you know of any place where one can get Double Gloster cheese. You will think I have gone mad – but all the articles of food G.B.S. likes best are gradually disappearing, & I feel at this rate he will disappear too! The delicious cheese we got him in Cornwall has ceased to come. He *says* he likes Double Gloster! Hence these entreaties!

C.F.S.

116 / To Barry Jackson Ayot St Lawrence, Welwyn, Herts.
   From Charlotte F. Shaw   1st December 1940

[ALS]

On 22 November 1940 Shaw complained to Gabriel Pascal about high taxation rates during the war: 'Only by living abroad in a neutral country could I escape this; and as they are all preparing for war I should as likely as not be bombed out of the frying pan into the fire' (Bernard Dukore, ed., Bernard Shaw and Gabriel Pascal *[Toronto: University of Toronto Press, 1996], 119). Charlotte explained the problem to Jackson, and added a few other wartime grumbles for good measure.*

Dear Barry

Thank you so specially much for your last letter. I do so heartily agree with what you express so well that now, when we most want our friends they are forced away from us. Here have we been down here for 3 months *exiled*, & seeing hardly anyone. It's a sort of solitary confinement & what can we do! *Not* go back to London; *not* an Hotel, even if I was well enough! Just sit & bear it. G.B.S. is luckiest, he has a never failing source of joy in his work!

It seems the very cruellest of irony that you should have seen the destruction of Birmingham from the Malvern Hills. I keep thinking of it & picturing it. How splendid of Dame Elizabeth about the Barn! She *is* a splendid old thing! We have just heard that the National Gallery (London) has had two direct hits. Our informant said 'It looks awful'!

You will be interested to hear the last achievement of 'that grand commercial industry – the cinema' as you call it! G.B.S. in the current year has made, or is to get, over £20,000 from Pygmalion. This runs his years income up to the highest figure of war taxation, with the result that he will be taxed 18/- in the pound. He will get 2/- out of every pound. And for surtax this involves *me*, as husband & wife are lumped together & my income is practically wiped out. They have made a really lovely film of Major Barbara so the same thing will probably happen next year. Pascal is going to start a studio in the Bahamas!

My love to you all & I don't forget dear Derrick. I am a little better if only I can keep so. Miss Patch is living down here with us: imagine the trio!

Your friend
Charlotte

Dame Elizabeth Cadbury (1858–1951) was the second wife of George Cadbury (1839–1922), son of the founder of Cadbury Brothers, chocolate makers. She had a country home in Malvern and regularly attended the Malvern Festival. It seems likely that she made a barn available to Jackson for storing BRT materials following the loss of the Birmingham storage building (Letter 114). **Derrick** has not been identified.

117 / To Barry Jackson Ayot St Lawrence, Welwyn, Herts.
From Blanche Patch 8th December 1940

[ALS]

Living at Ayot was far less dangerous than being in London, but life in the country had its own little adventures, as Blanche Patch explained to Jackson.

Dear Sir Barry

... Last night I was in bed soon after 10 & reading, when a sudden sharp rataplan noise like rifle firing under my window made me leap from my bed thinking any moment shots would be through the window. I went out & looked over the bannisters & there was Char[lotte] creeping about – he was in the dining room. She crept up to me & said 'What is it?' I didn't know so she decided it was *her shawl sweeping against the side of her chair*. I ventured to say that I'd hardly hear that in my room, but when I said I should return to my bed she thought she'd better go & sit in the study & see if anything else happened – *he* musn't be disturbed. I let her go & soon went to sleep & this morning the maid tells me it was our one barrage gun which, for the 1st time, had sighted a plane low enough to fire at. We'd had no Alert. He was vastly interested when I told him & thinks he must have been asleep though supposed to be working or listening to [the] wireless. This latter is the bane of my life. We have it some days all through lunch & dinner so those days we hardly speak as we live in different rooms at other times! Well, well, my Memoirs of the War might be amusing if we live through it.

My love to all.

Yours
B.P.

118 / To Barry Jackson　　　　　　Ayot St Lawrence, Welwyn, Herts.

31st January 1941

[APCS]

So Dame Elizabeth is lost to us.

No matter: we shall certainly meet her in heaven if ever we go there.

I have met only one other old woman who produced this conviction in me; and that was Krupskaya, Lenin's widow.

G.B.S.

Dame *Geraldine* Cadbury died on 30 January 1941. She married Barrow Cadbury, sometime Chair of Cadbury Bros., in 1891 and was active in Birmingham municipal politics, but she appears not to have had any connections with Barry Jackson. Her obituary was published in *The Times*, 31 January 1941. Shaw perhaps confused her with Dame **Elizabeth** Cadbury (Letter 116). Nadezhda **Krupskaya** (1869–1939), whom Shaw met in Moscow on 30 July 1931, was the wife of Vladimir Ilyich **Lenin** (1870–1924), leader of the Bolshevik revolution.

119 / To Barry Jackson　　　　　　Ayot St Lawrence, Welwyn, Herts.

31st March 1941

[TLS]

Having let off steam about Sunday performances (Letter 113), Shaw now gave Jackson his views on the distinction between amateur and professional theatre, particularly insofar as it affected, on the one hand, his royalty income and, on the other, the general health of British theatre. Giving so-called amateurs professional terms, as he was wont to do, actually cut into Shaw's income ('nimble ninepences' being less than the flat fee he could have charged and was encouraged to charge by the Society of Authors), but Shaw believed that it was in the best long-term interests of theatre to encourage and support amateurs, for it is they who 'keep the theatre alive at the roots, and not the West End big business.'

My dear Barry

I have fought the snobs of the Authors' Society for years against their ridiculous refusal to take copper or even silver fees from 'amateurs'. I ask them to define the word amateur. They reply, when they reply at all, that an amateur is an actor who is not paid for his work. I ask them was Irving an amateur when he not only did not make enough to pay his own salary but had to pay the other salaries out of his own pocket as well. That is a common experience of actors who finance their own plays.

What is a professional? Quite clearly and simply an actor who either puts his profits into the theatre's capital or else spends it in drink or some other form of self indulgence, and meets his losses by pawning his watch or his shirt or anything that is available.

An amateur is a person who gives away the profits of his performance (if any) to a charity, and repudiates the idea of his being a player instead of a gentleman, but wishes to shew how well he can act some fashionable actor's part in some fashionable play. He has to pay the author five guineas, which he can well afford.

The distinction is quite clear. It has nothing to do with salaries or no salaries. It turns on profits and losses. Any person or group of persons getting up and acting a play for their own profit at their own risk is a professional and is entitled to professional terms. The profession is open to everyone on these terms: there is no register or ordination or call to the bar. You as a Pilgrim Player were as indisputably a professional as the lessee of Drury Lane, though instead of being paid for your work it cost you £5000 a year.

Accordingly I charge the Women's Institutes and similar little ventures exactly what I charge you. If they perform St Joan (their favorite) and the gross receipts are fifteen shillings, they pay me ninepence, out of which I have to pay postage. I touch my hat and respectfully trust for a continuance of their custom. I get between two and three hundred a year in this way. It gives Miss Patch a lot of trouble; but no agent will take it on, as it would not pay them; and this is why agents stick so hard to the five guinea business. I, of course, look, not at the nimble ninepences, but at the fact that it is these little people – these real amateurs – who keep the theatre alive at the roots, and not the West End big business.

If they consult me I advise them to take some name like the Blank-town Players, and have a little constitution on paper to give them a permanent existence, and not on any account to call themselves amateur societies. Some of the big schools give public performances every year; but if they call themselves The Merchant Taylors Players or the like, and earmark their takings for wardrobe etc., they have professional terms.

As the poor foolish creatures still hanker after fashionable plays in which the players are the sole real attraction, and in which the local people are ghastly failures, it is well to advise them to stick to highbrow stuff that will hold an audience if only it is read audibly.

Charlotte still suffers horribly from her lumbago, and is more than half bedridden. I haven't tasted an orange for months. Starvation seems to be imminent; but since our village searchlight was taken away there are no more bombs: we contemplate London in flames as you contemplate Birmingham.

Scott [Sunderland] refused the brilliant part of Kneller in my Charles play. Why?

Yours always

G. Bernard Shaw

P.S. I may be wrong about the Women's Institutes just at present. They are getting up performances to give something to the Red Cross or some other war charity, and have no interest in the theatre *as such* at all. Miss Patch sends all these cases to the Society of Authors, which properly classes them as amateur, and I suppose charges them a guinea. If they would only say nothing about the Red Cross and call themselves the local dramatic club or the like, they would get professional terms.

The **Authors' Society** (Society of Authors) was founded in 1884 to promote and protect the business interests of authors, including playwrights. The part of **Kneller** in *In Good King Charles's Golden Days* was played by Denis Cannan in the 1939 world premiere at Malvern, and subsequently by Bruno Barnabe and Alec Clunes in 1939 and 1940 London productions.

120 / To Charlotte F. Shaw

Blackhill, Malvern

11 June [1941]

[TLU: BL]

The depression evident in this letter from Jackson to Charlotte did not last. In one sense – primarily financial – Malvern and London had been 'failures,' and Jack-

son had little to do as a producer after the war with either location: in London a
modern-dress Sheridan (The Rivals) at the St James's Theatre in June 1948,
Shakespeare's Henry VI at the Old Vic in July 1952 and July 1953, and Shaw's
Caesar and Cleopatra at the Old Vic in July 1956; and in Malvern a centenary
Shaw celebration in July 1956. But Jackson was a long way from his 'final exit
from the theatre.' The Birmingham Repertory Theatre reopened just six months
after he wrote this letter, and a turbulent Stratford adventure awaited him.

My dear Charlotte

... I am feeling rather weighed down by events. As you perhaps remember, the Birmingham Repertory Theatre closed down just after the bad autumn raids and now it appears we shall shortly have expended the all too small capital in meeting firewatchers, rates and other oddments. The Trustees had a palaver last Friday and quite calmly, under my very nose, talked of selling up all the moveables I had given to them! Common sense, no doubt, but rather crushing. If this happens my present frame of mind portends a final exit from the theatre. The failure in London, Malvern and now, possibly, Birmingham will weigh too heavily on any resilience that may be left – and there seems mighty little ...

Yours
Barry

121 / To Barry Jackson   Ayot St Lawrence, Welwyn, Herts.
    From Blanche Patch   4th July 1941

[TLS]

Having moved from the dangers of wartime London to live with the Shaws at
Ayot (see Letter 112), Blanche Patch had time and opportunity to report to Jack-
son on matters domestic and theatrical, and she did so with increasing frequency
(see, for example, Letters 128, 129, 139, 141).

Dear Sir Barry

... Katharine Cornell has done very well with The Doctor's D. in New York, which will help GBS to pay his monstrous Inc. Tax, and is now sending the play on tour. She has got Barry Jones in it as Blenkinsop. He and Maurice Colbourne were practically on the rocks out there and talked of coming home and trying to enlist, but I expect they'll stay put now as Colbourne is again with the Lunts – at least, I think he is.

We expect Pascal back about the 11th – flushed with success. His house at Chalfont St Peter has been let to Michael Redgrave while the latter was filming at Denham. Now finished.

Poor GBS was quite upset at having made the mistake of saying that Hitler would never dare attack Russia and has sent another letter to The New Statesman called My Mistake (it may be in this week's). He says that he never makes mistakes and has now lost prestige. I ventured to say that I could recall other mistakes, but he wouldnt have it ...

Yours
B.P.

Katharine Cornell produced and starred in *The Doctor's Dilemma* in New York in 1941. After 121 performances in New York, the production began a national tour in September 1941. Shaw complained frequently about his **monstrous** income tax. He grumbled, for example, that the £25,000 he earned in royalties from the film of *Pygmalion* (released in 1938) 'has ruined me by putting me into the class which is allowed to retain only sixpence of every pound it receives. My 25,000 sixpences did not pay the rent of my flat in Whitehall' (*Collected Letters*, IV, 610). (See also Charlotte's view of the tax situation, Letter 116.) The **Lunts** – Alfred Lunt (1892–1977) married Lynne Fontanne (1887–1983) in 1922 – were a successful acting and producing partnership in the United States. Gabriel **Pascal** had been in the United States for the opening (13 May 1941) of his film version of *Major Barbara*. **Michael Redgrave** (1908–85) was a British stage and film star. Shaw's letter on his **mistake** about Hitler and Russia appeared in *The New Statesman* 5 July 1941: 'I was wrong. I am always making mistakes by imagining that other people are as clever as I am myself.'

122 / To Barry Jackson　　　　　Ayot St Lawrence, Welwyn, Herts.
26th July 1941

[TLS]

In his early wartime correspondence Shaw had already given Jackson his views on Sunday performances and the distinction between amateur and professional theatre (Letters 113, 119). He now addressed the issue of audience behaviour in the theatre, specifically the 'detestable misbehaviour' of laughter. Happily, the reform proposed by Shaw has not been achieved.

My dear Barry

One of the greatest reforms we shall owe to the films is the abolition of applause while the curtain is up. My plays, exactly the right length at the dress rehearsals, have been interrupted, prolonged, and half spoiled by from 25 to 45 minutes of heehawing. I have circulated printed appeals to the audience not to keep themselves late for their last trains by this detestable misbehaviour, which is as inexcusable as brawling in church. I have instructed the company not to wait for the laughs so as to make the audience conscious that it is losing half the fun. Far from asking Pascal to leave time for the laughs, I shall suggest that we instal a controlled gramophone which on the slightest noise, utters a terrifying Sh-sh-sh, like the rending of the veil of the Temple at the crucifixion.

When The Apple Cart had acquired a settled congregation which came night after night and knew the play by heart, Lord Lytton brought a party to see it for the first time. They began laughing, and to their amazement, were immediately hissed into silence by the habitués.

The reform is quite practicable. Operas used to be interrupted by applause and encores; but Wagner made an end of all that: there is now no applause until the curtain falls. And people now never applaud between the movements of a symphony. So back me up.

G.B.S.

Lord Lytton, Victor Bulwer Lytton (1876–1947), grandson of playwright Edward Bulwer Lytton (1803–73), was a strong supporter of the arts and of women's suffrage. The operas of Richard Wagner (1813–83) were much admired by Shaw.

123 / To Barry Jackson   Ayot St Lawrence, Welwyn, Herts.
                                              2nd August 1941

[APCS]

Jackson apparently disagreed with Shaw about laughter in the theatre.

Yes; but, damn it, I always want to laugh at a funeral; but I don't guffaw.

I admit that some plays, like a clown's antics, would be nothing without the laughs; and I always laugh as loudly as possible to encourage the company; but at my plays the deader the silence the more terrific the effect. Tragedies can get on without tears and hysterics; and comedies can get on without roars of laughter.

I have no objection to smiles.

From the 12th to the end of the month our address will be c/o the Viscount Astor, Cliveden, Taplow, Bucks.

G.B.S.

The Shaws stayed at the home of Viscount and Lady **Astor** for three weeks while their house staff were on holiday.

124 / To Barry Jackson   Ayot St Lawrence, Welwyn, Herts.

[30th?] September 1941

[APCS]

The precise issue addressed by Shaw in this postcard is unclear (the letter from Jackson that prompted Shaw's response having been lost), but it related, it seems, to Protestant and Catholic attitudes towards theatre.

The distinction was made and imposed on his wretched children by an ultra-Protestant uncle of mine; but I never heard of it from a Catholic. Cardinal Richelieu wrote plays: Calvin didn't. The 'continental Sunday' is Catholic: the Scottish sabbath is Protestant.

This or that Catholic order may make a rule against theatregoing for its members (who can get dispensations) but the laity are much more free to enjoy themselves than their Protestant fellow creatures. Priests of my acquaintance have come to my plays, just as Mother Laurentia, Abbess of Stanbrook, an enclosed nun, can always drive into Birmingham with a hospital case or the like by dispensation.

When you have a free afternoon in town, take the train from Kings Cross to Welwyn Garden City or Hatfield and our car will pick you up there.

I have ordered a Brecon photograph for the R.A.D.A.

G.B.S.

Shaw's **ultra-Protestant uncle** was the Reverend William George Carroll, who both baptized Shaw and taught him Latin. **Cardinal Richelieu** (1585–1642), first minister of France, 1624–42, wrote plays by committee (les Cinq Auteurs) and founded the Académie Française. As Shaw says, Protestant reformer John **Calvin** (1509–64) didn't write plays, by committee or otherwise. **Mother Laurentia** (Margaret McLachlan, 1866–1953) was a Benedictine nun who became Abbess of Stanbrook Abbey, near Worcester. Shaw met her first in 1924 and maintained regular contact with her; 'I count my days at Stanbrook among my happiest,' he told her in 1944 (*Collected Letters*, IV, 723). Shaw and Jackson had visited the birthplace of Sarah Siddons, the great English actress (1755–1831), in **Brecon** on 9 February 1935. A photograph of them outside the birthplace, with Capt. Stanley Francis, president of the Brecon Chamber of Trade, was published in the *Western Mail & South Wales News* on 11 February 1935. Shaw and Jackson subsequently – in September 1941 – signed a copy of the photograph for Francis (Shaw's accompanying letter to Francis, 17 September 1941, with a note added by Jackson, is in the Hanley Collection, HRC). Shaw also, it seems, arranged for the photograph to be sent to RADA.

125 / To Barry Jackson   Ayot St Lawrence, Welwyn, Herts.

                                                    19th October 1941

[APCS]

The saw has arrived. It is fearfully effective; but it takes all the horse power I still possess (per minute) to keep it going. Still, the logs fall faster. So I am thankful.

Come again.

                                                    G.B.S.

126 / To Barry Jackson   Ayot St Lawrence, Welwyn, Herts.

                                                    29th November 1941

[APCS]

After being dark for a year the Birmingham Repertory Theatre reopened in December 1941, despite austere wartimes conditions. Jackson leased the theatre to a company managed by Basil Langton (b. 1912), whose Travelling Repertory Theatre had performed in the parks of Birmingham during the summer of 1941. Shaw's advice on how to keep the audience warm arose from his theatre-going in Beijing in February 1933.

In Pekin I had 15° of frost every night; and I went to the theatre all the same, though there were no heating systems there. My admission money entitled me to a small portable furnace which glowed very comfortably at my feet. The fuel seemed like charcoal and sawdust. If Langton lays in a supply of these and papers the house so that it is always full to capacity, taking care to stop all ventilation, the B. Rep. will be the most popular winter resort in the Midlands.

Aida was greatly improved by the omissions, the lady herself being a bore.

But did you listen in to Priestley on Colds. My God!!!

G.B.S.

Verdi's **Aida** was broadcast ('in full,' according to announcements in the *Radio Times*) by the BBC on Wednesday 19 November, with Eva Turner in the title role. Novelist and playwright J.B. **Priestley** (1894–1984) gave a weekly radio talk on subjects that took his fancy. The one referred to by Shaw was on Thursday 27 November.

127 / To Barry Jackson   Ayot St Lawrence, Welwyn, Herts.

8th May 1942

[TLS]

After a winter season at the BRT (which included a production of The Doctor's Dilemma*), Langton took his company back to the Birmingham parks, while other companies used the Rep. Shaw's views on the unsuitability of* The Devil's Disciple *for outdoor performance didn't prevail; the play opened Langton's summer season at Cannon Hill Park on 8 June. Nor did the 'political objection' prevail; Langton included* The Devil's Disciple *in his 1942–3 season at the Rep.*

My dear Barry

We ought to stop this silly selection of The Devil's Disciple for performances in the open air in Birmingham. Act I is in a dark ugly room at night. Act II is in a cosy room also at night. Both of these are as wrong for the open air as any two acts could possibly be. Act III requires two crowds of supers; and though I daresay the sort of people who dress up for pageants would oblige, they are just the people needed to fill the dearest seats and pay for them. I suppose it was this third act and its military band and crowds that attracted the management; and of course the other two acts can take place in daylight as well as at night; but their atmosphere will be gone.

However, I leave it to you: this is just to say that if you care to make them choose another play, you can put it on me. I stopped the play in America because its anti-British subject and feeling is just what we don't want at present.

Your letters to us and to Blanche are much relished here. Charlotte, who is just recovering from a bad relapse into her lumbago, wants her ashes sent to Ireland when she is cremated. As I doubt whether that will be practicable under the present regime I try to persuade her to be scattered over the Malvern hills, with you officiating.

We shall miss Gough at Tewkesbury.

I am working away getting my new book through the press. I had rather it was a play, but cannot deny that the people badly need elementary political instruction and have had quite enough of my plays to go on with.

G. Bernard Shaw

P.S. I licensed the D's D. for Birmingham – or rather Blanche did as a matter of routine; so perhaps the political objection is the one to urge. They should do The Simpleton, which is very open airy.

No doubt to Jackson's relief, alternative arrangements were made for the disposition of Charlotte's **ashes** when the time came (see Letter 135). **Gough** has not been identified. Shaw's **new book** was *Everybody's Political What's What?*, not published until September 1944.

128 / To Barry Jackson   Ayot St Lawrence, Welwyn, Herts.
     From Blanche Patch   14th May 1942

[TLS]

Blanche Patch continued to give inimitable reports to Jackson on wartime domesticity at Ayot. She also managed a theatrical outing to London from time to time.

Dear Sir Barry

Many thanks for your letter – the one to GBS arrived yesterday. It has now become a custom that when he has been summoned from his shelter by hand bell ringing to lunch he carries in the morning's letters with him so that they may be read aloud while he gets on with his first course – soup. This duty has devolved on Char[lotte] so that she shall not sit idly beside him and of late her voice has become more feeble, and he is deafer, and although I now give them 15 minutes start I often find that the reading has not progressed very far and I have to take it on. Always the case if there is a letter from Lady Astor in her own writing; some days I can hardly contain myself. As I say I don't join them for 15 minutes, but then there is the long business of handing biscuits and cheese and the eating thereof and when they are lucky (and this is happening just now) there are oranges which have to be cut in slices and then sucked and each day there is the remark that they are so dry that they are not *worth* eating 'but its nice to have a taste.' You may remember that I never eat oranges even when they are plentiful, so you will understand. And you are quite right about the uselessness of trying to simplify meals. Such suggestions are always taken as complaints ...

Poor Mrs S[haw] has had quite a bad turn in her left side and was in her own room for 3 weeks. She now creeps down for lunch and dinner returning above immediately after and its pathetic to see how shrunken she is when he arms her upstairs. And he looks too feeble to be doing such things. Last evening he fell asleep during the 9 o'clock news and I was able to remove the clock which he had been winding from his hand without his being conscious of what I was doing. As the clock has only recently returned from the mender I thought it a pity to let it crash to the ground – which it would have done.

I don't think I've written since I saw The Doctor's D. in London. I liked the whole thing, but wasnt impressed by Vivien Leigh's acting and thought Austin Trevor bad as B.B. The new Dubedat I liked. Did you hear that Cusack had to be sacked from the part owing to the curtain having to be rung down because he was so drunk? I lunched with Hugh Beaumont at the Ivy the day I returned and we motored down together. I saw Ivor Novello at the Ivy and Cicely Courtneidge, she looking old and thin, but casting kisses around ...

The country is looking lovely, but its devilishly cold and I've horrible rheumatism in my wrists.

Greeting to all.

Yours
B. Patch

The production of **The Doctor's Dilemma** seen by Blanche Patch opened at the Haymarket Theatre on 4 March 1942 and ran for 474 performances. It featured **Vivien Leigh** as Jennifer Dubedat. Leigh (1913–67) had married Laurence Olivier in 1940 and starred with him in London and New York in 1951 in *Caesar and Cleopatra*, two years after her famous performance as Blanche Dubois in Tennessee Williams's *A Streetcar Named Desire*. Irish actor **Austin Trevor** (1897–1978) was also in the cast of *The Doctor's Dilemma* as Sir Ralph Bloomfield Bonington. The **new Dubedat** was Peter Glenville (b. 1913), replacing Irish actor and *bon* *viveur* Cyril **Cusack** (1910–93). The **Ivy** was (and is) a fashionable restaurant in London's West End. Blanche Patch's lunch companion, theatre impresario **Hugh Beaumont** (1908–73), produced several Shaw plays, including *Heartbreak House* in London in 1943. Actor, composer, and playwright **Ivor Novello** (1893–1951) and actress **Cicely Courtneidge** (1893–1980) were leading theatrical personalities of their day.

129 / To Barry Jackson   Ayot St Lawrence, Welwyn, Herts.
      From Blanche Patch   18th June 1942

[TLS]

... It's a great regret to me that my last memories of them will be this extraordinary and not very happy life that they lead here. But, as I think I've said before, how the world would blast me if I ever wrote my reminiscences.

Yours
B.P.

Blanche Patch's **reminiscences**, *Thirty Years with G.B.S.* (ghostwritten by Robert Williamson), were published in 1951 (London: Gollancz), a year after Shaw's death.

130 / To Barry Jackson   Ayot St Lawrence, Welwyn, Herts.
                                 18th June 1942
[TLS]

Shaw had long advocated building a theatre in London to honour Shakespeare, but when he resigned from the Executive Committee of the Shakespeare Memorial National Theatre in July 1941 (at age eighty-five) little progress had been made. His 'comeback' a year later was prompted by negotiations between the Committee and the London County Council (L.C.C.) involving the exchange of a site in South Kensington owned by the Committee for a much larger site on the South Bank. A meeting was held on 9 June 1942; both Shaw and Jackson attended. Shaw opposed the proposed deal, holding out for a better site (Thurloe Square) in South Kensington, but later changed his mind, and an agreement between the L.C.C. and the Committee was eventually concluded. (See Geoffrey Whitworth, The Making of a National Theatre *[London: Faber, 1951].) As Shaw predicted, he had died by the time 'this business' was resolved; the resolution was the creation of a National Theatre in London, on the South Bank, but not one devoted to Shakespeare (see notes to Letter 25).*

My dear Barry

It was a fearful adventure for me, a ghastly old spectre, to stage a come-back with my lower teeth at the dentist's instead of in my mouth, and every likelihood that I should forget all the names of the places and people I should have to mention if I spoke. But I was so alarmed at the way in which the Committee were rising to the bait, and so puzzled as to why on earth the Council was offering us 2½ very valuable acres in a first rate industrial situation in exchange for a little wedge of an acre in Kensington, that I felt I must go.

I have drafted a report of the meeting for circulation to the Commit-tee. You will receive it presently. I now believe – or at least hope – that we shall get Thurloe Square if we hold on like grim death to our wedge until we get it.

In my speech I was not advocating the building of piles of flats; I was only facing the fact that the Council will have to build them when they carry out their improvement, as there is no practicable alternative way of housing the residential population, which is quite hopeless as an audience for our little theatre, essentially a national monument first, and a playhouse second. As such its situation is all important. You should explore the east end of London. One of the shocks you will get in the very slummiest depth of it is a magnificent Gothic dome, so incongruous and unexpected there that you will at first think you have gone mad and are having hallucinations. But go boldly up to and into it, and you will find that it is solid and real. It is Columbia Market, a folly of the Baroness Burdett Coutts. We could not afford anything so magnifi-cently architectooralooral; yet the place is utterly unknown except in the immediate neighborhood and to the handful of costermongers who infest its Puginesque chapels, because it is in the wrong place. Thou-sands to whom Westminster Abbey is a national Valhalla do not know that there is a cathedral in Southwark, nor care. The S.M.N.T. in South-wark would be another Columbia Market.

When this business comes to a point I shall probably be dead, and cer-tainly no longer able to tackle the L.C.C. You must take up my brief and fight the thing through.

As always
G.B.S.

132

Thurloe Square is in South Kensington, near the Victoria and Albert Museum. **Columbia Market**, a fish and vegetable market in the East End, with an incongruous Gothic design by Henry Ashley Darbishire, opened in 1896. It was funded by Angela Georgina, **Baroness Burdett-Coutts** (1814–1906), philanthropist granddaughter of banker Thomas Coutts. One hopes she appreciated the **Puginesque** influence identified by Shaw (British Gothic-revivalist architect Augustus Pugin, 1812–52).

131 / To Barry Jackson   Ayot St Lawrence, Welwyn, Herts.

24th June 1943

[APCS]

After two years during which the Birmingham Repertory Theatre was either closed or leased to other companies, Jackson resumed his own productions there in a season beginning on 17 November 1942. There was no Shaw in his repertoire in the winter of 1942–3 or in spring 1943, but after a summer break and some consultations with Shaw, Jackson selected Heartbreak House *for the new season, directed by H.K. Ayliff, who also played Shotover. It opened on 24 August 1943.*

You can do as you like with Methuselah; but as one of the two statesmen is stone dead, and the other has achieved a new and real success as a farmer, I have my doubts about the present topicality of Part II. At first I was about to suggest On the Rocks, which you have never touched; but unfortunately there is a war on and no unemployment; and a play all about unemployment and no war would hardly be more opportune.

Heartbreak, after a vainglorious beginning, is flopping. It is quite at your disposal. Ayliff would be all right.

I am glad you are back in Bghm at the old work. London is death to the theatre: the provinces and the real amateurs keep it alive.

G.B.S.

The **two statesmen** in Part II of *Back to Methuselah* ('The Gospel of the Brothers Barnabas') are Herbert Asquith (Henry Hopkins Lubin) and David Lloyd George (Joyce Burge). Asquith (1852–1928) was Liberal prime minister, 1908–16, succeeded by Lloyd George (1863–1945), also Liberal, 1916–22. Lloyd George farmed in retirement in Caernarvonshire, Wales. *Heartbreak House* ran at the Cambridge Theatre, London, 18 March–9 October 1943 (236 performances; see Letters 132, 133).

132 / To Barry Jackson   4 Whitehall Court SW1
                                              25th August 1943

[APCS]

It appears that the actor playing Hector Hushabye in the BRT production of
Heartbreak House *(Rod McPherson, who was new to the company) was having*
health problems, perhaps caused by service overseas, perhaps by German bombs in
Birmingham or London. Ariadne was played by Monica Stutfield, also new to the
company. Ariadne and Hector appear alone together late in Act 1.

I should have thought that a touch of shellshock is just what an actor
needs to qualify him for that scene. Its omission is hard on Ariadne, as it
is one of her best acting opportunities; but the scene is so episodic that
it can be cut out chock-a-block without being missed by anyone who
does not know the play. So cut it if you must.

We have been here in London since the 26th July, and seem likely to
have to stay through September if not longer, through a break-down in
our Ayot staff.

I have seen the London H.H. Half the parts are hopeless miscasts,
including Ellie and Hector, who suggest a faded maiden aunt and an
utterly unromantic village miller. Dresses and other details badly bun-
gled. Donat popular but transparently too young.

                                              G.B.S.

In the London production of *H.H.* (*Heartbreak House;* see Letter 131) Ellie Dunn was played
by Deborah Kerr (b. 1921), Hector Hushabye by Vernon Kelso (1893–?), and Captain Shotover by Robert **Donat** (1905–58). Several parts were subsequently recast (see Letter 133).

133 / To Barry Jackson   4 Whitehall Court SW1
                                              27th August 1943

[APCS]

In addition to Heartbreak House, *Jackson also included* You Never Can Tell *in*
the 1943–4 BRT season. But Shaw had some other suggestions. The world pre-
miere of In Good King Charles's Golden Days *had taken place at the 1939 Mal-*
vern Festival, produced by Roy Limbert, directed by H.K. Ayliff. Given Jackson's
resentment about the Festival after his departure (see Letters 101, 102), it would
have been rankling for him to 'borrow' the production from Limbert for the BRT.

In any event, it was idle to think of a BRT production of the play so soon after its revival at Birmingham's Alexandra Theatre (21 June 1943 for a two-week run). Jackson's production of Too True to be Good *(directed by Ayliff) had lasted for only forty-seven performances at London's New Theatre in 1942 (13 September–22 October), and* On the Rocks *(directed by Lewis Casson) had run for seventy-three performances in 1933–4 (25 November–27 January) in the aptly named Winter Garden Theatre.*

I forgot to say that though Ayliff would be a terrifically good Fox, Fox cannot carry the play, which requires a very strong cast, entirely beyond your present resources. If you cannot cast Hector how can you cast Charles and the brilliant painter [Godfrey Kneller] who picks up the play when the others are exhausted? It is an expensive play to dress, unless you borrow the production from Limbert. And it was produced only the other day in Birmingham, to Limbert's great disgust. Everything is against it except Ayliff's Foxiness; and as H.H. is dropping slowly in London I am half disposed to make the management recast it with Donat as Hector, a new Ellie (Freda Jackson or yours – what's her name?) and Ayliff as Shotover, but am waiting to see what happens to your production.

Have you thought of Too True to be Good? It was drawing a thousand a week in London when you dropped it. Or On the Rocks, which was literally frozen out of an unheated theatre, but always kept the audience amused? And there are other authors.

G.B.S.

The London production of *Heartbreak House* was substantially **recast**, as Shaw wished. Among several changes, Deborah Kerr was replaced as Ellie Dunn by Marian Manist and, subsequently, by Joan Greenwood (1921–87). Donat was replaced as Shotover by Mervyn Johns (1889–1992) and, later, John Laurie (1897–1980). But Vernon Kelso stayed on as **Hector** Hushabye. **Freda Jackson** (b. 1909) was not cast, nor was Jackson's **what's her name** (unidentified).

134 / To Barry Jackson   4 Whitehall Court SW1

5th September 1943

[ALS]

Shaw continued to find time to feed Jackson with ideas for productions in Birmingham, despite Charlotte's rapidly deteriorating health.

My dear Barry

I have just discovered the enclosed Sanskrit play, The Little Clay Cart, ideal for a characteristic Barry Jackson revival. No scenery: all described by the actors; consequently as varied and free from stage limitations as the cinema. Not a word need be altered. And quite charming.

The translator sent it to me four years ago; but it got overlooked until now.

The technique is perfect. No property man fooling about with a clappers to represent doors as in The Yellow Jacket and sham-Chinese plays. The storm is pure Shakespear, as in King Lear.

We are still in London and likely to stay here. Charlotte has visions like St Joan, and is gravely ill. You don't happen to know of a gifted psycho-therapist doctor, do you?

Edith was lucky to escape in good time. Dying by half inches is no fun.

G. Bernard Shaw

Shaw's copy of **The Little Clay Cart** was either a translation by Satyendra Kumar Basu (Calcutta, 1939) or by Revilo Pendleton Oliver (Urbana, Illinois, 1938). Jackson did not produce it. **The Yellow Jacket**, by George C. Hazleton and J.H. Benrimo, had premiered at the Duke of York's Theatre in March 1913. Jackson included it in the BRT's 1947–8 season. **Edith** (surname unknown) was a member of Jackson's household staff in Malvern.

135 / To Barry Jackson   4 Whitehall Court SW1
14th September 1943

[APCS]

Charlotte Shaw died on 12 September 1943. There was a brief announcement in The Times *on 14 September, and an obituary on 15 September headed 'End of a Felicitous Partnership': 'At literary parties and on the lawns of Malvern during the Shaw Festival she seemed to know by instinct when the subject engaging Mr Shaw and any group of admirers was exhausted, and with an unfailing air of inadvertance she would steer him towards some fresh controversial adventure.' Charlotte was cremated on 15 September at Golder's Green. Her ashes were eventually mixed with Shaw's and scattered in the garden at Ayot on 23 November 1950.*

By this time you will have read the news, as the papers got hold of it this morning.

I can't write; but I will tell you all about it when next you come to London. The story had a miraculously happy ending and must be told to you at full length; so do not be sad or sorry: rather rejoice greatly.

G.B.S.

You were – and are – one of her special friends.

136 / To Barry Jackson   4 Whitehall Court SW1
                                              8th October 1943

[APCS]

The gentleman operates not only at the Underground stations but at all the leading restaurants.

A day or two with you on the hills would be very agreeable; but I am tied here by a mass of business. Two big films, Caesar and St Joan, to be negotiated; Charlotte's affairs to be wound up; a new will to be executed (very complicated); and a book to be finished and seen through the press, make me busier at 87 than I ever was at 27.

We must wait until the long days return.

G.B.S.

The **gentleman** (presumably a busker) has not been identified. The film of *Caesar and Cleopatra*, directed by Gabriel Pascal, with Claude Rains as Caesar and Vivien Leigh as Cleopatra, was released on 13 December 1945. A film of *Saint Joan* was not made until 1957 (see Letter 98). According to Donald P. Costello, 'the British Ministry of Information is said to have demurred at the idea of a film in wartime showing the English burning a French patriot' (*The Serpent's Eye* [Notre Dame, Ind.: Notre Dame University Press, 1965], 112).

137 / To Barry Jackson   Ayot St Lawrence, Welwyn, Herts.
                                              20th February 1944

[ALS]

My dear Barry

Have you seen the enclosed friendly notice?

I was somewhat concerned about your indispositions: clearly you were overworking; but I think you are all right in respect of doing your proper and invaluable work, and no longer being swallowed up in London success, which is to me a delusion and a snare.

The distinction between educational plays and commercial ones serves our turn when we can escape entertainment tax through it; but it is utter nonsense, and the escape is pure chance.

I live here alone with nothing to do but work and cut up firewood with your saw; but this suits me exactly.

Making a new will is a very difficult job. I shall give this house to the National Trust. It is not a birthplace; but I have lived here longer than anywhere else – in the same house, I mean. The Trust will take it on with the furniture, and let it to someone who will shew it to pilgrims once a week or a month or so.

What will you do with Blackhill?

G.B.S.

The **friendly notice** has not been traced. Under the terms of the Trust established in 1935, the educational aims of the Birmingham Repertory Theatre were recognized by the British tax authorities, and the theatre was, therefore, exempt from paying **entertainment tax** (as was the Shakespeare Memorial Theatre at Stratford). Shaw gave ownership of his **house** in Ayot St Lawrence to the **National Trust** in June 1944 (while retaining the right to live there), and made provisions in his will for various contents of the house to be given to the Trust on his death. Jackson continued to live in **Blackhill**, his Malvern home, until his death in 1961. It remains a private home.

138 / To Barry Jackson   Ayot St Lawrence, Welwyn, Herts.
[23rd?] March 1944

[APCS]

Jackson continued to consult Shaw frequently on the repertoire of the Birmingham Repertory Theatre, in this case about Ibsen. Shaw had championed Ibsen's plays, which he knew through the translations of William Archer, since the 1890s. He lectured on Ibsen to the Fabian Society on 18 July 1890, and his influential Quintessence of Ibsenism *was published the following year. Jackson had frequently produced Ibsen over the years, and he heeded Shaw's advice to use the Archer translation for his production of* The Lady from the Sea, *directed by Peter Brook, in the BRT's 1945–6 season. It opened on 24 November 1945 with Paul Scofield as Dr Wangel.*

Don't listen to them about Archer being impossible. The tremendous impression made by Ibsen at his first impact here in the nineties was made by Archer's translations; *and it has never been repeated since* Archer was dropped and suburban small talk substituted for his dialogue. Archer was really half a poet, half a Norwegian, and wholly a Scot. Ibsen was wholly a poet, half Norwegian, half a Scot. Put his plays into common colloquial drawingroom English and they become sawdust – British sawdust. Archer kept as clear of that as Shakespear did: you never forget Norway and all its ghosts and poetry while you are listening to Archer-Ibsen: the great phrases haunt you afterwards. Of course it's as unlike modern back chat as Macbeth; but that is as it should be: it is a work of utmost art, not a photograph of Croydon. Make them stick to Archer and not change a word. The result will justify you. After a rehearsal or two the modern versions will become unbearable.

G.B.S.

139 / To Barry Jackson   Ayot St Lawrence, Welwyn, Herts.
    From Blanche Patch   26th July 1944

[TLS]

This letter from Blanche Patch to Jackson dealt with some business issues and some recent visitors to Ayot, but also gave Ms Patch an opportunity to give Jackson more details of wartime conditions at Ayot and in London. A German V-bomb fell near Ayot on 25 July, and in June another bomb had damaged Shaw's London flat.

Dear Sir Barry

... The enemy evidently thought to herald the 88th birthday and managed to pitch a 'Schicklgruber' (A.A. Milne's name for the brutes) in a spinney ¾ of a mile from us just before midnight, and the blast broke one of GBS's windows. The noise gave me such a shock that it was some moments before I had enough breath to get up (I now understand why one can die from shock), but when I did I found the old man in his dressing gown very interested as to how much glass was on the floor. A louder crash occurred while we stood together but didnt hit us so we decided to return to our beds, and he tells me he quickly went to sleep – which is more than I did ...

Did I tell you I came here because the windows at [the] Whitehall study were blasted, and also those in the diningroom at my hotel? Since I left there have been other hits in the latter district.

Yours
Blanche Patch

Alan Alexander **Milne** (1882–1956) is the author of *Winnie-the-Pooh* (1926) and other books for children.

140 / To Bernard Shaw   Malvern
                                    24th November [1944]
[TLU: BL]

Jackson's enthusiasm for the BRT – despite ill health and interfering bureaucrats – was back at full throttle, and he was eager to tell Shaw that the theatre was 'doing the best business of its career.' The distinction addressed in the letter between 'cultural' and 'non-cultural' plays was more than an aesthetic issue for Jackson. The BRT's exemption from entertainment tax (see Letter 137) depended on such arbitrary distinctions. The ellipses in this letter are Jackson's.

My dear G.B.S.

Though very often in my thoughts I have refrained from adding to your letters which must be endless and often troublesome – at least many of mine are. Now that the book is off your hands and, to judge by its frequent appearance, in those of a large public, perhaps you have a little leisure to spare for generalities. Cedric Hardwicke is the last individual I have met to have seen you and it was good to learn you are well. To return to the book for a moment, I endeavoured to send a copy to my Belgian friend but none were available; surely some more will be coming along soon. Judging from experience with a short book on the BRT published eighteen months ago the binding problem is as acute as the paper shortage.

The theatre has been doing the best business of its career. Being anxious to obtain the good will of what is clearly a new audience I have refrained from a too adventurous programme. 'Getting Married' was enormously popular. 'Autre temps, autre moeurs.' I recollect our first production which was received in stony silence. You are invariably about twenty to thirty years in front. A waitress from a tea shop told one of our company that 'Getting Married' was the kind of play she liked as it gave her something solid to bite on ... a very different point of view to that of the critics of the Haymarket production. Can this be accounted for by some growth in the general level of intellect? Or is the waitress a freak? I cannot believe in the latter because audiences were invariably large and, what is more important, enthusiastic. Last Tuesday we produced a new play by Andrew Leigh all about King Stephen and the Empress Maud. It is in modern idiom and has every symptom of success – but – again and again Ayliff, who produced, agreed with me that the subject was worthy of your handling. One might have imagined the period to be too remote to be of interest to-day, but – in spite of the waitress – mankind changes mightily little and Maud's supposition that her title of Empress of Germany would endear her to the citizens of London has an odd tang. All I ever learned about her was the fact that she escaped from Oxford in the snow camouflaged in a nightgown ... as Leigh points out, warmly clad underneath.

The wear and tear of Birmingham, for conditions are anything but easy, put me out of continuous action some six weeks since and I have been idling up here. Though the medicine man, or witch doctor, did not put it in so many words it was obvious to me that nervous energy had out-paced physical strength and quiet is the only remedy for that. I had mis-givings some months back but like a fool did not heed the warnings.

Have you come across the astonishing lists of plays that Customs and Excise accept as cultural and non-cultural? A light affair for the young-sters' Christmas entertainment, by Cicely Hamilton, has been turned down though I had accepted it for production. I have suggested to her that she gets the Society of Authors to work. Any addition to the existing difficulties that lie between a dramatist and his audience is a menace.

Yours

Barry

The **book** that was now off Shaw's hands was *Everybody's Political What's What?*, published by Constable on 15 September 1944 (85,000 copies). Jackson's **Belgian friend** has not been identified, but see Letter 111 for his interest in the Belgian artist Gustave de Smet (who was dead at the time of this letter). The **short book on the BRT** is T.C. Kemp's *Birmingham Repertory Theatre*, published in Birmingham by Cornish Bros. in October 1943. Jackson's **first**

production of *Getting Married* was at the BRT in 1921; the **Haymarket production** opened on 12 May 1908, directed by Harley Granville Barker. Critic H. Hamilton Fyfe described the play as a 'medley of stale argument and cheap jest' (*The World*, 20 May 1908). **Andrew Leigh** (1887–1957) had a versatile career as actor, director, and playwright. His **new play** was called *The Empress Maud*. **Cicely Hamilton** (1872–1952), actor and playwright, was the original Mrs Knox in *Fanny's First Play* (1911).

141 / To Barry Jackson　　　　　Ayot St Lawrence, Welwyn, Herts.
　　From Blanche Patch　　　　　　　29th November 1944

[ALS]

Amid grumbles about her health and impatience at the intrusions of various visitors, Blanche Patch continued to provide Jackson with her own special insights into Shaw's domestic and professional circumstances.

Dear Sir Barry

... GBS tends to become more & more silent & some days pass with hardly any speech between us. At meals he is quite capable of surrounding himself with papers & letters & is so slow chewing his victuals that I could rap the table with annoyance! If it wasn't for the fact that he looks so *old* some days & London isn't pleasant just now (nasty V2 in Holborn last week & another at New Cross) I'd go back tomorrow ...

Pascal has practically finished Caesar, & Rains goes back to USA next week. As a spectacle its really magnificent & I think it would be a mistake to damn it by saying its not the play. GBS likes it though he admits that owing to wartime difficulties some of the people in the cast are not right, but it certainly shews that we can do things as well, if not better, than Hollywood. It should be ready about Feb ...

Limbert was very keen to revive King Charles in London, but GBS won't have it. Thesiger is now too old & the suggested Cedric [*sic*: Godfrey (Kneller)] wouldnt do. Personally I doubt if the play would run more than 6 weeks at most. Ellen Pollock's shows at the Lyric, Hammersmith are doing very *poor* business. GBS takes next to no interest in the returns so I say nothing ...

　　　　　　　　　　　　　　Yours
　　　　　　　　　　　　　　B. Patch

The **V2** (Vergeltungswaffe-2, 'revenge weapon 2') was a German ballistic missile first used against Britain in September 1944. Gabriel Pascal's *Caesar* film wasn't released until December 1945 (see Letter 136). **Ellen Pollock's** (b. 1903) Shaw season at the Lyric, Hammersmith (October–December 1944), consisted of *Too True to be Good, Candida, Village Wooing,* and *Pygmalion.*

142 / To Barry Jackson Ayot St Lawrence, Welwyn, Herts.
28th October 1945

[TLS]

This letter marks the beginning of an important new phase of the relationship between Shaw and Jackson, encompassing Jackson's somewhat turbulent three-year spell as director of the Shakespeare Memorial Theatre at Stratford-upon-Avon. Jackson's appointment was announced in The Times *on 9 October 1945. Initially Jackson was appointed director of the Stratford Festival; he was subsequently made director of the Shakespeare Memorial Theatre as a whole, not just the festival presented there each spring and summer (see Letter 146). Jackson had not consulted Shaw about taking the position, but Shaw was not reluctant to give his advice on any number of theatrical, administrative, and political issues that faced Jackson at Stratford. He began by lecturing Jackson on the mistakes of his Stratford predecessors in the new theatre (opened in 1932), with particular disdain for Komisarjevsky's* Macbeth *(1933) and* King Lear *(1936) and W. Bridges-Adams's* Love's Labour's Lost *(1934, the notorious tree designed by Aubrey Hammond). And for good measure Shaw added some criticism of Jackson's modern-dress production of* Macbeth *(London and Birmingham, 1928, actually directed by H.K. Ayliff, not Jackson; see Letter 23). This opening salvo set the tone for a series of feisty exchanges between Shaw and Jackson on Stratford matters.*

My dear Barry

I was surprised to learn from the papers that you had taken on Stratford, and very much interested.

In the days when the S.M.N.T. financed Stratford I used to go there and see the whole set of productions regularly every year until the Charity Commissioners stopped the subsidy and I was no longer responsible for the use that was being made of it.

The performances were all more or less provincial and amateurish because nobody knew the Shakespearean stage technique. And it was most unlucky that when the new theatre was complete with plenty of modern machinery for scene changing a fashion had set in of doing the whole play in one scene. Macbeth and Lear were played without a change. Love's Labor had an enormous practicable tree in the middle of the stage. You could see nothing and think of nothing but this arboreal monstrosity from the rise of the curtain until its final fall. When the interval came in Lear for tea Charlotte rose and made for the hotel. I warned her that the interval would last only fifteen minutes. She turned and said incredulously 'Havnt you had enough of this drivel?' That was what they made of Lear in one scene.

What they did not understand was that scenery can be dispensed with if the play is presented on a magnificent architectural tribune without any pictorial suggestion whatever as the Greek plays were, or on an Elizabethan stage with traverses and a balcony but no scenery, or like Punch & Judy; but the moment you add a picture of any sort you must go the whole hog and have a new picture for every scene.

Make a note therefore to exploit all the change resources of Stratford to the utmost, competing with 'the pictures' on their own ground. Think of what a Shaw-Pascal film is like, and has taught playgoers to expect.

The stage technique is enormously important. When you produced Macbeth in modern dress you were so preoccupied with that novelty that you killed Maturin (he has never been heard of since) by letting him try to get his big climaxes by shouting himself down, up and up and up. Of course he was out of his range, or any human range, in no time, and like nothing but a very drunk and disorderly common soldier.

The skilled tragedian of the grand school begins the technical study of his part by marking, not the top notes of it, but the points at which he can drop to absolute zero so as to keep the climax well within human voice compass. He knows that when he has hurled the last word of a ranting climax at the audience he must do a walk down stage in terrible silence and throw himself into a chair, bringing down the temperature to one degree centigrade, so that his next utterance will be a whisper, and not à la Maturin a louder shout than the last.

This is only one of the tricks. There are half a dozen ways of getting back to zero and persuading the audience that they are extra strokes of great acting; but it illustrates what I mean and how you murdered Maturin.

I learnt the business from Barry Sullivan, Salvini, and Ristori. Forbes Robertson learnt it from Phelps. Coquelin was, within his limits as a comedian (and beyond them as Cyrano, which he played without tiring himself in the least), a master of it. Your job will be to get Stratford back to it and let your pictorial taste and ingenuity rip with the machinery that has never yet been fully exploited. If you succeed you will be the first really competent Shakespear manager that this generation has seen.

It may end in your selling Blackhill and going to live on the Avon. It is the only way you can get on top of Malvern, which you may leave to Limbert, who is more biddable than you, and may get on if well advised.

I had my last tooth pulled yesterday. I am very groggy on my legs, but otherwise as well as one can expect to be on the verge of 90.

G.B.S.

Excuse my blotchy typing. It is the best I can do at 89¼.

For Shaw's involvement with the **S.M.N.T.** (Shakespeare Memorial National Theatre) see Letter 25. Jackson's modern-dress *Macbeth*, with Eric **Maturin** as Macbeth, was at the Court Theatre in February 1928 (see notes to Letter 23). Italian actors Tommaso **Salvini** (1829–1915) and Adelaide **Ristori** (1822–1906) enjoyed international reputations, as did the leading Molière actor of his day (also famous for his **Cyrano** in Edmond Rostand's *Cyrano de Bergerac*) Constant-Benoît **Coquelin** (1841–1909). Samuel **Phelps** (1804–78) produced and acted in Shakespeare for some twenty years at Sadler's Wells Theatre in London.

143 / To Barry Jackson   Ayot St Lawrence, Welwyn, Herts.
5th November 1945

[TLS]

Jackson's defence of Eric Maturin hasn't survived, but it evidently didn't convince Shaw. Shaw's acknowledgment, however, of the 'rough truth' of the New Statesman *article on Stratford reveals his sense of the challenges facing Jackson in his new position. The article ('Shakespeare and Stratford-on-Avon' by John Garrett, 3 November 1945) doesn't mention Jackson, but argues that Stratford 'is held in low esteem by the theatrical profession,' that 'mediocrity is not enough,' and that 'the moment is ripe for a new deal.' Stratford should strive for 'the best that scholarship, production, acting, and setting can achieve for Shakespeare's work.'*

My dear Barry

You havnt taken my point. You say that Maturin was a good actor as if I had said he was a bad one. He was an exceptionally good actor: nobody could have bettered him in Heartbreak or in Galsworthy's Loyalties.

Why then did he wreck himself and give a pitiful and ridiculous performance in Macbeth? Not because he acted it badly: he did not act it at all. Simply because he did not know the stage tricks of heroic acting, in which the actor has to produce an illusion of superhuman strength with only human resources. When Salvini, as Samson, picked up his father and threw him over his shoulder and carried him off like a feather, he seemed to be the strongest man on earth; but he was only doing what every fireman is taught to do, and nobody not so taught could possibly do. Macbeth, skilfully played, seems to be piling one climax on top of another, and reaching Alpine summits; but he really gets down to zero between each of them and can play the whole last act without turning a hair, and go through the final combat as fresh as paint. There is no question of fine art or good or bad acting here: it [is] a matter of pure technical trickery, of illusion, not of personification.

Now this is your weak point. Heroic acting was dead with Barry Sullivan before you began playgoing; the only exponent of it in your time was Chaliapin, an opera singer. But I was nursed on it, and on Italian opera: actors who cannot declaim are of no use to me. You must pick up the tricks and teach them in Stratford or you will wreck all the Macbeths as you wrecked poor Maturin.

As to the fine art of the business you need not worry. It will be all right when you get there: your high faculty for it is a proved fact; and it will not fail you when it comes to the point.

There is an article in The New Statesman about Stratford which is the rough truth about it. Ask Ayliff how utterly impossible it is to produce six plays in one week with a picked-up company and a few weeks rehearsal. And if a permanent one is engaged you will have to take it to America and lecture there about it.

You are right, of course, about playing with only one interval (sanitary); but the Stratford machinery, which has never been fully exploited, will make that easy without the shifts to which Paul Shelving was put.

I regard your transfer to Stratford as an event of first class importance.

> In haste
>
> G. Bernard Shaw

Eric Maturin played Randall Utterword in the English premiere of *Heartbreak House* at the
Court Theatre, 18 October 1921, and Captain Ronald Dancy in the premiere of John
Galsworthy's *Loyalties* at St Martin's Theatre, London, 8 March 1922. Shaw, recently
arrived in London from Dublin, probably saw **Salvini** perform **Samson** (in Ippolito d'Aste's
Sansone) on his 1876 British tour.

144 / To Barry Jackson   Ayot St Lawrence, Welwyn, Herts.

5th January 1946

[APCS]

I see that Cymbeline is on the Stratford program. What about my variation on the fifth act? The original is an interpolated masque forced on it
by the expensive fashion that swept the theatre away under James. Cut
the masque out and play what is left as usual and the result is a dismal
boresome failure, mere perfunctory denouement without a touch of
character except in one page which I have retained. Do the masque
thoroughly regardless of expense and the audience will be intrigued
and amused, besides being faithful to Shakespeare. My variation is a
gem, brief, easy, inexpensive and effective to the end. The Stratford
Committee asked for it and then funked it. At the Swiss Cottage Theatre
it was a complete success. It has had to wait in Stratford for you.

By the way there can be no Art Director Absolute but you. Leefe
should be Resident Director.

> G.B.S.

Cymbeline opened the 1946 Stratford season, directed by Nugent Monck. Shaw wrote his
variation, *Cymbeline Refinished,* with a rewritten fifth act, in late 1936, in anticipation of a
Stratford production. That production never materialized; nor did Jackson take up Shaw's
offer on this occasion. It was, however, produced at the Embassy Theatre, **Swiss Cottage**,
on 16 November 1937, directed by Ronald Adam. It ran for twenty-four performances.
Reginald **Leefe** designed regularly at Stratford, including *Love's Labour's Lost* for Peter
Brook in 1946.

145 / To Barry Jackson   Ayot St Lawrence, Welwyn, Herts
23rd January 1946

[APCS]

The Times reported on 22 January 1946 on a lunch held the previous day in London hosted by Lord Iliffe, president of the Stratford Memorial Theatre. Fordham Flower, chair of the governing council, was not present, but his sister read a statement on his behalf that addressed some concerns about the situation at Stratford. The governors, the statement said, 'were determined that quality in acting and production should take precedence over profits, and to prove that the charge of complacency was no longer valid.' As a first step, the director, Jackson, was to be given 'more latitude and power than had been the practice at Stratford.'

There was a handsome middle article in The Times yesterday on you and Stratford. Did you see it?

As to Cymbeline, what you must bar at any cost is a cut last act with the masque left out. That is a far worse departure from Shakespear than mine; and it makes the end a failure. The alternative to mine is the masque as S. wrote it line for line, with Jupiter as *deus ex machina*, eagle, doggerel verses, comic jailer, all complete. They supply entertainment and spectacle and save the play; but they cost a lot. Mine costs nothing; and is quite successful as a finish, besides being a feature for the press. The actors love it.

And for heaven's sake don't let your artistic interest in the acting blind you to the purely physical training and trickery without which the big parts are impossible and ridiculous.

Priests can get indulgences to see St. J.

G.B.S.

146 / To Barry Jackson   4 Whitehall Court, SW1
14th September 1946

[TLS]

After his first summer at Stratford – a season noted both for the young Peter Brook's successful production of Love's Labour's Lost *and for the largest deficit ever recorded at Stratford – it became clear to Jackson that radical administrative reform was necessary if artistic standards were to be improved. That would take time and authority. He therefore sought and received from the board an extended contract (now to include the 1948 season) and greater control: he was appointed director of the Shakespeare Memorial Theatre itself, in addition to his position as director of the annual Shakespeare Festival. As* The Times *explained (30 August 1946), 'The change will involve a complete overhaul of the present administrative machinery since, under the new organization, all departments will come under the direct supervision of Sir Barry Jackson.' A major implication of the change was that Jackson now had year-round control of the Memorial Theatre, including off-season events – previously controlled by the board through a general manager (Henry Tossell, who left Stratford at the end of the 1946 Festival). If not quite the 'Perpetual Grand' that Shaw dubbed him, Jackson now had the kind of responsibility he was accustomed to at Birmingham and Malvern. Amid Shaw's many questions and comments in this letter about Jackson and Stratford is the revealing paragraph on Harley Granville Barker, who died in Paris on 31 August 1946, survived by his second wife, Helen Huntington, the woman who, in Shaw's view, and to his deep chagrin, caused an irreparable rift between the two men who had been so close, personally and professionally (see Letter 19). It was, however, this rift that consolidated Shaw's 'second alliance,' this one with Barry Jackson.*

Dear B.J.

I was much satisfied when I read in The Times that they had made you Perpetual Grand at the theatre. Nothing remains but to shoot Mrs M. and cut the National Anthem out of every performance, a most annoying feature, but the old lady insisted on it after 1918.

The little monthly paper is very useful: I read it from end to end. It is friendly and not negligibly critical.

How will the new permanence affect your movements? You must have a home at Stratford. Will you keep Blackhill for Sundays or sell it?

The death of Granville-Barker, premature at 68, gave me a shock which made me realize that I had never abandoned the hope that the death of his wife, who was older, might bring us together again; for she, who divided us, was older than he. But of course that was not possible: she had dragged him back into her own period of Meredith and Henry James; and I had formed a second alliance (with you) and gone on to Heartbreak (which he actually thought immoral) and Methuselah. I have sent a picture of him and a few lines to The Times Literary Supplement.

Are you going to carry on the Theatre between the festivals or to leave Tossell to let it to touring casuals? The difficulty is that the war has revived the ancient vagabondage of the profession. In my old days at the Court Theatre employment was so precarious that players would take less than half their nominal salaries if they were guaranteed a few months. I think it will come to that again when the dozens of mad little theatres are wound up and unemployment hits the players again; but for the moment permanence does not tempt them.

What happened to the last act of Cymbeline? Was the masque faithfully done? Nobody seemed to know that it had never been done within living memory and that I had written a new version which had made a success of the last act at the Embassy Theatre. I wrote it for Stratford; but they funked it at the last moment. You must try it some day.

The birthday business and making me an honorary Freeman by the City of Dublin has been unspeakably trying and tedious; but at last it is over and the spotlight has been lifted to Wells, whom I am trying to get into Westminster Abbey.

Don't answer for some months. The papers keep me *au courant* in public matters; and you have plenty else to do.

Recorded music cannot be turned on by the nearest nobody. It must be in charge of a conductor who can set the right speeds, which are never the marked ones.

The excellent Festival Souvenir has just arrived. The L's L. L. [*Love's Labour's Lost*] ladies look like Tissot's pictures of the fashions of 50 years ago. None the worse for that. The Macbeth-Macduff costumes are ridiculous. They should both be rugged kilted caterans. The words 'Before my body I cast my warlike shield' are better omitted; but to insist on them and arm poor Macbeth with a soup plate is too silly.

G.B.S.

Mrs M. (Eleanor Melville, 1864–1954) was an influential Stratford governor and wife of the Rev. Canon William Melville, Vicar of Stratford. The **National Anthem** was played before performances at Stratford until dropped by Peter Hall, director of the Royal Shakespeare Company at Stratford, 1960–8: 'It is not a good tune to raise a curtain; and it was only introduced in the 1914–18 war to encourage patriotism' (*Peter Hall's Diaries*, ed. John Goodwin [London: Hamish Hamilton, 1983], 222). The **little monthly paper** was the *Stratford-upon-Avon-Scene*, '[t]he Magazine ... for people interested in Shakespeare and Shakespeareland.' Jackson sent Shaw a copy of the first issue (September 1946); it contained, among other things, an article by Ruth Ellis (theatre critic for the *Stratford-upon-Avon Herald*) that criticized the performances of Robert Harris (Angelo) and Ruth Lodge (Isabella) in Stratford's 1946 *Measure for Measure*. Shaw's **few lines** about Granville Barker appeared in the *Times Literary Supplement*, 7 September 1946: 'We clicked so well together that I regarded him as my contemporary until one day at rehearsal, when someone remarked that I was fifty, he said, "You are the same age as my father." After that it seemed impossible that he should die before me. The shock the news gave me made me realize how I had still cherished a hope that our old intimate relationship might revive.' Shaw was made an **honorary Freeman** of the City of Dublin in a ceremony in his Whitehall Court flat on 26 July 1946 (his ninetieth birthday). H.G. **Wells** died on 13 August 1946 and was cremated at Golder's Green on 16 August. Given Wells's unconventional moral values and behaviour, it is not surprising that Shaw's efforts to get him a memorial in Westminster Abbey were unsuccessful. James **Tissot** (1836–1902) painted scenes of Victorian life in London. The **Macbeth-Macduff costumes** were designed in Jacobean style by Frederick Crooke. The photograph in the souvenir program that prompted Shaw's ridicule does indeed show shields resembling a **soup plate**. The **Macbeth** line is a slight misquotation of his 'Before my body I throw my warlike shield' (V. x. 32–3).

147 / To Barry Jackson

Ayot St Lawrence, Welwyn, Herts.
20th September 1946

[ALS]

Jackson faced enormous challenges at Stratford: a crumbling physical plant, a stagnant artistic reputation, and board members and citizens hostile to change. It could not have helped, then, to receive a barrage of criticism from Shaw, much of it, it must be said, hasty and ill informed, though Shaw himself seems to have been misled (perhaps deliberately) on the issues on which he here challenges Jackson (see Letters 148–52).

My dear Barry

Your shutting the theatre to the touring companies between the festivals has an unforeseen result, because there is an agreement in existence which you probably know nothing of. Certainly I never heard of it. By it the cinema, which has a stage and 12 dressing rooms, is not to perform plays and the M.T. [Memorial Theatre] not to shew pictures. Consequently no plays except Shakespear's can now be acted in Stratford. This is monstrous; and I am going for the Council with all my guns to have the agreement cancelled.

If the M.T. wants to tie its hands as to pictures it should bind the cinema to house the tours for some months every year.

The immediate victims of the agreement are my important self, my Charles II latest play being stopped in Stratford, and Limbert, who wants to produce it there. He is taking it lying down; but I shall raise hell. So be prepared for an atomic bomb at the next Council meeting.

The final solution must be winter seasons of modern drama at the M.T. by its own company.

Meanwhile Charles must wait; but the agreement must go. It is now quite indefensible.

A dramatic school with a theatre will finally be needed; but if it is let to commercial strangers it will be rated.

G.B.S.

148 / To G. Bernard Shaw   [Shakespeare Memorial Theatre
Stratford-upon-Avon]
23rd September 1946

[TLU (c)]

My Dear G.B.S. (Before launching your thunderbolts)

The Memorial Theatre was built and endowed for the express purpose of presenting Shakespeare's plays, and all its activities should be directed to this end.

The production of eight major plays is not the work of one week, but more probably eight or 10, and it is imperative for me to have complete use of the building for that period before production in March or April.

Hitherto, the winter season's programme has been almost entirely in the hands of a London agent, for whom, incidentally, I have the very greatest respect. As you will see from the enclosed list, there is no lack of variety and no mention of closing.

Your letter gives the first information to reach me of 'In Good King Charles's Golden Days,' and I can only surmise that Limbert had approached the agent in regard to early Spring booking, and I am convinced that you will realise the impossibility of housing visiting companies during our rehearsal period.

Except for contracts already existent, there is not the slightest doubt that we could have continued with the present repertoire for at least another month, thereby fulfilling the purpose for which the theatre was erected.

Over and above the necessity for preparation of the season's work by

152

the company, I find the Memorial Theatre and all its contents are badly in need of complete overhaul – a formidable task of great magnitude, because, as far as I can make out, very little has been attempted since the theatre's inception. I am envisaging a forced closure in the winter of 1947/8 to accomplish this.

It is most certainly not my intention to close the theatre to touring companies and I cannot think where you obtained your information. Heaven alone knows whence it came.

Yours ever,

[Barry Jackson]

The **enclosed list** of winter productions has not survived, but they included Shaw's *Devil's Disciple*, Gilbert Murray's translation of Euripedes' *Electra*, Noël Coward's *Private Lives*, *Lorna Doone* (William Deneen's adaptation of R.D. Blackmore's novel), and a D'Oyly Carte season of Gilbert and Sullivan. There was no **forced closure** of the 1947–8 winter season; a full repertoire was produced.

149 / To Barry Jackson   Ayot St Lawrence, Welwyn, Herts.
25th September 1946

[ALS]

My dear Barry

Wake up: you havnt given my letter a moment's attention.

I am not taking the slightest exception to your policy or proceedings. But I have discovered an agreement which you evidently knew nothing of any more than I did.

It was harmless as long as the M.T. was available for the tours and trifles. Without this it is scandalous and must be cancelled. You cannot defend it.

Cancel it: that is all.

My information, founded on a correspondence with the cinema management, is unquestionable.

Don't argue. Keep your eye on your father and he'll pull you through.

G.B.S.

150 / To G. Bernard Shaw   [Shakespeare Memorial Theatre
Stratford-upon-Avon]
26th September 1946

[TLU (c)]

Shaw's 'letter of the 23rd' appears to have come into Jackson's hands inadvertently (because of the staff 'change over'). The letter (now in BCL MS 2129/5/1–2) describes the alleged agreement between the Stratford cinema and the Memorial Theatre (Letter 147) as 'intolerable' and requests the governors to cancel it. 'It was reasonable only while the Memorial Theatre was open to modern drama. It is now entirely indefensible. That Stratford should become the only place in England where my plays ... cannot be performed make[s] it not a centre of British culture, but a disgrace to it.'

My Dear G.B.S.

As a result of the change over, your letter of the 23rd, addressed to the Secretary, has come to me.

Having already put some of the facts before you in my last letter, dated the 23rd, is it still your wish that I bring the matter to the notice of the Council?

It would be as well to make my own position quite clear. If I am to be deprived of the use of the theatre for the preparation of what is probably the most arduous undertaking in the theatre world, I shall have no alternative but to resign. The too prevalent notion that we who work on the stage gather together in the morning and say, 'Let us perform "Back to Methuselah" to-night. It would be fun,' has got to be scotched – firmly – every time it occurs, which is all too frequently.

As I mentioned in my previous letter, there are many vital replacements required through lack of attention during the war years. A touring company would not think too well of us if they were precipitated into the cellar during their performance.

Yours ever,
[Barry Jackson]

151 / To Barry Jackson   Ayot St Lawrence, Welwyn, Herts.

                                                27th September 1946

[ALS]

My dear Barry

You are overworked, and possessed with an incurable delusion that I am trying to shove Methuselah into the M.T.

   Put it all out of your head. I will get Fordham Flower to deal with it. It will not interfere with your arrangements in the least, and is necessary *for your protection.*

                                                G.B.S.

152 / To Barry Jackson   4 Whitehall Court SW1

                                                22nd October 1946

[TLS]

Shaw's concession in this letter of 'much ado about nothing' concerning his complaints about lack of opportunities for non-Shakespearean productions at Stratford brought to an end the escalating and unnecessary quarrel with Jackson. In view of the bad blood that was already developing between Jackson and some members of the board and the Stratford community, one might well share Shaw's puzzlement about the mis-information he had apparently received. In the meantime Peter Brook, whose Love's Labour's Lost *had been well received at the 1946 Stratford Festival, had, at Jackson's suggestion, visited Shaw in preparation for his 1947 Stratford production of* Romeo and Juliet *(which was not nearly so well received). Brook wrote to Jackson on 10 or 12 October (the dating of the letter is unclear) to tell him that the meeting with Shaw gave him 'the thrill of my life.' 'G.B.S. was in bed – as you may have seen in the papers he fell over the other day (he slipped out of a new swivel chair) and hurt his leg. However, he seemed full of beans' (BCL MS 2129/3/1–2).*

My dear Barry

Brook was a surprise. He is obviously not an actor, and looks anything but an artist of any sort. This is all to the good, as his productions will not be a string of imitations of himself. He must have a strong vocation or he would not have taken to the business. I put him up to the tricks of

Romeo's top scene at Mercutio's death, and he was convinced, or pretended to be.

Tybalt need not be much of an actor; but he must be a safe fencer.

At Covent Garden in De Reszke's time there was only one singer who could fence well enough to parry De R's furious thrusts; and he was a rival tenor named Montariol who considered it beneath his dignity to play second (not to say sixth) to Jean. They had to announce that he had 'condescended' to play Tybalt.

You will have to get some honorary librarian, or even a bibliographer to tackle the hidden treasures of the library and museum. Jaggard ought to have discovered and tackled them long ago.

F.F. [Fordham Flower] now tells me that there is no agreement with the cinema people. If so, the whole matter drops; but why do they specifically state that there is an agreement. They wrote this to Limbert, who sent me their letter. F.F. tells me also that they have abolished the adaptations they made for stage plays. But why didnt they say so instead of alleging an agreement, and running me into much ado about nothing?

My fall in London kept me in bed for a week; but that was perhaps what I needed. I am now back in Ayot crawling about on two sticks, but mending satisfactorily, and not otherwise the worse.

G.B.S.

Polish tenor Jean de **Reszke** (1850–1925) frequently played Romeo in Gounod's *Roméo et Juliette*. His **rival**, **Montariol**, like de Reszke, appeared regularly at the Royal Italian Opera House and other leading European venues. Jackson appointed Levi Fox, a qualified **librarian**, to organize the Memorial Theatre's library, which opened in 1880. Fox also assumed responsibility for the library of the Shakespeare Birthday Trust. The collections were merged in 1964 in the new Shakespeare Centre in Stratford. William **Jaggard** (1867–1947), the Shakespearean bibliographer, did much of his research at Stratford; he was also a member of the Stratford board of governors. Shaw was made an Honorary Freeman of the Borough of St Pancras on 9 October 1946 (he served as a Council member from 1897 to 1903), but a **fall** (see headnote) prevented his attending the ceremony. His acceptance speech was broadcast from his bed by the BBC.

153 / To Barry Jackson 4 Whitehall Court SW1
20th February 1947

[TLS]

The squabble over access to the Memorial Theatre now resolved (though not to Shaw's satisfaction), Shaw pursued other paths of advice and commentary on

Jackson's responsibilities and challenges at Stratford: the new rehearsal and production schedule (in which Jackson staggered the openings rather than crowding them all into the first few nights, as had been the practice); the relationship between the proposed Shakespeare Memorial National Theatre in London and the Shakespeare Memorial Theatre at Stratford (see also Letter 25); the Memorial Theatre's library (see Letter 152); and refurbishment of the Memorial Theatre. Shaw also now revealed to Jackson that he had a new play, Buoyant Billions. *He had told Roy Limbert about it several months before, anticipating its premiere at the 1947 Malvern Festival. But no Festival occurred in 1947, or 1948, and the world premiere took place in Zurich on 21 October 1948 in a German translation* (Zu viel Geld). *The British premiere came the following summer at the 1949 Malvern Festival (13 August 1949). Jackson's thoughts on the play are given in Letter 154.*

My dear Barry

I am fortunate in this weather that frost, though not comfortable, agrees with me and keeps my spirits up. I hope it does the same for you.

The arrangements for the next festival will certainly mean better rehearsed production; but the drawback will be that it will be impossible during the first week to see all the plays in one week as I did for so many years when the London S.M.N.T. was subsidizing Stratford.

I agree that London and Stratford institutions should not have the same name. The word National is the disputable one for Stratford; but for London it is the word Shakespear because a national theatre must play all authors and may never play Shakespear at all. It is for London to change. The titles should be The National Theatre for London and for Stratford The Shakespear Memorial Theatre.

Even if it involves new building I think the precedent of the British Museum should be followed by combining the library with a reading room and the museum, and under the library heading claim insertion in The World of Learning, published by Europa Publications Ltd, 19 Bedford Square, W.C.1. This is really important.

Nothing can make the Palladian entrance hall Elizabethan. Arras would make it ridiculous. I think any changes must be invisible structurally.

The library must be under a single command. So must the theatre.

Study how Montgomery cleared the dug outs for Alamein. Archie is a reasonable man: he will make you C. in C. painlessly.

And now for a secret: a copy, most private, of my latest attempt at a new play for the Malvern Festival. It is pretty pitiable. Read it and tell me whether I ought to burn it or not. At 90 I cannot trust my own judgment. Certainly not Limbert's, for he must take anything he gets.

G.B.S.

The World of Learning, an annual directory of universities, colleges, libraries, and other educational institutions, began publication in 1947. Presumably, Shaw had recently seen the first issue. Shaw's military allusions are to Bernard Law (later Viscount) **Montgomery** (1887–1976), Second World War commander of the allied 8th Army in North Africa, where he defeated German Field Marshall Erwin Rommel (1891–1944) at El **Alamein** in 1942. **Archie** Flower had been chairman of the Stratford governing council until April 1944, when he was succeeded by his son, Fordham Flower.

154 / To G. Bernard Shaw   [Shakespeare Memorial Theatre
Stratford-upon-Avon]
[? February 1947]

[TDU]

These are Jackson's views on Shaw's new play, Buoyant Billions.

The first act aroused my keen interest and I felt assured that we were going to see the world-betterer's plans unfold for good or ill, for world betterers have a way of creating as much misery as happiness. Without giving us a taste of his capabilities he immediately falls victim to the Life Force and vanishes, to all intents and purposes, from the play. We finish with a sort of compromise by which he will carry on the good work by means of his wife's fortune. The moral of this implies that to be a world betterer the first step is to marry a wealthy wife and as any such is not easy to come by in present times he and his kind will presumably vanish from the earth. Both courses are possible as is instanced by Jesus and Mahomet, the latter rather overdoing the matrimonial aspect. I always have a conviction that it is most dangerous to interest an audience in a personage that fades away. What would have happened had you switched the main theme of St Joan over to the Dauphin after the second act? It appears to me that a play should have a centre that is constant with every ramification of action and dialogue definitely linked to that centre. Change of direction is apt to confuse the audience.

But all this is by the way for dramatically you are a law to yourself. 'The Buoyant Billions' should be listened to in acting. I purposely do not use the all too familiar term – 'seen.'

[Barry Jackson]

155 / To G. Bernard Shaw   [Shakespeare Memorial Theatre
                                        Stratford-upon-Avon]
                                        11th November 1947

[TLU (c); original TLS is in HRC]

My dear G.B.S.

On Wednesday, 19 November, the Midland Regional Service of the B.B.C. are giving a programme, lasting an hour and a half, which will incorporate excerpts from past work at the Birmingham Repertory Theatre. [Cedric] Hardwicke, Gwen Davies and Ralph Richardson, and many others, have made recordings and it has been suggested that you be asked to read the speech that you made at the conclusion of the first English performance of 'Back to Methuselah.'

The complete speech is, of course, in existence and consists of from 200 to 250 words. If you would consent to reading this any time between now and next Monday, 17 November, the B.B.C. would put every available resource at your disposal by bringing the recording apparatus to Ayot.

As time is short, I enclose a telegraph form, and your reply – whether yea or nay – would be to hand almost immediately.

Yours ever,

SIR BARRY JACKSON

The radio **programme** was called '"The Mighty Line": History of the Birmingham Repertory Theatre' and was broadcast, as Jackson says, on 19 November 1947, 7:20–9:00 p.m. The transcript of the broadcast is in the BCL MS 978/4. Among the participants was **Ralph Richardson** (1902–83), who had first performed at the BRT in 1925. He was knighted in 1947. The **speech** referred to by Jackson was given by Shaw from the BRT stage on 12 October 1923 following completion of the British premiere of the full cycle of *Back to Methuselah*: 'I know my place as an author, and the place of an author is not on the stage. That really belongs to the artistes who give life to the creations of the author, and are the real life of the play. I have had the luxury of seeing my own play, which only existed until they took it and made it live. I should like to ask one question, and that is whether, apart from a few personal friends of mine, there are any inhabitants of Birmingham in this house? This has been the most extraordinary experience of my life. I have had five magnificent performances in four days, and, what is more extraordinary, this has been done in Birmingham. I remember Birmingham when it was, dramatically and theatrically, the most impossible place in the world for work of this description. That is why I ask – Are you all pilgrims or strangers here, or are there one or two genuine inhabitants of Birmingham? It is astonishing to me that this, perhaps the crown and climax of my career as a dramatic author, has been seen in Birmingham. I suppose Mr Barry Jackson must be a changeling, or is it that there is occurring in Birmingham some change such as that in this play? The first two of the people who live 300 years are people who never imagined it would be possible, and people whose friends never imagined it would happen to them. Their surprise can be compared to my experience, for Birmingham, the last place in the world one would imagine to become the centre of dramatic art, has produced a play of an intensity I think unparalleled. Without the cooperation of the audience such a feat would have been impossible' (Matthews, 110–11).

156 / To Barry Jackson   [Ayot St Lawrence, Welwyn, Herts.]
                                                          13 November 1947
[TEL; original ANS is in HRC]

Shaw's response to Jackson's request was prompt – and firm.

FINALLY NO AM WRITING TO EXPLAIN – SHAW

157 / To Barry Jackson   Ayot St Lawrence, Welwyn, Herts.
                                                        13th November 1947
[APCS]

NO, for the following reasons:

1. I have been on the air twice this week, first from a record several years old, and second from one made a fortnight ago. The difference between the former voice and the present senile croak was obvious. I cannot now recapture my Methuselah voice.

2. The speech as I recollect it was too topical and tricky for reproduction effectively today.

3. As you were the real hero of the occasion I am quite determined to leave the spotlight entirely to you. Your voice is still the same.

I will croak no more.

                                                              G.B.S.

Shaw's broadcasts **twice this week** were on 11 November in a program called 'Voices: Memories of Great Occasions and Personalities in Broadcasting,' part of a series celebrating the twenty-fifth anniversary of the BBC, and on 12 November in a program called 'London Theatre: A Pageant of Plays and Players 1922–1947,' written by St John Ervine and also featuring Alec Guiness, Edith Evans, John Gielgud, Lewis Casson, Emlyn Williams, Irene Vanbrugh, and others. In an article in the *Radio Times*, 7 November 1947, Shaw is credited with being 'one of the first to perceive the immense potentialities of broadcasting, and over the years he has contributed notably to its development.'

158 / To G. Bernard Shaw

[Shakespeare Memorial Theatre
Stratford-upon-Avon]
26th November 1947

[TLU (c)]

The program that Jackson listened to was a repeat of the one first broadcast on 12 November (Letter 157). Jackson's Shakespearean quotation is from A Midsummer Night's Dream *(III.i.122); the Jackson/Shaw:Titania/Bottom pairing is fascinating. The doubts about a Malvern Festival for 1948 were justified; the first post-war Malvern Festival was delayed until 1949 (see also Letter 159).*

My dear G.B.S.

When I heard your voice over the air on Sunday night – and this is no mere compliment – I was astonished by its vigour and vitality. If that was 'croaking,' I prithee croak again for 'mine ear is much enamoured of thy note.'

I do not know whether you were able to hear the Birmingham Repertory Theatre broadcast, but, considering the innumerable difficulties, it seems to have been successful and aroused what seems unavoidable with so many – nostalgic memories. For myself, I hate nostalgic phenomena, and I believe that you do too.

From local newspapers and gossip, I gather there is some doubt about a festival at Malvern next year. If production of 'Buoyant Billions' is to be held up, remember the B.R.T.

With every good wish,

Yours,
SIR BARRY JACKSON

159 / To Barry Jackson   Ayot St Lawrence, Welwyn, Herts.
30th November 1947

[APCS]

Roy Limbert's efforts to revive the Malvern Festival after the war were frustrated by municipal parsimony and community scepticism. An editorial in the Malvern Gazette *on 15 November 1947 advised against a 1948 Festival: petrol rationing and 'national economic troubles' would make it 'sheer madness' to proceed. And the* Gazette *reported on 29 November 1947 that the Malvern Urban District Council had unanimously decided that Limbert 'would be well advised to postpone the Drama Festival originally proposed for the year 1948.' Shaw continued to be supportive, but recognized that without Jackson's personal munificence a public subsidy was essential. His telegraph to this effect was also published in the* Gazette *on 29 November: 'Festival will bring money to Malvern but as little of it will go to the Theatre box office it must be postponed unless the Council guarantee the Theatre's risk.' Shaw further supported Limbert by leaving* Buoyant Billions *unproduced in Britain (despite Jackson's express interest in it for the Birmingham Repertory Theatre [Letter 158]) until the Festival resumed in 1949. Limbert subsequently took the production to London, where it opened at the Prince's Theatre on 10 October 1949 and ran for forty performances.*

You have no doubt seen in the Malvern Gazette that the Council advises Limbert to defer the Festival until 1949, not being prepared to guarantee him financially. I cannot but agree, though I do not see how 1949 will be any better than 1948.

I foresee that L. will try to get the required capital if I let him take B.B. [*Buoyant Billions*] to London. If he succeeds I cannot reasonably object, but I shall do nothing that can cut out the B.R. It must, however, act in before L. takes the road after London, as he certainly will if the play does not flop.

G.B.S.

160 / To G. Bernard Shaw   [Shakespeare Memorial Theatre
Stratford-upon-Avon]
4th December 1947

[TLU (c)]

Jackson's rather casual reference in this letter to the ending of his term of office at

Stratford concealed a good deal of personal distress and impending controversy. He was stoically taciturn at this stage of the unpleasant affair, but as it boiled into a public ruckus, he took Shaw more and more into his confidence. Jackson's interest in a play based on the legend of seven persecuted Christians who were sealed in a cave by the Roman Emperor Decius and slept for 187 years may or may not have reflected in some way (consciously or unconsciously) his own psychological state as relationships with his employer deteriorated, but the idea was in any event given short shrift by Shaw (Letter 161).

My dear G.B.S.

I only mentioned the possibility of your play [*Buoyant Billions*] being welcomed at the B.R.T. if all other outlets with Limbert proved fruitless. It is more than probable that if the Malvern project falls through, a production in London will materialise. Indeed, I hope so.

When you have time and inclination – and the latter is the more important – can you offer a word of advice? My term of office here will terminate next October when I shall be sixty-nine years of age. At the time of writing, I find myself heading for at least 12 months' immunity from theatrical wear and tear, and planning a long holiday whilst I can still enjoy travel and my box of water colours. Against such a pleasant prospect, I have set the fact that I am running away from responsibilities and a path where I might still be of some service. As I set down before, your advice, provided you have the inclination, would be welcome.

I am haunted by the possibility of the old legend of 'The Seven Sleepers of Ephesus' being a good peg on which to hang a play. I mentioned this to you years ago and my memory received a reminder when, last week-end, I opened that queer volume of Edwards entitled 'Words, Facts and Phrases' at the very page where the variants of the story were given. Think about it.

The local bus services are doing excellent work in bringing patrons to the theatre here from the surrounding countryside. Without their help, the petrol cut would put us in a very bad way.

Yours,

[Barry Jackson]

Jackson was an enthusiastic and accomplished painter, especially of landscapes, and his **box of water colours** was never far from his side. The **queer volume of Edwards** is Eliezer

Edwards's *Words, Facts, and Phrases. A Dictionary of Curious, Quaint, and Out-of-the-Way Matters* (London: Chatto & Windus, 1882; reissued 1911). In October 1947 a **petrol cut** was imposed by the British government that made 'pleasure motoring' (such as driving to Stratford) virtually impossible (*The Times*, 1 October 1947).

161 / To Barry Jackson

4 Whitehall Court SW1
10th December 1947

[TLS]

This letter is dated 10 December 1947 on Whitehall Court letterhead. The envelope is postmarked from Welwyn, 11 December 1947. And there is a reference in the letter to an article in The Times *'today (6th Dec).' All of which may simply mean that Shaw used Whitehall Court letterhead at Ayot and posted the letter from there the next day – and that he didn't read the 6 December issue of* The Times *until 10 December. In any event, the article in question is headed 'Sir Barry Jackson's Strong Company for 1948' and lists, among others, Diana Wynyard, Godfrey Tearle, Robert Helpmann, Anthony Quayle, and Paul Scofield as members. 'Such a strong team has not been assembled for the festival since the new Shakespeare Memorial Theatre was opened [in 1932].'* The Times *offers no advice to Jackson about staying on at Stratford beyond 1948; that suggestion comes from Shaw. But neither* The Times *nor Shaw knew the full and deeply ironic truth that lay beneath the praise for Jackson. The company was indeed strong: Diana Wynyard (1906–64) spent the early years of her acting career at the Liverpool Repertory Theatre, moved to New York and Hollywood in the 1930s, and after the 1948 and 1949 seasons at Stratford went on to a major career in film and theatre; Godfrey Tearle (1884–1953), born in New York, was knighted in 1951 after a distinguished acting career; Australian-born Robert Helpmann (1908–86), knighted in 1968, was a lead dancer with Sadler's Wells Ballet from 1933 to 1950, and also acted and directed extensively in the West End and in film; Anthony Quayle (1913–89) had a flourishing West End and New York career interrupted by war service and went on after eight years at Stratford to international success in theatre and film; and Paul Scofield (b. 1922) established his reputation at the Birmingham Repertory Theatre before joining Jackson at Stratford in 1946 and subsequently achieving international acclaim as an actor in the classical and contemporary repertoires. The irony was that while the press gave Jackson the credit for all of this, he was not in fact responsible for attracting some of the key company members named by* The Times *(and other papers). It was not that Jackson willingly accepted undeserved credit; he believed, rather, that manoeuvring in the summer of 1947, led by Quayle and Michael Benthall (1919–74), who had directed* The Merchant of Venice *for Jackson at Stratford in 1947, had put him in an impossible position as director. Jackson never spoke publicly about this, but revealed all to Shaw in June 1948 (Letter 173).*

My dear Barry

The late Lord Haldane used to advise me not to take long holidays but frequent short ones of a few days. I took long holidays with Charlotte, going round the world and the like; but I worked all the time or I should have gone mad. Haldane smoked himself to death with enormous cigars.

There is an article about you in The Times today (6th Dec) which suggests that you ought to give Stratford another year unless you have trained a capable deputy to carry on. It is not easy to travel just now. Suppose you try the short and frequent plan. But Heaven forbid that I should put you off a long rest if you really need it. You must have had the devil of a time getting the theatre out of its rut, to say nothing of your own rut between Birmingham and Blackhill. Stepney or Limehouse might be the right relief after Malvern.

I have no use for the Seven Sleepers. Their opinions are not mine: I am trying to make people see that personal immortality (their pet fad) is a horror. Besides, what little faculty I have left must be reserved for XXI century plays, as my XX ones were written in XIX. Why not write it yourself: that may prove the right holiday for you.

G. Bernard Shaw

Richard Burdon **Haldane** (1856–1928), Viscount Haldane of Cloan, served as Lord Chancellor 1912–15 and again, briefly, in 1924. He was one of the founders of the London School of Economics. **Stepney** and **Limehouse** were working-class districts of East End London, far removed, socially speaking, from the middle-class gentility of Malvern.

162 / To Barry Jackson   Ayot St Lawrence, Welwyn, Herts.
10th January 1948

[ALS]

Despite complimentary stories in the press about the 1948 Stratford company, rumours that Jackson was not to continue at Stratford after the end of the 1948 season began to circulate early in the new year. On 7 January 1948 there was a report in the Daily Mail*: 'Sir Barry Jackson retires from the directorship of the Shakespeare Memorial Theatre ... when the 1948 season ends on October 2 and his three-year contract expires, it was announced yesterday ... No successor to Sir Barry has yet been nominated.' There was no hint of controversy in the* Daily Mail *article, but there was in an editorial in the* Birmingham Mail *on 7 January and in a long article on 8 January. A pencilled note on the envelope containing this letter to Jackson indicates that Shaw sent clippings of these* Birmingham Mail *pieces to Jackson. The editorial spoke of Jackson's 'retirement' as 'a bad business,' and the article said that the retirement was 'unknown to many members of the Executive Council of Governors' and that 'all officials associated with the administration were greatly disturbed' by the news. The* Birmingham Post *also came to Jackson's defence, an editorial on 7 January arguing that '[t]he Governors did themselves honour when they appointed Sir Barry as director,' but adding that '[m]any will wonder why he has not been asked to continue.' Shaw wondered too and, smelling a fight, promptly offered to enter the fray on Jackson's behalf.*

My dear Barry

What does all this mean? Would you like to say anything through me when I reply to the Mail. The notion that there has been a quarrel, and you have been sacked as a failure must give way to the real situation. What shall I say – if anything?

1. Having cleaned up and put the business in order for your successor you are making way for a younger man (or woman).

2. The experience of the Festivals has proved that a change of artistic direction every three years is the right system.

3. Having founded the Pilgrim Players, built the Rep, established the Malvern Festival, and put Stratford on its legs, besides making a success in London and finding it an *ignis fatuus*, you have still energy enough left for some new and needed theatrical enterprise.

4. That you cannot be hampered for a fourth year with all the old cats and fossils that barnacle Shakespear at Stratford.

5. That it is your inveterate habit to chuck all your enterprises for no discoverable reason whatever.

Which shall it be?

G.B.S.

Like an *ignis fatuus* (will-o'-the-wisp), Jackson's 'success' as a producer in London had been but fleeting. Or perhaps Shaw had in mind Falstaff's description of Bardolph and his nose running up Gad's Hill in the dark: 'an *ignis fatuus* or a ball of wildfire' (*1 Henry IV*, III.iii.37).

163 / To G. Bernard Shaw   [Shakespeare Memorial Theatre
Stratford-upon-Avon]
12th January 1948

[TLU (c)]

Jackson wasn't looking for Shaw's help – at least not publicly – because Jackson himself was the source of the newspaper articles. As he explains in this letter to Shaw, a reporter from the News Chronicle *had picked up a rumour about Jackson's departure from Stratford and had telephoned him on 6 January. Based on a letter he had received in November 1947 from the chairman of the governing council, Fordham Flower, Jackson made the announcement that was carried in the press the next day. The* News Chronicle *embellished the announcement with some commentary on Jackson's 'pride' in running deficits: 'Sir Barry's view was that he could see no point in the comfortable surplus which had cropped up year after year before his arrival on the scene. He wanted to see Stratford as the home of the most experimental and lavish productions of Shakespeare.' In a subsequent interview with the* Birmingham Post *(9 January 1948) Jackson elaborated on his situation (and added fuel to the speculation about what was going on) by declaring that he was willing to consider an extension to his contract beyond the 1948 season. No such offer, however, was made, and by the middle of January Fordham Flower had already secretly offered Jackson's position to Anthony Quayle and Quayle had accepted (Beauman, 193–4), although the appointment was not publicly announced until June (Letter 173).*

My dear G.B.S.

The facts of all this hullabaloo are as simple as ABC. I was appointed as Director of the Memorial Theatre for three years, which time expires next October. At a meeting of the Executive Council of the Governors, last November, it was decided not to invite me to continue. This information was conveyed to me by Fordham Flower in a letter, though the decision does not appear to have been communicated to those members of the Governors not at the meeting.

Last Tuesday, 6 January, a representative of the 'News Chronicle' said that his office had received news that I was not to continue at Stratford and made it clear that in default of any official statement, some announcement would be made next day. So that there should be no garbled version, I authorised a simple statement of the facts as given above and this statement has since been endorsed by the chairman, though I was unable to consult him before it was issued. But had it been made clear to me by the Executive Council that my continued holding of office would be for the good of Stratford and the theatre, I would have, unhesitatingly, very seriously considered the proposition, though I must confess that the undertaking is extremely arduous and fraught with possibilities of criticism from the uninformed.

And now to the points in your letter.

1. Having cleaned up and put the business in order for your successor, you are making way for a younger man (or woman).

   I have absolutely no notion as to whom the next will be to fill my place, and, in any case, I much doubt whether any amount of training would inspire even the few qualifications that I possess, for I am acutely aware of my deficiencies.

2. The experience of the Festivals has proved that a change of artistic direction every three years is the right system.

   In this suggestion, I am up against a dilemma which has puzzled me for years, as my ideal is a theatre such as, say, La Comedie, that has static qualities, but which, at the same time, must possess no small amount of elasticity in direction and programme.

3. Having founded the Pilgrim Players, built the Rep., established the Malvern Festival, and put Stratford on its legs, besides making a success in London and finding it an *ignis fatuus*, you have still energy enough left for some new and needed theatrical enterprise.

   In the realm of adventure, it is quite possible that I have shot my bolt, but as I experienced this sensation long before Stratford came my way, like everyone else, I am in the dark as to the future. After my many vicissitudes, I would always be happy to do something for the theatre with such literary powers that I possess – and there is always B.R.T. which at the present moment is feeling both hurt and neglected.

4. That you cannot be hampered for a fourth year with all the old cats and fossils that barnacle Shakespear in Stratford.

It is only you who dares to put this down in black and white!

5. That it is your inveterate habit to chuck all your enterprises without notice for no discoverable reason whatever.

The only enterprise in which I firmly fixed my teeth and retained complete grasp is the B.R.T. though, both there, in London and in Malvern, the pricks and lack of understanding of what my work represents often caused me to accept both the towel and the sponge. In one of the more difficult crises at Birmingham, one of my trustees, before my very face, proposed selling the entire building and all it contained! I was so deeply shocked that this left me completely speechless. I would like you to know that one of the final straws at Malvern – and I am sure you have forgotten the incident – was when dear Charlotte had to come to you for a penny in order to enter the lessees' 'cloakroom.' To many less sensitive than myself, this may mean nothing, but such a deplorable state of affairs quite shuts me up and I can never forget it, nor will it ever be excused. In short, I am not of the mental build that can walk through the brick and concrete walls erected by the visionless and stupid.

I had intended replying to your kind response to my request for advice about retirement during a fortnight's stay in Cornwall. When you pointed out that you found short holidays more congenial than lengthy trips to foreign places, the scene between Bellarius and the twins in 'Cymbeline' came to my mind:–

Arviragus: What should we speak of
              When we are old as you? when we shall hear
              The rain and wind beat dark December, how

In this our pinching cave shall we discourse
The freezing hours away? We have seen nothing;
We are beastly; subtle as the fox for prey,
Like warlike as the wolf for what we eat;
Our valour is to chase what flies; our cage
We make a quire, as doth the prison'd bird,
And sing our bondage freely.

Yours ever,
[Barry Jackson]

Jackson's ideal theatre, **La Comedie** (La Comédie Française), was founded in Paris in 1680.
The speech by **Arviragus** is from *Cymbeline*, III.iii. 35–44.

164 / To G. Bernard Shaw Shakespeare Memorial Theatre,
Stratford-upon-Avon
2nd April 1948

[TLU (c)]

*Jackson's responsibilities at Stratford left little time for any active involvement
with the Birmingham Repertory Theatre, and as he recognized in his previous letter to Shaw (Letter 163), the BRT was feeling 'hurt and neglected.' The 1946–7
season was directed by William Armstrong, the 1947–8 season by Willard Stoker,
but this letter to Shaw (concerning a play by Bernard Lytton Jaeger,* Let the People Live) *shows Jackson's ongoing interest – and he returned to the BRT at the
end of his Stratford contract to take charge of the 1948–9 season. The letter also
reflects positively on Jackson's professional integrity. Despite his distaste for what
he considered underhand behaviour by leading individuals in the company and
governance of Stratford (see Letter 173), Jackson remained committed to the artistic success of the 1948 Festival. Anthony Quayle knew at this point that he would
replace Jackson; Jackson didn't know until late May (Letter 173).*

My dear G.B.S.

If my memory serves aright, you are credited with the statement that
English audiences prefer lectures to plays. The theory, if one calls it so,
has always caused some doubt in my mind for I am convinced that the
spring-board of drama was the story-teller. However, you went your way

and in more than one instance proved your point. Now come the imitators. Among these was a man who submitted a play in about 1940. His dialogue was far above the average and his theme the town-planners. The play was of inordinate length and, like his model, he refused to have a line excised. He was a victim of the war and left his work in the hands of a sister; with her help we have got the play going at BRT where, after a severe trouncing by the critics, it is attracting large and most enthusiastic audiences. Yet it is neither more nor less than a prolonged discussion which vividly shows the stupidity of these garden-city maniacs using up first-class agricultural land for villa residences. In the course of a scene representing a town meeting, the Vicar rises up on his hind legs and denounces the representative of the Government as an agitator of class warfare in the pay of the Communists; this remark is greeted with applause from his very few stage supporters and a veritable salvo from the audience. Which all goes to prove that you were correct in the assumption that our public enjoys lectures.

The new company here is working harder than anything in my experience and the productions should be extremely interesting. The 'Hamlet' is inspired by Winterhalter and is very opulent. Advance booking is as heavy as in previous years and if the basic ration is restored we are in for an excellent season. If I have any fear, it is caused by the inclusion of three plays that have never been very popular with the greater public – 'John,' 'Winter's Tale' and 'Troilus and Cressida'. However, unusual production, as in the case of Peter Brook's 'Love's Labour's Lost' may at least inspire curiosity.

Scott joins in love and best wishes for your welfare.

BARRY

I read some 'Methuselah, Part I' to a group of French teachers, last night, with what appeared to be very satisfactory results.

The **severe trouncing** of *Let the People Live* (which opened at the BRT on 16 March 1948) included comments such as this: 'The growing habit of using the theatre as a forum for these exercises in political polemics greatly alarms me, and I await with no little apprehension the inevitable dramatic argument on domestic sanitation and the play dealing with the case for proportional representation' (*Birmingham Mail*, 17 March 1948). The **new company** at Stratford for the 1948 Festival (see also Letter 161) included directors Michael Benthall (*Hamlet* and *King John*) and Anthony Quayle (*The Winter's Tale* and *Troilus and Cressida*). The acting company included Paul Scofield and Robert Helpmann (who alternated as Hamlet), and Claire Bloom, Diana Wynyard, and Quayle. Franz Xaver **Winterhal-**

ter (1806–73) was a German artist who painted a number of royal portraits (including Queen Victoria).

165 / To Barry Jackson   Ayot St Lawrence, Welwyn, Herts.
                                                    3rd April 1948
[TLU]

The previous letter showed how Jackson kept part of his mind in Birmingham, however complex and demanding his Stratford duties. This one contains a brief reminder from Shaw of Jackson's Malvern connections. Jackson still had his home in Malvern (Blackhill), but had severed his relationship with the Malvern Festival in 1937. His successor, Roy Limbert, mounted Festivals in 1938 and 1939, but had been frustrated in his efforts to revive it after the war (see Letter 159). Shaw's 'stinger' of a letter to the Malvern Gazette (3 April 1948) attacked the ratepayers of Malvern as 'too small-minded' to appreciate the value of the Festival: 'Wake up Malvern!' was his concluding exhortation. He had some exhortations for Jackson as well about Stratford's 1948 season, particularly concerning the Victorian setting (designed by James Bailey) for Hamlet *and director Michael Benthall's approach to* King John.

My dear Barry

Do not for a moment dream of Hamlet in crinolines. Hamlet in modern dress is an excusable experiment with which your name is associated. But Hamlet in a period that is not either Hamlet's period nor Shakespear's is indefensible ugly nonsense, and would be used to justify your dismissal as a faddist with an unpleasant complex.

I mean this most seriously. Countermand the crinolines at once; and order the usual pseudo-Danish costumes, on which the fancy may have boundless range.

John is sweepingly magnificent in its verse. If it be properly declaimed, with Faulconbridge as the big bowwow star part, it is as sure fire as Hamlet. If your producer is so utterly off the mark as to imagine that he has a poor play and must aim at illustrating history by shabby clothes and worn-out paint on the walls, pitch him into the Avon or cast him for Barnardo or Marcellus. These young fools do not understand their job.

I have written a stinger of a letter to The Malvern Gazette in which you figure, about the opposition to the Festival.

An author who will not alter a word knows nothing about the stage. I have done a lot of it. But it is a highly skilled business, though everyone in a theatre, from the leading tragedian to the most casual extra, and from the producer to call boy, considers himself perfectly qualified for it, and would have botched my plays as Irving and Daly botched Shakespear's if I had let them.

Any subject on earth can be dramatized: that is, made the matter of a dialogue. If in that dialogue every speech *provokes* the next, you have a good play. If not, no matter how beautiful as poetry or eloquent as prose the speeches may be, the author is no playwright.

You have not told me how matters stand between you and the old Stratford gang. Are they going to chuck you out? If they do, what then?

My letter will be in the M.G. next week.

G.B.S.

The **star part** in *King John* (Falconbridge) was played by Anthony Quayle. Henry **Irving** and American playwright and director Augustin **Daly** (1838–99) both 'botched' Shakespeare – Shaw's view on this is not now considered eccentric – by privileging scenic effect over textual integrity (Irving) and taking gross liberties with textual adaptation (Daly).

166 / To G. Bernard Shaw [Shakespeare Memorial Theatre
Stratford-upon-Avon]
6th April 1948

[TLU (c)]

My dear G.B.S.

I was profoundly touched that you should seize your typewriter and reply to my letter of last week with such celerity. It is too late to do anything drastic in regard to 'Hamlet'; we can only await results. As I think I told you, the general effect is opulent, and as Edward Wadsworth, the artist, who paints sea-shells, screwdrivers and sextants in tempera, said to me, '"Hamlet" is a very *chic* play.' The trouble with the pseudo Danish-Viking costuming is that poor Ophelia's funeral invariably looks like a Victorian fancy dress ball, savouring of the Prince Consort more than any Winterhalter!

I am in entire agreement with you about 'King John.' The designs for this are of superb barbarity and should satisfy the eye. During rehearsals the play has risen considerably in the esteem of the company.

When I got home at five o'clock on Saturday, your letter in the local paper caught my eye immediately. You have far more knowledge of the whole idea from its inception than anyone else for I distinctly recall discussing the notion of a Festival at Malvern with you long before it assumed any tangible shape. Directly it began to be something more than a dream, the first step was to consult whoever was in control of what was then called a 'Super Talkie Theatre.' It was entirely at my instigation that in later years this designation was dropped in favour of 'Festival Theatre'. The man in charge was a little startled at first, but on being assured that he would receive a very adequate rental and rehearsals cut to allow him to use his Super Talkie machinery, and that he would have very little to do except sit in his office (my side of the affair had no office), agreement was reached with one condition – that all printing carried the phrase, 'in association with'. Hence the association of two individuals by nature as remote from each other as Uranus and Earth. I have told you what eventually caused my demission, but there were many episodes equally galling and at last I could bear it no longer. So far as the present situation goes, there is absolutely nothing to prevent the Festival from being held this year. The theatre is, at least, very little worse than when I put on plays there and the suggestion that nothing is possible without expending £12,000 is fantastic. It appears to me to be little more than subterfuge on the part of an individual, or individuals, lacking courage and pluck.

Nor can much be expected of the town itself. You once said to me that the perfect State would never come about unless blood were shed; I feel very strongly that no amount of blood-shedding will ever promulgate vision and intelligence, but rather the reverse. Malvern is neither better nor worse than any other place. If it ever resumes its Festival activities (which I doubt), the incentive will not be local for, beyond the possibility of putting some money in their pockets, the inhabitants have not the least notion of what it is all about. On more than one occasion I was frankly told that the whole thing was a nuisance.

One of the organisers of the Edinburgh Festival informed me that it is almost hopeless to build anything of the kind without a name. Malvern had two names – Edward's [Elgar] and your own and the place was honouring itself in honouring both of you. I feel nauseated when I think of lost opportunities. So much could have been accomplished with full co-operation.

I must tell you more about Stratford another time and, at this point, confine myself to expressing fear of the Family Saga. There is something more to the running of an International affair than pride of race – a procedure which is dying before our eyes almost hourly.

Yours ever,

[Barry Jackson]

Edward Wadsworth (1889–1943), a member of the influential London Group of artists (founded 1913), specialized in tempera. The **designs** for the Stratford *King John* were by Audrey Cruddas. The **man in charge** at Malvern when Jackson began the Festival there was Roy Limbert. The immediate cause of Jackson's **demission** from Malvern is described in Letter 163. Jackson's anxiety about the **Family Saga** of the Flowers perhaps alludes – intentionally or otherwise – to the tribalism of Galsworthy's Forsytes.

167 / To Barry Jackson　　　　　Ayot St Lawrence, Welwyn, Herts.

7th April 1948

[TLU]

The dilemma facing Roy Limbert at Malvern was that Ministry of Health regulations necessitated considerable expenditure (about £12,000) on improvements to the Festival Theatre. Since Limbert lacked the personal resources of Annie Horniman (see Letter 24) – derived from the tea trade – or Jackson – derived from the Maypole chain of grocery stores – Shaw, unlike Jackson, thought he deserved some sympathy and support. Shaw also thought that Jackson himself deserved some sympathy and support at Stratford in his wrangle with 'the family' (the powerful Flower family and their circle), but he was overly optimistic in thinking that a design change for Hamlet *could save Jackson's job, whatever 'public opinion' might be.*

My dear Barry

I still urge you to give up the crinolines and Dundreary whiskers. They are utterly indefensible, and will give the family a valid excuse for discarding you and damaging you. It must still be possible to alter them into purely fancy unperiodic costumes which will be quite in order.

You are too much accustomed to do just as you like, as Miss Horniman was. With the Maypole at your back (in her case it was tea). You have never understood the straits of the poor devils who have nothing behind them, and are in constant dread of being left destitute by a week's bad business. The penny in the slot seemed to L[imbert] to be his mother's daily bread. To you it was unpardonable – as indeed in fact it was. But courage and pluck will not produce twelve thousand pounds. Only the Maypole can do that.

Besides, you had a free hand. Nobody could make you put the theatre in safe and decent repair behind the scenes. And you didnt. But now the State comes in and says to L. 'If you don't spend £12,000 on such repairs you shall not give any performances.' In vain he pleads that he has spent £3,000 and can spare no more. Even you have little to spare now. I collect taxes for Cripps who allows me a commission of sixpence in the pound. You are only a Festival manager at a salary. As such you must keep up at least an appearance of carrying out the policy of the Council. No doubt they hanker after Benson cutting down Coriolanus to an hour. Still, though they pay the piper they dare not call that scandalous tune. You have public opinion at your back so far. But it would be at their back if you made Hamlet a Dundreary.

Therefore perpend, unless you are prepared either to retire or to buy the Festival theatre lock stock and barrel, and spend twelve or twenty thousand pounds on it. All this in hottest haste. I am up to my neck in work publishing and proof reading.

G.B.S.

Dundreary whiskers (side-whiskers worn without a beard) became fashionable from E.A. Sothern's portrayal of Lord Dundreary in Tom Taylor's play *Our American Cousin* (1858). Sir Stafford **Cripps** (1889–1952) was Chancellor of the Exchequer 1947–50; Shaw's tax rate was nineteen shillings and sixpence in the pound (97.5%). Sir Frank **Benson** (1858–1939) directed all but five of the Shakespeare seasons at Stratford between 1886 and 1916. He was enamoured of cutting Shakespeare's texts. Among other things, Shaw's **publishing and proof reading** involved working on rehearsal copies of *Buoyant Billions*.

168 / To Barry Jackson   Ayot St Lawrence, Welwyn, Herts.
                                                          4th May 1948
[TLU]

William Poel (1852–1934) had a major influence on twentieth-century theory and practice of staging Shakespeare. He was an unflagging advocate of unclut-

*tered, unspectacular productions, freed from the restrictions of the proscenium
stage. In 1894 he founded the Elizabethan Stage Society and for ten years experimented with Shakespeare and his contemporaries in a variety of unconventional
performance spaces. Poel's Measure for Measure was seen at Stratford in 1908,
and in 1913 his Troilus and Cressida was performed there on a virtually bare
stage, with the parts of Aeneas, Paris, and Thersites all played by women. Barry
Jackson saw and admired the production, but Poel was never invited back to
Stratford. Jackson held Poel in considerable respect, and wanted to ensure that his
achievements were adequately documented and recorded (see Letter 169). Hence
his request to Shaw for his views on Poel.*

My dear Barry

Enclosed is all that there is to be said about Poel. Probably nobody else
will say it.

As far as I have seen you have had a very good press for Hamlet, proving that Shakespear and a promising actor will pull you through anything. Pascal has his eye on the young man.

I do not trust the Old Gang; but I think you are now in command of
the situation.

G.B.S.

The **young man** in *Hamlet* was Paul Scofield. He appeared at the Birmingham Repertory
Theatre in 1942 as Stephen Undershaft in *Major Barbara* and went on to become an international star on stage and screen – though not with Gabriel Pascal.

Included with this letter are Shaw's views on William Poel:

William Poel was an extraordinary and incalculable Adult Phenomenon, in appearance so like a crushed tragedian that I once, on Margate
Sands, mistook Irving for him. Born stage struck, he studied Salvini to
acquire his method and succeed to his eminence; yet he was almost
ridiculous as an actor, and when he read a play he began too fast and
was presently gabbling prestissimo quite unintelligibly. In the teeth of
Irving and Augustine [*sic*] Daly, who cut Shakespear's plays to pieces to
accommodate the refreshment bars and transfer all the best lines to the
stars (Daly for Ada Rehan and Irving for himself) Poel devoted his life
to the restoration of the plays to the stage in their integrity; and yet no

actor-manager ever dared to take such liberties with them as he did. When he played Polonius and was duly stabbed by Hamlet he made Hamlet carry his corpse from behind the arras to the front of the stage and play the rest of the scene kneeling with Poel in his arms and the queen, the ghost, and Hamlet himself nowhere. When he produced Troilus & Cressida with a beginner (Edith Evans) as Cressida, he cast another actress (Mrs Robertson Scott) for Thersites, dressing her fantastically as a zany, and making her speak in his notion of a Somerset dialect, not one word of which was intelligible.

How then did he, the perpetrator of these monstrous aberrations, initiate the Shakespear Restoration afterwards consummated sanely and completely by Granville-Barker, who as a juvenile, acted for him and was supposed to be his pupil? Simply by sticking to the text, the whole text, and nothing but the text; doing without scenery; and exploiting a wardrobe of more or less Elizabethan costumes he had picked up. The text pulled him through. His other resources were so slender that as a producer he could achieve only sample scraps of what he aimed at, and let the rest of the acting go hang; but the samples were so convincing that a thoroughpaced young Shakespearean like Granville-Barker went ahead with the good work with a success far beyond Poel's means; for Barker had Lord Howard de Walden's millions at his back; and Poel had nothing but his rather impossible self.

I tried to get him a knighthood, and had all but succeeded when Poel, whose formal consent was necessary, announced that he could accept nothing from the British Government because it had not conferred a title on his father Reginald Pole [sic] for the light he had thrown on Mozart's Requiem.

What could be done with such a man?

Personally he was likeable. Abstractly he was incurably cantankerous. Many reformers are like that.

G.B.S.

Shaw's concept of Poel as an **Adult Phenomenon** perhaps draws on Dickens's 'infant phenomenon' in *Nicholas Nickleby*. **Ada Rehan** (1860–1916) first acted with Daly's company in New York in 1878. She stayed with him until his death in 1899, frequently appearing in London. **Mrs Robertson Scott**, an amateur actress, was Secretary of the London Shakespeare League; 'Poel entrusted her with the part because "a man would be sure to over-act"' (Robert Speaight, *William Poel and the Elizabethan Revival* [London: Heinemann, 1954], 196).

Shaw's version of Poel's refusal of a **knighthood** does not accord with the version given by Poel in a letter (10 January 1930) to his biographer: 'I was too painfully conscious that my labour to secure recognition for the Elizabethan stage as a proper method for presenting Shakespeare's plays was not approved of among those who control our public stage. It was inconceivable to me that my name could be added to the long list of theatrical knights not one of whom was in sympathy with an Elizabethan method of presentation' (Speaight, 254).

169 / To G. Bernard Shaw   [Shakespeare Memorial Theatre
                                                                    Stratford-upon-Avon]
                                                                              6th May 1948

[TLU]

The ellipses in this letter are Jackson's.

My dear G.B.S.

Your immediate acquiescence to my request in relation to Poel leaves me with no alternative but to express my gratitude with all possible speed – a speed somewhat hampered by a ribbon that ties itself into unending knots.

All the artists I have approached have added to the store of Poeliana in varying degrees, the majority expressing admiration for a wayward genius. When the time comes for a 'Life' to be compiled, the Memorial Library will be able to supply much first-hand information. I learn that the magnificent Library in Birmingham, which, according to Allardyce Nicoll, is second to none in Shakespeariana, has many programmes and cuttings. Gabrielle Enthoven also has photographs. I am rather worried about these photographs for photography in Poel's day was by no means as scientific as to-day and there are obvious signs of fading. I gather there is some process by which the prints could be intensified, but that it is a costly matter.

The Old Gang flourishes and my position is not altogether happy. Blatant stupidity is an enemy that is difficult to counteract. Like the Boyg, it gives at every touch.

It will not be long before I shall be in a position to put the whole story before you ... at least I hope it will not be long. Fordham made an entirely tactless speech on the Birthday night and has avoided me persistently ever since. The Press was furious and all my supporters [are] seething with bitterness.

Do you know if there is any truth in the story, related to me, that Harley Barker walked out of a meeting with the Governors?

It is common knowledge that every individual put in control has left in an atmosphere of unpleasantness. I hoped and prayed that this would not happen in my case.

'More than this I cannot tell you,' as the old melodramatic actor said when he dried up ... but before long, you shall know all.

Yours

BARRY

A comprehensive **'Life'** of William Poel remains to be written, but Robert Speaight's *William Poel and the Elizabethan Revival* (London: Heinemann, 1954) made good use of the materials Jackson collected at Stratford. They are now in the Shakespeare Centre Library, Stratford, MS 83.6/Poel/JAC. In a review of Speaight's book (*Shakespeare Quarterly* 6 [1955], 89–90) Jackson calls Poel 'a genius,' and praises Speaight's portrait of him: 'The inspired drive, the strange and inexplicable idiosyncrasies are all set forth with admirable and perfect honesty.' The **magnificent library in Birmingham** is the Birmingham Shakespeare Library, founded in 1864, and now part of the Birmingham Central Library. **Allardyce Nicoll** (1894–1976), prolific theatre scholar, taught at London, Yale, and Birmingham universities and established the Shakespeare Institute at Stratford in 1951. **Gabrielle Enthoven** (1868–1950) donated his extensive theatre collection to the Victoria and Albert Museum in 1924; it is now housed at the British Theatre Museum in Covent Garden. The **Boyg** is a symbolic, ectoplasmic figure in Ibsen's *Peer Gynt.*

---

170 / To G. Bernard Shaw

The Shakespeare Memorial Theatre
Stratford-upon-Avon
12th May 1948

[TLU]

Jackson knew Shaw's views on William Archer as a translator of Ibsen (see Letter 138), but Jackson tested Shaw, nonetheless, about the Peer Gynt *translation, used for a Birmingham production directed by Willard Stoker. It was, said critic J.C. Trewin* (Birmingham Repertory Theatre, *144), 'a hazard bravely faced.' The critics and Jackson were of one mind about the 'young men's' production of* The Taming of the Shrew *at Stratford, directed by Michael Benthall (aged twenty-nine).*

My dear G.B.S.

The B'ham theatre made a brave effort last night to perform 'Peer Gynt' in the Archer translation. It played for the best part of four hours and there was very little cutting. But much of the text bewildered me – a bewilderment which may be explained that, as a member of the audience, my mind becomes akin to that of a rather undeveloped adolescent. Again and again I found that I was conscious of Ibsen's thought, glimmerings, as it were, but remained defeated by the words which give it expression. I still think that there is room for a translation that will make all clear. What puzzles me is the fact that the Pastor's long speech at the burial of the man who hacked his fingers off stood out like a trumpet blast – the second time in my experience that this has occurred. Did WILLIAM write it? It is lucid, pleasant to the ear and concise. This cannot be claimed for many of the other long speeches so far as I am concerned.

Our young men's production of 'The Shrew' took place last Friday, a completely wild farrago of nonsense in which the appearance of the Marx Brothers would create no surprise.

Audiences continue vast. Charabancs pour up from all over the country side. How those who, apart from the organised parties, fill in the odd seats get to and from Stratford passes my comprehension. A dozen or so cars only now appear. The theatre is full, full, full.

Scott joins me in love and remembrances.

BARRY

171 / To Barry Jackson   Ayot St Lawrence, Welwyn, Herts.
                                             17th May 1948

[TLU]

Once more, Shaw came to Archer's defence.

My dear Barry

Do not dream of using any translation of Peer Gynt except Archer's. The understanding will come to you as it never came to Archer himself, who was no Ibsenist, and was scandalized by my interpretations. But he was more than a bit of a poet, and, having Norwegian cousins and knowing the language, the Norwegian atmosphere was familiar to him, and he was deeply moved by Ibsen's poetry. So was I: I caught it from him. The play is a great dramatic poem; and all the attempts to turn it into a dry treatise in colloquial English (there have been several) are depoetized deIbsenized bores. They all fail, like the recent Broadcast, which might as well have been written by the call boy. Archer uncut never fails: it alone has the Ibsen touch.

G.B.S.

There had been no **recent Broadcast** of *Peer Gynt.* Shaw may have been referring to a BBC radio production of Ibsen's *Rosmersholm,* adapted by Cynthia Pugh from Archer's translation, broadcast on 28 November 1947.

172 / To G. Bernard Shaw   Shakespeare Memorial Theatre
Stratford-upon-Avon
27th May 1948

[TLS] (copy)

My dear G.B.S.

Thanks, indeed, for the letter from Poel. I note that he mentions his prompt books which you advised him to keep. I have fears that these have vanished into the limbo of oddments which appears to be the fate of so much theatrical history. Gabrielle Enthoven managed to collect relics from Mrs Poel but I am ignorant of their character.

As I write I see that odd figure, Percy Allen, wandering about in front of the theatre. He now has visions and spends much time conversing with spirits of the Elizabethans who assure him that the plays were written by the Earl of Oxford.

'Peer Gynt' is proving attractive to evening audiences though the female element which patronizes matinées leaves it severely alone.

The audiences at Stratford are fantastic and the money that has to be turned away quite heart breaking.

Our President, Lord Iliffe, is, as the French say, 'offering' me a lunch at Claridges. Being well aware of your aversion to such entertainments, an aversion shared by myself, I wish you could be present to support me.

I began with thanks for the very valuable Poel letter & finish with renewal of gratitude.

Yours,
Barry

I shall make endeavour to come to see you before the summer ends. After next week we shall be given a little more freedom on the roads.

The Poel **letter** to Shaw is in the Shakespeare Centre Library, Stratford (1 August 1932, MS 83.6 Poel/JAC): 'I am happy to follow your kind advice of years ago – that I should keep a few of my prompt copies for possible use by others in days to come. If I can get them into Book form it is the last thing I can expect to do.' The Enthoven Collection at the British Theatre Museum contains several Poel **prompt books**. **Percy Allen** argued his case for the Earl of Oxford in two books: *The Case for Edward de Vere 17th Earl of Oxford as 'Shakespeare'* (London: Cecil Palmer, 1930) and *The Oxford-Shakespeare Case Corroborated* (London: Cecil Palmer, 1931). The **lunch at Claridges** (the fashionable London hotel) was held on 25 June 1948 (see Letter 173). On 1 June 1948 post-war petrol rationing became less restrictive, allowing **more freedom** of travel.

173 / To G. Bernard Shaw [The Shakespeare Memorial Theatre
Stratford-upon-Avon]
11th June 1948

[TLU (c)]

On 11 June 1948 there was finally a public announcement that Anthony Quayle was to take over from Jackson as Director of the Shakespeare Memorial Theatre, a position Quayle held until 1956. Jackson said little publicly until the luncheon given in his honour at Claridge's on 25 June, and not much then. Lord Iliffe was generous in his praise. Barry Jackson, he said, 'has succeeded in infusing a note of great distinction into the theatre's work, heightening immeasurably public interest in the annual Shakespeare festivals.' 'Indeed,' he continued, 'the Shakespeare Memorial Theatre is today occupying its rightful place as a theatre of national dignity and international importance, and this is principally due to Sir Barry Jackson.' Jackson's response was decidedly cool. He 'was glad,' he said, 'to feel that the Memorial Theatre now seemed to be flourishing,' and he 'hoped his successors would find everything in order' (The Times, 26 June 1948). To Quayle, Jackson's taciturnity carried a clear message: '[M]anifestly I had Jackson's curse and not his blessing' (Anthony Quayle, A Time to Speak *[London: Barrie and Jenkins, 1990], 320). In the same book (316), Quayle describes Jackson as 'an enormously esteemed old bird with a rather academic turn of mind, but immensely distinguished.' The public announcement of Quayle's appointment provided the impetus and opportunity for Jackson to deliver on his promise (see Letter 169) to give Shaw his private view of the unseemly circumstances that had led to his departure from Stratford.*

My dear G.B.S.

You will have seen the announcement of my successor and I can now give you a précis of the events of the last months.

During the summer of 1947, the growing reputation of this place attracted the attention of some of the more ambitious and younger members of the stage. Anthony Quayle, whose record can be seen in *Who's Who in the Theatre*, and Michael Benthall, who had produced *The Merchant* for me, presented themselves with a proposal for this year.

They had approached Diana Wynyard, Robert Helpmann and Godfrey Tearle. All this was presented to me 'on a plate,' to use a rather vulgar expression. Had I rejected the scheme, the reputation of the Memorial Theatre would have sunk among the gossips and paragraphists of the West End. For the good name and almost certain expedient welfare – for the public will swallow almost anything provided names are forthcoming – I felt it incumbent to accept.

From that moment, I became submerged in a sea of underhand dealings accompanied by ill-manners. Fordham fell an easy prey to Quayle for they speak the same language and, like many climbers, the latter has an insinuating manner. Surreptitious meals and drinks at a distance from Stratford – a childish and ridiculous attempt to camouflage what was writ large – played a part.

Fordham saw me in October, 1947, and hinted that no invitation to continue after my term of three years would be forthcoming. I told him that if such experience as I had would be of help in making a new appointment, it was entirely at his service. Never a word.

During the rehearsal period of 1948 and the first months of the Festival, gossip and rumour left no doubt as to future events. Oddly enough, word came to me that a friend of the new Director described the appointment as 'in the bag,' an expression which, small as it is – and as I have told you, trivialities of life mean much to me – completely sums up the atmosphere which will prevail after my departure.

Fordham gave me no direct information until three weeks ago, though in the customary speech on the Birthday night, he implied what was in the air. This speech was so unfortunate in regard to myself and raised such a storm of protest and indignation that Lord Iliffe is giving me a luncheon at Claridges on 25 June, an exceedingly well-intentioned endeavour to make matters even. The good man has no notion what discomfort and misery this gesture causes me. But for his sake, I must go through with it; to refuse would only to be associated myself with the tactless ill-manners I have experienced.

That, I think, is a brief outline of the story.

The upshot of all this is that the parochial control of Stratford must go. So long as this has the upper hand, there can be no surety or satisfaction. The majority of our Governors have not an atom of artistic perception, no academic qualification, no knowledge of the theatre and its perplexing ramifications. Their main interest is a free seat now and again.

Events here and at Malvern are leading me to demand a complete understanding with authority at Birmingham. The rise of costs is playing havoc with work in such a small house and unless some guarantee is forthcoming, I begin to feel – a sensation due to advancing years – that the struggle is too arduous. If the future of the B.R.T. is to be disintegration, I would rather set the time bomb myself – first retiring to a safe distance.

Yours ever,

[Barry Jackson]

The implication of Jackson's reference to Quayle's **record** is, perhaps, that it did not qualify Quayle for the Stratford directorship. Certainly it could not compare with Jackson's experience (Quayle was only thirty-five years old), but as given in the *Who's Who in the Theatre* (10th ed., 1947) that Shaw might have consulted the record is quite impressive: significant experience as actor and director at the Old Vic, the West End, and New York, with lots of Shakespeare and Shaw, and then war service in the Royal Artillery. For **Michael Benthall, Diana Wynyard**, **Robert Helpmann**, and **Godfrey Tearle** see headnote to Letter 161. Quayle and Fordham Flower shared a military background and hence to the non-military Jackson spoke **the same language**, as did Michael Benthall who, like Quayle, had served in the Royal Artillery.

174 / To Barry Jackson   Ayot St Lawrence, Welwyn, Herts.
16th June 1948

[TLS]

Distanced as he was from the situation at Stratford, Shaw oversimplified the reasons for Jackson's departure, and his well-intentioned advice about what Jackson should say at the June 25th luncheon, while appreciated by Jackson (see Letter 175), was not adopted (see headnote to Letter 173). Nor was Jackson in the mood to bail out the Malvern Festival. His theatrical future was, rather, with his roots, the Birmingham Repertory Theatre, to which he returned to take charge of the 1948–9 season. But that future, as Shaw predicted, involved, in the long term, a new, larger, municipally supported BRT.

My dear Barry

I have read your letter very attentively. By and large it comes to this: that the issue was between your complete mastery and management of the theatre and that of the Council. It has got rid of you on your overwhelming merits, not on your demerits. It was *aut Caesar aut nihil*; and they preferred *nihil*.

The difficulty now is what you are to say at the Iliffe banquet, to which I have just been invited but cannot go. You will be in the same predicament as Lord Melbourne when he said to his Cabinet 'I don't care what damned lie you tell; but you shant leave this room until you are all agreed to tell the same damned lie.'

If I were in your place I think I should say 'My record must speak for itself; but how, at my age, could I resist the appeal to make way for younger men and initiate a policy of triennial changes of artistic direction to prevent the business from falling into a rut, as it had done before I was called in? I could not have gone on for many years without falling into a rut myself. That is why I have given every assistance and encouragement in my power to the change, and am returning to my work in Birmingham full of hope that Mr Quayle's success may surpass mine. He will have the advantage of all the spring cleaning I have had to do.'

And now, what next? Will you put your foot down and announce that you must either chuck the B.R.T. or be provided with a municipal theatre large enough to pay its way with popular prices, practically free of rent and rates?

What would suit me best personally would be your putting down the £13,000 to repair the Malvern theatre, and resume the Festival there; but I presume that the war taxation has left you, as it has left me, without a penny to spare, and that you could not be bothered with the management of the theatre nine months in the year and would have to leave it to Limbert.

Altogether a series of dilemmas. Such is life.

G.B.S.

Lord Melbourne (1779–1848) was British prime minister in 1834 and again 1835–41.

175 / To G. Bernard Shaw   [The Shakespeare Memorial Theatre ·
Stratford-upon-Avon]
19th June 1948

[TLU (c)]

*Having given Shaw (Letter 173) his unfettered views on the Stratford debacle,
Jackson, prompted by Shaw's ongoing interest in the Malvern Festival, now wrote
candidly – and with some bitterness – about his Malvern experiences.*

My dear G.B.S.

Your regret regarding the events at Malvern is shared by me. It was not
without certain pangs that I saw nine years' hard and costly work go
down the drain leaving, it would seem, little trace beyond stray laments
for 'the good old days.'

My position was irksome and nothing was done to offer the most commonplace amenities for myself or an extremely loyal and very hard
worked staff.

Immediately I departed, alterations to the building were put in hand.
Now comes a demand for more with a half-veiled threat that unless
these are done no Festival can take place. It does not appear to have
occurred to anyone that I was able to get the plays on during my years
and have them performed with a certain amount of credit.

The expenditure now asked for is puerile. Nothing but complete
demolition and re-building will ever make the place worthy of the seed
we sowed together. Even if this gigantic task were achieved, the question
of control would arise and this would be attended with all the thorns
and dangers (I listened to 'Hamlet' last night) which appear to be part
and parcel of the job.

It appears that I am that rara avis, a disinterested individual whose
only ambition is to serve. Had Limbert been imbued to meagre extent
with the same purpose, the story would have been entirely different.

Robert Louis Stevenson asked that some day the world should return
to the word *duty* and be done with the word *reward*. Though in agreement with you that a man must live, there must be some limit to reward.
Had I been in the lessee's place, I should have said to myself, 'Here is a
madman with visions. He may be right, he may be wrong. So long as I

am under no pecuniary loss – and I will take good care that this does not happen – I will give all possible help and also be content to serve.'

Forgive me if I quote again, but most sayings thought to be original have an unexpected source. This time it is Cecil Rhodes, who said, 'You can make your book with roguery, but vanity is incalculable and will invariably let you down.'

Directly I heard that Malvern – perhaps on Bridie's suggestion for he had proposed to me a Festival devoted to six original plays – was to be turned into a shop-window for the possible exploitation of at least one play in the West End, I knew that the end was in sight.

Limbert used this argument recently by calling Malvern's attention to the fact that 'The Barretts' had proved a very remunerative proposition, carefully avoiding any reference to other works which failed and proved very costly.

It is a source of sorrow to me that the scheme did not die the quick and dignified death we all aspire to. This dribbling away into obscurity only intensifies the regret and renders more remote the possibility of a re-birth under better conditions – with duty rather than reward uppermost.

Intimates tell me that it is fortunate that I am the happy possessor of a calm and very simple philosophic nature, perhaps my saving grace. Like you, I tell myself that such is life and that if one's work has failed in leaving the world a little better, we can at least pray that we have left it no worse.

With gratitude for your advice as to a line at Friday's lunch.

Yours ever,

[Barry Jackson]

There is some slight confusion about dates with this letter. It is dated 19 June, and Jackson says he 'listened to' (his usual term for seeing a play) *Hamlet* 'last night' (presumably at the Memorial Theatre – it wasn't playing at the BRT). But *Hamlet* played on June 17th, not 18th, and in any event **thorns and dangers** are from *King John* ('I am amaz'd, methinks, and lose my way/Among the thorns and dangers of this world') – which played on 19 June. The quotations from Scottish novelist **Robert Louis Stevenson** (1850–94) and South African statesman **Cecil Rhodes** (1853–1902) have not been located. The plays of James **Bridie** (Osborne Henry Mavor, 1888–1951) had been frequently performed at the BRT and Malvern. *The Barretts of Wimpole Street* had been a success at the 1930 Malvern Festival and enjoyed further success in London (see Letters 42, 48).

176 / To Barry Jackson Ayot St Lawrence, Welwyn, Herts.

21st June 1948

[TLU]

Perhaps reacting to the despondency of Jackson's previous letters about Stratford and Malvern, Shaw attempted to cheer him up with a reminder of what he had accomplished. But if Shaw recognized that Jackson was no longer interested in Malvern – artistically or financially – he kept a close eye on the situation there for his own interests: he was still holding the British premiere of Buoyant Billions for Limbert (Letter 159). In this regard Shaw would have read in the Malvern press of promising developments concerning renovations to the Festival Theatre. There were some local political tantrums about who should pay for the renovations – at a meeting of the Malvern District Council on 1 June the mayor 'removed his chain of office and walked out' after he was accused of bias in handling the debates about the theatre – but work began in July (ten new dressing rooms, eight bathrooms, two wardrobe rooms, and a greenroom) when it looked likely that the government would provide funding, as it formally did in October. This ensured that there would be a Malvern Festival in 1949.

My dear Barry

When I came to know William Morris I was a generation ahead of him, and found that he was unaware of the weight of work he had done as a political and aesthetic propagandist.

Now, a generation behind you, I find you imagining that all your work at Malvern has been thrown away. Not a bit of it. If Malvern were atom-bombed out of existence tomorrow your activities would still have made a prodigious difference, all to the good. No man has less reason to look back on his life as wasted.

It looks as if the Festival is pretty sure to be resumed next year. The £12000 will patch up the theatre quite sufficiently to carry on. But however great the work you have done I don't think you should lose any more money.

Malvern should not be pauperized, especially now that the changes that have banned the unrepaired theatre have also made public finance possible.

G.B.S.

Shaw was a close friend and admirer of **William Morris** (1834–96), craftsman, printer, decorator, and socialist (see also Letter 82).

177 / To Barry Jackson Ayot St Lawrence, Welwyn, Herts.
24th June 1948

[TLU]

There had been a contretemps between Shaw and Jackson in the autumn of 1946 (Letters 147–52) about Shaw's plays (or the absence of them) at Stratford, particularly concerning Roy Limbert's frustrated efforts to produce In Good King Charles's Golden Days *at the Memorial Theatre. Limbert tried again, and thought he had an agreement to produce the play in Stratford in November 1948. The deal fell through, however, because the governors wanted 'lighter plays' in the off-season and didn't believe that Shaw could attract audiences. Limbert sent the correspondence to Shaw, with a covering letter, on 22 June 1948. Shaw sent it on to Jackson, who, happily, didn't tear it up. It is now in the Birmingham Central Library, MS 2129/1/2.*

The enclosed, which you can tear up, was a surprise. I did not know I was blacklisted at Stratford.

As the modern Shakespear I consider that a season of Shaw plays in the off season should be a permanent feature there.

The kick-out is pretty complete now.

G.B.S.

178 / To Barry Jackson [Onslow Court Hotel, Queen's Gate, SW7]
From Blanche Patch 12th January 1949

[TLS]

Having spent most of the war at Ayot St Lawrence, Blanche Patch returned to live in London, whence she continued to give Barry Jackson accounts – often acerbic – of Shaw's activities. Among the 'parasites' around Shaw were neighbours Clare (1894–1989) and Stephen Winsten (1893–1991). Clare painted Shaw's portrait and was commissioned by Shaw to sculpt a statue of Saint Joan for his garden at Ayot, while Stephen wrote and edited books about Shaw, including the one described in this letter, Days with Bernard Shaw *(New York: Vanguard*

Press; London: Hutchinson, 1949). Even more parasitical, in Blanche Patch's view, was F.L. Loewenstein (1901–69), a German refugee who wheedled his way into becoming Shaw's official bibliographer.

Dear Sir Barry

I was very pleased to have news of you; but sorry to know you have had such a worrying time. For myself I seem to have slipped into a sort of backwater away from all the parasites who gather round G.B.S. He still pours out quite a lot of shorthand which he sends to me for typing and this with a certain amount of the business side of his work keeps me pleasantly busy during the mornings. I go to him for occasional weekends and recently motored down there for an afternoon visit with Fanny Holtzman of New York.

My feeling about the Winsten book is that if G.B.S. really sat down in a house and answered every question at such length he would be rather a bore; but I think a good deal of the material is just lifted from his writings. The photographs are quite good and one can see that Winsten is an educated man, but he would have needed a stenographer behind him so as to be able to report the conversations at such length – memory wouldnt go to that length. I fancy that Loewenstein is protesting somewhat that he has overstepped his right of quotation; but now that the book is out and Winsten is G.B.S.'s friend nothing will be done. It is of course sad that there should be all this unpleasantness around the old man in his latter years. Loew and the Winstens are not on speaking terms and now and again Nancy Astor dashes down and creates scenes because she says Charlotte left her in charge of G.B.S. This he denies quite rightly ...

Yours
B.P.

Jackson's **worrying time** probably arose from the illness with cancer of his partner Scott Sunderland. **Fanny Holtzman** (1903–80) was a New York lawyer who had tried – unsuccessfully – in 1948 to persuade Shaw to authorize a musical version of *Pygmalion*. Shaw had told her in October 1948 'It is not worth coming to England to see the little that is left of me; but come if you will' (*Collected Letters*, IV, 830). She did.

179 / To Barry Jackson   Ayot St Lawrence, Welwyn, Herts.
                                      5th March 1949

[ALS]

Jackson had settled back into his post-Stratford responsibilities at the Birmingham Repertory Theatre, though he had taken care on his return there, as Shaw notes, to arrange for additional administrative support ('acting lieutenants'). Jackson was hardly in straitened financial circumstances, but it seems he was considering switching from his regular Birmingham base at the Queen's Hotel to the less expensive Temperance. Shaw wasn't short of money either, but since he hadn't been in London since late 1946 (and was never to return) there was no point in keeping his Whitehall flat. (And Blanche Patch, to Shaw's evident consternation, was quite comfortable in a hotel in fashionable Kensington.) At Ayot, however, Shaw remained astonishingly busy. Although nothing came of Quayle's interest in a Stratford production of Cymbeline Refinished *(see also Letter 144), there was much activity at Malvern in preparation for the 1949 Festival, as well as new work.*

My dear Barry

I was on the point of writing to you for news of yourself when your letter arrived. On the whole, the news is not bad now that you have acting lieutenants. On the other hand you have, I suppose, less money, as to which see enclosed card. Probably you *ought* to put up at the Temperance and not at the Queen's. I have myself put up there in my Socialist tours. It was quite comfortable.

I have had at last to face the folly of paying £1000 a year for the Whitehall flat when I have not been there for years and may never see London again – at least I hope not. So it is now to let; and the furniture is to be auctioned except enough to furnish a smaller and cheaper flat as an office for Blanche Patch, and a bed for me in case I should be burnt out here, or my domestics all laid up and in hospital.

I have only one Stratford item. Quayle wants to do Cymbeline with my fifth act at least once.

Limbert keeps me bothered about Malvern. The Festival now seems certain to take place in August, July being too soon for the builders. The *pièce de résistance* will be Buoyant Billions; but I have written two later plays. The first is Farfetched Fables: six scenes in the guessed future to be played by the same group of players. Useful perhaps for amateurs.

The second and probably the last is a masterpiece. Lanchester, at the Marionette Theatre, sent me photographs of two puppets: one of myself and one of Shakespear, with a request for one of my celebrated dramas for them, to last 10 minutes. Which I accordingly did, in blank verse. Title SHAKES & SHAV.

A collector's edition of B.B. with pictures by Clare Winsten, limited to 1500 copies at 6 guineas, is in the press.

My new book 16 Self-Sketches will reach you next week when I get a batch of copies.

G.B.S.

PS Patch lives at Onslow Court Hotel!!!!!

Shaw's standard printed **card** rejected appeals from 'charitable institutions, religious sects and Churches, inventors, Utopian writers desirous of establishing international millennial leagues, parents unable to afford secondary education for their children: in short, everybody and every enterprise in financial straits of any sort.' *Buoyant Billions* opened the Malvern Festival on 13 August 1949 (six performances). *Farfetched Fables* was first produced by the Shaw Society at Watergate Theatre, London, on 6 September 1950, designed by Felix Topolski, directed by Esmé Percy. It ran for thirty performances. Waldo S. **Lanchester** (1897–1978) founded the Lanchester Marionette Theatre in Malvern in 1936. *Shakes versus Shav* opened there on 9 August 1949. The **collector's edition** (1025 copies) of *Buoyant Billions* was published by Constable on 15 May 1950. Not many collectors were interested, and most copies were remaindered. *Sixteen Self Sketches* was published on 3 March 1950.

180 / To Barry Jackson Onslow Court Hotel, Queen's Gate, SW7
    From Blanche Patch 19th January 1950

[TLS]

On the surface not much had changed at the Malvern Festival. The 1949 program included a good dose of Shaw (The Apple Cart *and* In Good King Charles's Golden Days *as well as* Buoyant Billions *and* Shakes versus Shav), *music, lectures, and the usual round of social events. Administratively and financially, however, there were some significant developments, including co-production arrangements with the Cambridge Arts Theatre and, through the Cambridge Arts, support from the Arts Council of Great Britain. The arrangement with the Cambridge Arts Theatre took two of the Festival's plays –* Buoyant Billions *and* Max, *a new play by Denis Cannan – to Cambridge, where* Buoyant Billions *opened on 5 September 1949 and* Max *a week later. Reviews in the*

Cambridge Daily News *spoke of a 'successful' and 'memorable' Festival, but Limbert lost money. When his request for a subsidy from the Malvern Urban District Council was rejected, he decided he could not continue. In the* Daily Express *article (19 January 1950) referred to by Blanche Patch at the beginning of this letter Limbert explained that he was dropping the Festival for three reasons: 'The urban council's decision not to give adequate financial assistance'; 'The time wasted in "wrangling"'; and 'The endeavour of the Malvern public to pry into private affairs' – i.e., to see Limbert's account books. Shaw was sympathetic to Limbert's situation, telling the* Birmingham Mail *(16 December 1949) that the citizens of Malvern 'like to have something for nothing,' but when Blanche Patch read of Limbert's decision in the national press she was far less sympathetic, a sentiment she knew that Jackson would share.*

Dear Sir Barry

I see in today's Daily Express that Limbert states definitely that there will be no Malvern Festival this year. What puzzles me is how he can afford to lose the money he does when he takes Shaw's plays to other Repertory theatres. I believe he made a trifle when he took his company on to Cambridge after the Festival, but he must have lost quite a packet when he did a 6 weeks season at Harrogate. But he has a share in the Westminster Theatre present affair (Daphne Laureola) and that is still doing well. However I'm sure he is wise to cut out the festival. What he lacks is the machinery to attract well-known visitors and performers to the place. Yours was a very different sort of affair. Another thing no one has much spare money nowadays and hotels are very expensive ...

GBS has just issued a dictum that there are to be no visitors until after Easter. This is because Greer Garson got lost in a fog on her way back to London and was wandering about in her car for 2 hours or more. He says she would have been frozen to death had she not been wearing her mink mantle which must have cost *millions*. But that is his usual exaggeration, as there has been no frost until last night. Should you happen to be here towards the end of February we might get down to Ayot one afternoon ...

Yours
Blanche Patch

Limbert presented a season of Shaw plays at the Royal Hall, **Harrogate**, in the summer of 1948. He also co-produced a play by Lesley Storm, *Black Chiffon*, which had a successful run of 416 performances at the **Westminster Theatre**, London, beginning on 3 May 1949. (Blanche Patch's reference to **Daphne Laureola** has not been identified.) **Greer Garson** (1903–96) had acted at the Birmingham Repertory Theatre in 1932 and had toured the U.K. in the same year as The Patient in *Too True to be Good*. She subsequently went on to a major film career in the United States.

181 / To Barry Jackson Onslow Court Hotel, Queen's Gate, SW7
From Blanche Patch 7th May 1950

[ALS]

Jackson's final meeting with Shaw, arranged by Blanche Patch, took place at Ayot on 17 May 1950 at 4 o'clock in the afternoon. 'The last time I saw him,' Jackson recalled, 'he was transparently frail; he had become almost disembodied thought. Nevertheless, within half an hour he touched brilliantly upon half a dozen vital topics of the moment, and I left him marvelling' (Mander and Mitchenson, 2).

Dear Sir Barry

I think it should be possible for us to go to Ayot on Wed. the 17th. I was there last week with Nicholas Davenport (*almost* father-in-law to Gorgeous Gussie) & one now sees that an hour's visit to GBS is about as much as he can stand – & he didn't come out to wave us through the gate. Still, mentally he's still very bright & still turns out long letters & short articles in his shorthand.

You will have read the somewhat mixed criticisms of the London production of 'The Cocktail Party,' the general opinion being that Rex Harrison is miscast. I haven't seen it yet.

Yours
B. Patch

I'll let you know definitely when I've spoken to Mrs Laden about the 17th. One never knows what dates are fixed for Pascal. Sometimes he's in Mexico fixing Arms & the Man, or Rome with Androcles & the Lion, & next day in his flat in South Street ...

Nicholas Davenport (1895–1975) was a financial backer and economic adviser to Gabriel Pascal. His son, it seems, had been romantically involved with the Australian tennis star

Gorgeous Gussie Moran. T.S. Eliot's *The Cocktail Party* opened at the New Theatre on 3 May 1950 with **Rex Harrison** as the Unidentified Guest. 'It seemed both interesting and prestigious,' Harrison recalled, 'so I agreed to do it, but in the event I hated doing so' (Nicholas Wapshott, *Rex Harrison: A Biography* [London: Chatto & Windus, 1991], 135). Alice **Laden** was Shaw's housekeeper and cook, known locally in Ayot as 'the Dragon.' On Shaw's death the National Trust appointed her custodian of the Ayot house ('Shaw's Corner'). Pascal's film of *Androcles and the Lion*, starring Jean Simmons and Victor Mature, was released in 1953. Pascal never completed a film of *Arms and the Man*.

182 / To Barry Jackson   Ayot St Lawrence, Welwyn, Herts.

17th August 1950

[TLU]

This is the last letter that Shaw wrote to Jackson, and one of the last of his life. To the end, he was reporting on his work and quizzing Jackson about his own new interests, in this case the plays of Jean Anouilh (which Shaw had a good shot at spelling correctly). The 'half length attempt at a little comedy' was Why She Would Not, *which was not published until August 1956 (in the* London Magazine *and in* Theatre Arts*). A typewritten note attached to this letter characterizes it as '[a] reply to a note suggesting that if G.B.S. would take a theme and embroider it in his own illimitable manner he would turn out the best play ever.'*

My dear Barry

I am dead as a playwright. On my birthday I managed to send off to the printer a half length attempt at a little comedy; but it is a pitiful senile squeak. I shall probably burn it. My big plays did not blaze a trail to greater heights: they reaped the harvest and cut down the trees, leaving nothing but a desert with a silly old stag trying to browse in it.

Still, I am content to have said my say and shot my bolt. I have done a good day's work; and now I must put up the shutters.

All this drivel you have provoked by expecting another Heartbreak House.

I never heard of the unpronouncable and unspellable Anhouilh. Is he published and buyable in French? Are you translating?

I cant think of anything more to say. The pump is dry: I can spout nothing but metaphors, well mixed.

G.B.S.

183 / To G. Bernard Shaw [no address]
21st August 1950

[TLU (c)]

This is Jackson's last letter to Shaw. Three weeks later, on 10 September, Shaw fractured his thigh in a gardening accident. After hospital treatment he returned to Ayot, where he died on 2 November 1950. The obituary in the Birmingham Post *the next day quoted Jackson on Shaw: 'One of the greatest and kindest of men has gone from us, and I can only be grateful for his friendship and wise counsel ... I always found G.B.S. the kindliest and most human creature it has been my fortune to meet.'*

My dear G.B.S.

I regret to say that I find it difficult to believe in the sentiments expressed in your letter. Your well will never be dry as long as you have breath in your body. If Verdi could transmute Otello and Falstaff, and Wagner the Sleeping Beauty, I do not see why you could not give the world something equally great, even though founded on something like Dick Whittington, which has always been one of my pet stories. The final indignity of his being made Lord Mayor of London would, I feel sure, appeal to you! Whether the cat could be transformed into a go-getting blonde is another matter which would have to be left to you.

Jean Anouilh is considered a figure of the avant-garde in the French theatre. He is, I imagine, in his middle forties and although I do not think him to be [one] of the great figures in the drama, he certainly has an amazing gift of theatre. His present success in London is 'Ring Round the Moon,' a translation by Christopher Fry of 'L'Invitation au Château,' produced by Peter Brook, with my protégé, Paul Scofield, in the leading role which happens to be twins.

Most of his works are published in French. Like you, he has published and had played, plays both pleasant and unpleasant or, as he himself says, 'Pièces Roses et Pièces Noires.' Among the latter, is his 'Antigone,' which has had great success in London, New York, Paris and elsewhere. The play 'Ardèle ou la Marguerite' which we are proposing to give here in the autumn, and which has been translated by one of the company, had great success in Europe, but failed completely when given recently in New York where apparently 'a spade is not called a spade, but a bloody shovel.' I will send you a copy of the translation later on.

Scott joins in love and good wishes.

Yours,

[Barry Jackson]

Christopher Fry's (b. 1907) translation of **Jean Anouilh**'s (1910–78) *L'Invitation au Château, Ring Around the Moon*, opened at the Globe Theatre, London, on 26 January 1950 and ran for 682 performances. *Ardèle, ou la Marguerite* opened at the BRT on 24 October 1950. In an adaptation by Cecil Robson, *Cry of the Peacock*, *Ardèle* opened at the Mansfield Theatre, New York, on 11 April 1950. Critic Brooks Atkinson thought it 'inept and muddled' (*New York Times*, 12 April 1950).

Afterword

On the evening of 2 November 1950 Barry Jackson, Scott Sunderland, and the staff who looked after them in their Malvern home gathered round the radio to listen to St John Ervine's tribute to Bernard Shaw. They were all, Jackson wrote to Ervine the next day, 'profoundly moved.' Ervine paid tribute as well to Charlotte, whose contribution to Shaw's achievements had been overlooked in the 'Press welter' about Shaw's death – a 'lamentable omission' in Jackson's view. 'Well – it has come at last and there is a void that cannot be filled, for us, at least,' Jackson told Ervine (Ervine Collection, HRC). And indeed, with Charlotte's death in 1943, and now Shaw's, Barry Jackson had lost two close friends and intimate correspondents. From the Shaw household there remained Blanche Patch, with whom Jackson had corresponded regularly for some years. No letters from Jackson to Blanche Patch have survived, but extant letters from Miss Patch to Jackson date from December 1940. The correspondence continued after Shaw's death, though with less frequency and, almost certainly, with more enthusiasm from Miss Patch than from Jackson. The last known letter from Blanche Patch to Barry Jackson is dated 9 December 1956 and concerns, among other things, legal disputes between Shaw's estate and the producers of *My Fair Lady*. Blanche Patch died in 1966, five years after Jackson.

Jackson's professional life after Shaw's death focused on the Birmingham Repertory Theatre. As the end of his tenure at Stratford approached and his return to a full commitment to the BRT was imminent, Jackson told Shaw that '[t]he rise of costs is playing havoc with work in such a small house and unless some guarantee is forthcoming, I begin to feel – a sensation due to advancing years – that the struggle is too arduous. If the future of the B.R.T. is to be disintegration, I would rather set the time bomb myself – first retiring to a safe distance' (Letter 173). The 'guarantee' that Jackson had in mind was adequate municipal funding for the existing theatre, but Shaw was more ambitious. 'Will you put your foot down and announce that you must either chuck the B.R.T. or be provided with a municipal theatre large enough to pay its way with popular prices, practically free of rent and rates?' (Letter 174). It may be that Jackson reached this conclusion – the need for a new, larger, subsidized Birmingham Repertory Theatre – independently of Shaw, but whatever the origin of the idea Jackson began actively to promote it. On his seventieth birthday, in 1949, Jackson told a reporter for *Illustrated* that his 'only remaining ambition is to see the erection of a Civic Theatre in the city which he has so loyally served. "But sometimes I fear I shall never live to see the foundation stone laid"' (22 October 1949). His fear was justified. The new Birmingham Repertory Theatre, with more than double the seating capacity (about 900) of the old one, did not open until 1972. It remains one of Britain's leading regional theatres, while the revered old Rep stays in service as a venue for a variety of community and professional theatre events.

Jackson continued to live in Malvern, his personal life saddened by the death of his partner Scott Sunderland in December 1952. Jackson's resolve not to provide any further support for the Malvern Festival was not altered by Roy Limbert's decision to withdraw. Limbert's 1949 Festival proved to be the last of its kind during Jackson's lifetime. Malvern hosted a number of summer theatrical and musical events in the 1950s, including a 'Bernard Shaw Centenary Week' in July 1956 organized by Jackson and the BRT, but a full-scale Festival was not held again until 1977.

In 1960 Jackson's health began to deteriorate seriously. Suffering from leukemia, he began a routine of dividing his time between hospital in Birmingham, his home in Malvern, and his office at the theatre. The last play he saw was *Antony and Cleopatra* at the BRT in March 1961, though he wasn't well enough to stay beyond the first intermission. Barry Jackson died on Easter Monday, 3 April 1961.

Table of Correspondents

Unless otherwise noted the letters were written by Bernard Shaw and Barry Jackson.

23 To Barry Jackson 13 February 1928   27
24 To G. Bernard Shaw 8 June 1928   28
25 To Barry Jackson June 1928   30
26 To Barry Jackson 13 July 1928   34
27 To Barry Jackson 14 November 1928   34
28 To Barry Jackson 21 November 1928   35
29 To Barry Jackson from Charlotte F. Shaw 6 January 1929   36
30 To Barry Jackson [January 1929]   37
31 To Barry Jackson 10 February 1929   39
32 To Barry Jackson from Charlotte F. Shaw [19 February 1929]   40
33 To Barry Jackson 6 April 1929   40
34 To G. Bernard Shaw 9 April 1929   41
35 To Barry Jackson 13 May 1929   42
36 To Barry Jackson from Charlotte F. Shaw 21 May 1929   43
37 To Barry Jackson 20 July 1929   44
38 To Barry Jackson 23 July 1929   45
39 To Barry Jackson 29 July 1929   46
40 To Barry Jackson 31 July 1929   46
41 To Barry Jackson 19 January 1930   47
42 To Barry Jackson 2 March 1930   48
43 To Barry Jackson 2 May 1930   49
44 To Barry Jackson 13 May 1930   50
45 To Barry Jackson from Charlotte F. Shaw [16] May 1930   51
46 To Barry Jackson 26 May 1930   52
47 To Barry Jackson 25 October 1930   52
48 To Barry Jackson 17 November 1930   53
49 To Barry Jackson 13 July [1931]   54
50 To Barry Jackson 5 October 1932   55
51 To Barry Jackson 19 April 1933   56
52 To Barry Jackson 28 April 1933   57
53 To G. Bernard Shaw 30 April 1933   60
54 To Barry Jackson from Charlotte F. Shaw 27 November 1933   60
55 To G. Bernard Shaw 1 December 1933   61
56 To G. Bernard Shaw 5 December 1933   62
57 To G. Bernard Shaw 11 January 1934   62
58 To Barry Jackson 11 January 1934   63
59 To G. Bernard Shaw 12 January 1934   63

Index

Since the names of Shaw and Jackson appear on most pages of this volume they are not included in the index except where their works are mentioned. The location of theatres is London unless otherwise indicated.